JESUS

AND THE *gods*
OF THE
new age

JESUS

AND THE *gods*
OF THE
new age

Ross Clifford
Philip Johnson

The Bible Teacher's Teacher

An Imprint of Cook Communications Ministries •
Colorado Springs Colorado

Victor is an imprint of
Cook Communications Ministries, Colorado Springs, Colorado 80918
Cook Communications, Paris, Ontario
Kingsway Communications, Eastbourne, England

JESUS AND THE GODS OF THE NEW AGE
© 2003 by Ross Clifford and Philip Johnson (U.S.)
© 2001 by Lion Publishing (U.K.)

First Printing (U.S.), 2003
Printed in the United States of America
1 2 3 4 5 6 7 8 9 10 Printing/Year 08 07 06 05 04 03

Library of Congress Cataloging-in-Publication Data

Clifford, Ross.
  Jesus and the gods of the New Age
  ISBN 0-7814-3943-4
  1. New Age movement. 2. Christianity and other religions--New Age
movement. 3. New Age movement--Relations--Christianity. I. Johnson,
Philip, 1960- II. Title.
  BP605.N48C57 2003
  261.2'993--dc21

                        2003010230

Contents

Preface

No one can doubt that the church is having a hard time in Western cultures today. Attendances are falling in all denominations and traditions. Even people in mid-life, who have been part of the church all their days, are moving out to look elsewhere for spiritual answers to life's questions. Sadly, it seems to be taken for granted among younger people that, whatever church might be about, it is not concerned with anything spiritual.

It is this last view that makes today's decline in church commitment a completely new phenomenon, quite different from anything our forebears ever encountered. There have always been those who were not interested in Christianity and so adopted a completely non-religious lifestyle and worldview. Today, though, things are very different. Huge numbers of people are quite open about the fact that they are searching for something spiritual, and they are not interested in the church because they believe that Christians are the last people to be interested in such things.

Christians, for their part, have not been slow to respond to today's spiritual searchers. They have mostly discounted what is going on as superficial and meaningless, maybe even demonic. As a result, the gap between Christian faith and the new spirituality is far wider than it needs to be. The people who search for meaning in neo-paganism or the human potential movement or channeling or encounters with angels are not monsters, but, according to the very first page of the Bible, women and men made in God's image. They are seeking to discover how they can become most truly human, fulfilling their destiny within the cosmos, and will use whatever stories and methods seem to produce positive results. That, in essence, is what the teaching of Jesus is also about—so why do Christians find it so hard to relate to these people?

Ross Clifford and Philip Johnson start with some down-to-earth observations about this situation. They are right to suggest that Christians do far too much talking, and too little listening.

As they unpack their own biblically inspired apologetic approach, they emphasize the importance of hearing what is being said. If we Christians do not understand the questions that others are asking, how can we ever point them in the direction of useful answers? If we are so resistant to anything new in our own spiritual experience, how will we ever have anything worthwhile to share with our companions on life's journey?

In this helpful book, we are introduced to today's spiritual searchers—their worries and fears as well as their discoveries and aspirations. In the process, we meet actual people, for it is a significant strength of this book that it is based on real-life case studies, not just imaginary characters nobody ever meets. Those who are genuine in their concern to share their experience of Christ will find many helpful practical pointers here, as well as insights into the sorts of things that others now find it possible to believe.

Australians have a reputation for being blunt, and this book, by two Australians, presents some awkward questions to the church, for its authors accept that many of the criticisms directed at Christians are in fact valid. However, they also point to innovative forms of communication being used by Christians around the world that are rooted in the biblical traditions as well as being relevant to people's lives. Throughout, they constantly refer back to the Scriptures for guidance and inspiration. This is what makes their arguments so challenging and their analysis so perceptive, for they constantly connect what they know about contemporary culture to the message of the Bible in a way that will, at the very least, make you think.

John Drane
University of Aberdeen
Adjunct Professor, School of Theology
Fuller Seminary

Introduction

You are about to embark on a challenging journey that will take you into the mindset of today's spiritual seekers. You actually rub shoulders with them every day—on the bus, ferry, and train; at the theater, fast-food restaurants, gym, Internet chat rooms, school, supermarket, university, and workplace. They are numbered among your relatives, friends, neighbors, and work colleagues. Rarely do they bother with the church. Instead, they pursue spirituality by traveling along avenues such as alchemy, angels, astrology, Celtic paganism, channeling, clairvoyance, gnosticism, hermeticism, meditation, the power of the mind, reincarnation, sacred sex, spirit guides, tarot, witchcraft, and yoga.

Both of us have spent more than a decade witnessing to New Age seekers of the spiritual at psychic fairs and spiritual exhibitions. Being in such unusual venues has not only placed us on the evangelistic coalface but has also touched us in significant ways. After our initial encounters, we quickly realized how unfruitful it is to approach seekers with the objective of debunking, deconstructing, and demonizing their worldview. We had to stop holding up the cross in protest at them and start introducing seekers to the Jesus who hung on that cross and rose again. Amazingly, when we stopped being defensive and began to approach seekers using incarnational principles of mission, we discovered how open many of them are to following Jesus. Who we are, what we do and say to them, makes all the difference in communicating Christ to this spiritual supermarket.

Of course there is already a top-heavy pile of books that describe and analyze New Age and postmodern spiritualities, many of which have valuable insights. Have you noticed, though, that very few books take you into the marketplace with models or good advice on how to share? What distinguishes our book is that it presents a practical, field-tested model of how to share your faith, and demonstrates how you can apologetically direct conversations towards Jesus' call to discipleship.

We feel you will greatly benefit from our experiences. We shall introduce you to fifteen seekers who are among some of the more memorable characters with whom we have shared the gospel. In the chapters, apart from our dialogue, we also include pertinent information that will assist in understanding the issues for sharing faith. The seekers were really thrilled to talk with us, knowing that we are committed Christians. Here was a chance for them to pose their many unanswered questions, as well as challenging us to seriously consider what they had found.

These seekers brought us into very serious dialogues. Some of their questions reflect our common quest for meaning, while others relate to claims or objections to Christianity. By and large, most of these issues are not dealt with in introductory evangelism and discipleship courses. Today's seeker wants to know the answers to questions such as these:

- How can I be the best person I can possibly be?
- How can I find my place in the cosmos?
- Who am I anyway, and who might I become?
- Where do I find release from my brokenness?
- How do I cope with my illness?
- Where do I find peace?
- Where is the heart of love and acceptance?
- How can I reconnect my soul with the divine source of all life?
- What path should I choose?
- What kinds of values should I embrace?
- How is it that the cosmos I inhabit, which appears to have order and design and ought to be harmonious, is so screwed up?

Before we meet the seekers, we start with a foundational chapter that explains how and why we use an incarnational approach in order to reach seekers. We briefly map out the territory for this spirituality and its connection to postmodernity. We consider the strengths and weaknesses of existing Christian responses to New Age ideas and set out the biblical basis for our incarnational approach. To comprehend the remainder of this book you must first read this chapter.

Between chapters 2 and 11 you will meet our cast of characters and hear their challenges, objections, and questions concerning Jesus, the Bible, and Christianity. In these chapters we will show you how to find points in common or agreement on which you can build up to the gospel. We address the typical issues that a seeker will raise and show you how to give a reason for your faith "with gentleness and respect" (1 Peter 3:15, NIV-UK).

Some of the major topics we tackle include angels, astrology, complementary healing techniques, Jesus' missing years, power of the mind, near-death encounters, reincarnation, and Wicca. We also deal with various popular psychotechnologies and spiritual tools such as alchemy, auras, clairvoyance, feng shui, numerology, Qabalah, t'ai chi, tarot and yoga. With all of these topics we demonstrate how you can affirm the seeker as a person and, without being derogatory or dismissive of their search for meaning, positively introduce them to Jesus Christ.

Today's seekers are accustomed to participating in spiritual exercises. They will try almost anything that can connect them with the Creator. So, in chapter 12, we present Christian spiritual disciplines, exercises, and God-given tools that we all need on our journey with Jesus. These are practical and experiential entry points for encouraging them to become disciples of Jesus. In our closing chapter we offer some practical advice on how to conduct a ministry at festivals, together with a model sermon for preaching in today's spiritual supermarket.

Our book closes with three appendixes. The first underscores critical areas of mutual challenge that seekers and Christians alike need to address. The second appendix reproduces the personal journey of a young woman who explored Christianity, became disenchanted and now embraces Wicca. Her story is a sobering and provocative case study. It is designed for either group discussion or individual reflection. At the end you will find both a bibliography of Christian, secular, and New Age texts for each chapter as well as notes. *Jesus and the gods of the New Age* is a completely revised, updated and expanded version of our previous book *Sacred Quest*.[1]

[1] Ross Clifford and Philip Johnson, *Sacred Quest*, Sutherland, New South Wales: Albatross, 1995—first issued in 1993 under the title *Shooting for the Stars*.

Chapter 1
Incarnating the Good News

The key message now is that we should all seek to be visionaries ourselves, to explore every possible way of expanding our spiritual horizons. Each of us will find that sacred source in different ways. It may be that some of us will embrace the infinite through some form of guru or spiritual teacher. Some will reach spiritual realms through meditation, shamanic journeying or devotional prayer, and others by wandering in wilderness regions, mountains or rain-forests—opening their hearts and minds to the rhythms and harmonies of Nature.[1]

It is fair to say that most modern errors are only ancient heresies and doctrines in a different guise, tailor-fitted for the age in which we live. Therefore it should not surprise us that the old answers from the accumulated wisdom and theological expertise of the apostles, church fathers, and reformers are the best means of fighting ancient occultism in its modern forms. It is difficult, if not impossible, to improve on what the historic scholarship of the Christian church has to say about the revival of occultism in this New Age.[2]

The advent of the New Age can be seen as a mixed blessing for Christians who are called upon to respond in faith to the presence of new religions towards the end of the 20th century. While the New Age may be drawing away from traditional faith many dissatisfied individuals who have embarked on a personal religious quest, it might also be doing a service to Christianity by encouraging Christians to delve deeper into their religious tradition and rediscover its treasures.[3]

The 21st century has opened with a widespread resurgence of interest in spirituality. This has been spurred on by the colossal degradation of human existence that occurred during the two World Wars, the Holocaust and other tragedies. Secular philosophies that were founded on rationalism and scientific naturalism failed to furnish any substantial meaning for life. For so long, spiritual and religious thought were disparaged as archaic and intellectually primitive. The past century's denial of the spiritual is now being reversed.

This surge of spiritual exploration is being made in several different places, but today's seekers do not normally include the church on their "shopping list" of places to investigate because they regard the church as being devoid of true spirituality. This is further compounded in North America, Britain, Europe, Australia, and New Zealand, where church affiliation is, in many places, static or in serious decline. Some Westerners are attracted to Buddhism, Hinduism, and Islam. Others seek fulfillment in a myriad of new religions—those groups popularly branded as cults. However, the greatest and most popular impulses are found in a do-it-yourself spirituality, where belief and practice occur outside the bounds of organized religion. This do-it-yourself spirituality began blossoming in the latter decades of the 20th century and used to be called New Age.

Nowadays the expression "New Age" is rather hackneyed. Just like the word "fundamentalist," it didn't take long for the cynics to pour contempt on it as representing something superficial, ephemeral, or silly. Although the whole New Age thing did attract a lunatic fringe, there was a deeply disciplined side to it. Phil Rickman in his best-selling novel *Midwinter of the Spirit* neatly sums up through the character Jane what New Age spirituality means to so many people:

---◆---

The New Age is about…It's about millions of people saying: I want to know more…I want an inner life…I want to commune with nature and the cosmos and things, find out about what we're really doing here and who's running the show, and like what part I can play in the Great Scheme of Things.[4]

---◆---

Jay Kinney, editor of *Gnosis* magazine, suggested in 1998 that the New Age as a movement has started to reposition itself. He compares it to the civil rights and women's movements. Just as these movements started on society's fringes, so too New Age originally looked offbeat, but soon became normative. Although New Age jargon initially seemed odd, it was suited to the temperaments of the time. By the late 1980s this avant-garde movement had touched many people. It spilled over into many facets of society, such as business, counseling, education, and medicine. By the century's end, it had so saturated the culture that New Age jargon and ideas had become interwoven into the fabric of mainstream social discourse.[5] Even though New Age spirituality has now leveled out, the spiritual surge continues to spread far and wide.

The growing Christian concerns about reaching New Age seekers coincides with it becoming mainstream, but just as the term is falling out of favor with seekers and scholars alike. As Francis Schaeffer was fond of saying, the church specializes in being behind. The current expressions now preferred include *Aquarian Age, New Consciousness, New Edge, New Sense, New Spirituality, Next Age, Next Stage,* and *Postmodern Spirituality.*[6] These expressions reflect more recent developments in this spiritual and cultural ferment. Throughout this book, we will use the term "New Age" for the sake of simplicity, but we suggest that either *New Spirituality* or *Postmodern Spirituality* may end up being the preferred or most commonly used label in the 21st century.

Signposts of New Age spirituality

A little later in this chapter, we will consider how the church has responded to New Age spirituality. After that, we will explain why we use incarnational mission principles to reach today's seekers. However, right now we want to identify some easy-to-recognize signposts of New Age spirituality and briefly consider why they have arisen.

The obvious signposts of New Age spirituality can be seen in books, magazines, festivals, radio, TV, movies, and on the Internet. A quick visit to a secular bookshop reveals a large selection of titles under the rubric "Mind, Body, and Soul." Some of the most popular and influential authors include Fritjof Capra, Deepak Chopra, Shakti Gawain, Louise Hay, Shirley Maclaine, James Redfield, Anthony Robbins, and Marianne Williamson.

Peruse the mainstream women's magazines and note the regular columns devoted to astrology, feng shui, and tarot. Radio and TV chat shows and lifestyle programs reflect these same interests. Cult TV shows of the likes of *Buffy the Vampire Slayer*, *The X-Files*, and *Star Trek Voyager* touch on spiritual and paranormal themes. Movies such as *The Matrix* readily spring to mind as further indicators of these concerns. Internet sites devoted to angels, astrology, paganism, spirit guides, tarot, and Wicca abound, many of which record high numbers of daily hits.

Perhaps the most visible indicator of interest in this area is the alternative lifestyle and spirituality exhibitions. Each year The Whole Life Expo crosses several cities from California to New York and draws in thousands of patrons. The International Festival for Mind-Body-Spirit convenes in London, Manchester, Brisbane, Sydney, and Melbourne, and its annual combined attendance rates reputedly makes it the world's largest spiritual trade exhibition. Similar New Spirituality exhibitions will be found in such diverse cities as Adelaide, Auckland, Dublin, Johannesburg, and Toronto. Psychic fairs and neo-pagan gatherings will be found in many urban and rural districts, especially where alternative/counter-culture lifestyles prevail. The common feature of these exhibitions is the do-it-yourself nature of the quest and that what counts is what works best for you.

The mindset of modernity

This New Age thinking has probably arisen for many historical and sociological reasons. One that commentators such as John Drane point to is that it represents a reaction to the mechanistic and rationalist outlook that has dominated the past four centuries of Western history. That outlook, which pulsed through the European Enlightenment and beyond, is referred to as modernity. Advocates of modernity redefined reality in non-spiritual ways and treated both humans and the cosmos as mere objects for scientific analysis.[7]

The primary method of thought in modernity, which can be traced to philosophers such as Descartes (1596-1650), was grounded in doubt or skepticism. Added to this were the scientific discoveries made by Galileo and Newton, which made a lot of previously held views about the cosmos untenable. Darwin's thesis overturned many other long-held beliefs about the creation. Naturalism became the prevailing dogma.

So, in North America and Europe, parts of the intelligentsia developed a mindset that trusted in human rationality and science as providing ultimate meaning in life. Many chided religious beliefs as primitive superstitions, casting doubts on the Bible and miracles as being rationally and scientifically impossible. The very assumptions of Christian belief were challenged and discarded in many quarters.

Of course, this mindset did not spell the end of religion at all. It led to intellectual jousts between Christians, agnostics, humanists, and skeptics. Some theologians acceded to modernity's criticisms of the Bible and miracles and sought to accommodate or reinterpret the faith along rationalist and scientific lines. Others sought to uphold and defend orthodox belief by using the critical tools of modernity.

The epitome of modernity is its tendency to both dismiss spiritual viewpoints as incredible and reduce life and meaning to behavioral, economic, rationalist, or scientific explanations. One of the clearest examples of a modernity-based philosophy is Marxism, with its primary emphasis on economic explanations of human life and activity. It is not surprising that some see the collapse of Marxism throughout Eastern Europe in 1989 as signifying the very end of modernity.[8]

Spiritual undercurrents in modernity

Even as humanist and Christian thought jostled each other for 400 years throughout North America and Europe, alternative spiritual views percolated below the surface. Elements of these spiritual undercurrents have survived and been freely adapted by today's seekers. To put New Age spirituality into perspective, let's briefly note a few of the influential figures and movements that precede it.

After the Reformation, a period of political, social, and religious upheaval ensued throughout Britain and Europe. Apart from movements revitalizing the established church, other spiritual options quickly emerged. Two early visionaries were the Swedish scientist Emanuel Swedenborg (1688-1772) and the English poet William Blake (1757-1827).

• Swedenborg first had a distinguished career as a mathematician, engineer, inventor and politician; then he became a clairvoyant seer. He abandoned his Lutheran background and reinterpreted the Bible as a "parable" of the spiritual realm. The spiritual realm has its exact correspondences in the physical world, "as above, so below" (this is technically known as hermeticism).

His reinterpretation of the Bible and Christian belief appealed to notable figures such as the German romantic Goethe, the American jurist Theophilus Parsons, and Helen Keller (the famous deaf-blind woman whose remarkable life was cinematically portrayed by Patty Duke). Among Swedenborg's many books are *Arcana Coelestia* and *Heaven and Its Wonders and Hell*. After his death, his followers in England formed the Church of the New Jerusalem.

- Swedenborg also influenced William Blake. Like Swedenborg, Blake communicated with angelic beings and also with his dead brother's spirit. Blake's poetry and art reflected these visionary experiences. Blake's and Swedenborg's ideas have poured into the streams of New Age spirituality.[9]
- Freemasonry and Rosicrucianism also became attractive options for those disenchanted with orthodox Christianity. Freemasonry is a speculative ideology based on moral and spiritual allegories that are expressed by means of a symbolic system of ritual degrees. It sprang out of the 14th-century stonemasons' guilds and started with a basic Christian ethos. However, by the early 18th century, it evolved into an esoteric organization.

  Allegations of Luciferian and satanic rituals in the highest degrees stem from the French hoaxer Gabriel Jogand-Pagès (alias Leo Taxil).[10] While we have objections to its compatibility with authentic Christian discipleship, nothing worthwhile comes of bearing false witness about Freemasonry.[11]
- Rosicrucianism emerged out of Lutheranism in the last decades of the 16th century and began to flourish in the early 17th century in Germany and then England. It espoused secret wisdom that saw itself as superior to orthodox Christian belief. The key German figures to shape it were Simon Studion, Julius Sperber, and Aegidius Guttmann. In England, the healer Robert Fludd and the astrologer William Lilly amalgamated Rosicrucian teaching with alchemy and astrology. These movements later died out, but a variety of new Rosicrucian-based orders were created in the 20th century, drawing on the traditions of magick, parapsychology, Freemasonry, and theosophy.[12]
- France proved to be fertile ground for occult thinkers such as Jean-Baptiste Alliette (alias Etteilla) and Eliphas Levi. They were the first to associate tarot cards with fortune-telling and the Qabalah.[13] British esotericists such as Arthur Edward Waite (1857–1942) and Francis Israel Regardie (1907–85) exerted great influence in the 20th century. Waite was a prolific writer on the hermetic arts of alchemy and Qabalah. He had a background in Catholicism and embraced a mystical approach to spirituality. He once belonged to the Order of the Golden Dawn, which was an influential magickal group. He later established his own Brotherhood of the Rosy Cross. He devised the Rider-Waite tarot deck,

which became the most widely used deck of the 20th century. He translated some of Levi's books into English. Regardie was a practicing alchemist and prolific writer on Western esotericism. He wrote a four-volume work on the Order of the Golden Dawn.[14]

- Several American writers and poets who favored a romantic philosophy unleashed a different set of impulses. A group of them, known as the New England Transcendentalists, included Ralph Waldo Emerson (1803–82), George Ripley (1802–80) and Henry David Thoreau (1817-62). They embraced an intuitive, experiential approach to spirituality, rejected orthodox Christian beliefs, and were among the first Americans to study the then newly translated Hindu text the Bhagavadgita.[15]

- A number of American metaphysical healers and thinkers have contributed another stream of thought. The best known was Mary Baker Eddy (1821–1910). She was the founder of Christian Science. In *Science and Health with Key to the Scriptures*, she taught that the material world, evil, pain, sickness, and death are an illusion of mortal minds. God was a principle in everything. Sickness and evil are overcome by recognizing that they are illusory. Her teachings either influenced or were paralleled in metaphysical groups of the likes of New Thought (Warren Felt Evans), Religious Science (Ernest Holmes) and the Unity School of Christianity (Charles and Myrtle Fillmore).[16]

- Theosophy, which literally means "divine wisdom," forms probably the most influential source for today's New Age spirituality. It combined elements of the Western esoteric traditions with Buddhist and Hindu concepts, creating new spiritual myths about a brotherhood of ascended masters, the lost years of Jesus, and offering the universal wisdom of the world's faiths.

- Helena Blavatsky (1831–91) was a Russian-born psychic and medium, and a co-founder of the Theosophical Society. Her most influential book is *The Secret Doctrine*.

- Annie Besant (1847–1933) was a prolific author, campaigner for social reform and independence in India. As Blavatsky's successor in theosophy she established the Order of the Star of the East to promote the coming Lord Maitreya, who she believed was Jiddhu Krishnamurti (1895–1986). Krishnamurti eventually rejected this mantle and become a popular yogic philosopher-teacher in his own right.[17]

- Charles Leadbeater (1854–1934) was a leading British theosophist who became the first bishop of the Liberal Catholic Church in Australia. He was closely associated with Annie Besant and sponsored Krishnamurti as the promised Lord Maitreya. Many of his ideas have had a seminal impact on New Age spirituality. Greg Tillett observes:

  The modern occult revival owes more to him than to anyone else; his concepts and ideas, his popularizing of occult and theosophical terms and principles run through all modern works on these subjects—Words like karma, chakra, chela, Mahatma, atma, Buddhi, manas, Maitreya—have continued to be used in the sense in which he used them, regardless of their original meanings by writers and theorists who give no acknowledgement to Leadbeater as the origin of their ideas.[18]

- Alice Bailey (1880–1949) began in theosophy, but left to create the Arcane School and Lucis Trust. She claimed her teachings came from an ascended master, Djwhal Khul. She believed in the coming of the World Teacher, Lord Maitreya, who would usher in the New Age. She wrote the "Great Invocation," a prayer used by her followers. Benjamin Creme, a Scottish devotee of Bailey's teachings and founder of the Tara Centre, in 1988 identified a Pakistani mystic as Lord Maitreya in Nairobi, Kenya.[19]

- Rudolf Steiner (1861–1925) began in theosophy but left to establish anthroposophy. Steiner preferred a mystical-occult reinterpretation of Christianity, teaching that the earth had passed through seven epochs with the Eastern religions preparing the way for Christ. He believed in spiritual evolution and reincarnation, advocated herbalism, and created the sacred dance called eurhythmy. He developed biodynamic farming where specially consecrated manure is diluted, buried according to astrological settings so as to activate the "universal life force," re-exhumed, and then sprayed over crops. The Steiner schools are based on his ideas, and there is a church gathered around his teachings known as The Christian Community.[20]

- Beyond theosophy we have the contribution of Carl Gustav Jung (1875–1961) the Swiss psychotherapist. His ideas about the archetypes of the collective unconscious have been formative influences in New Age spirituality. Jung's views were shaped by his interests in occultism,

Swedenborg, neo-paganism, evolutionary biology, Aryan racial theories, and monistic religious thought. Joseph Campbell (1904–87) popularized Jung's thought about mythic archetypes.[21]

Although these spiritual thinkers and their movements were sometimes marginalized, many of their ideas and practices would eventually find widespread acceptance in the closing decades of the 20th century. By that time most of the assumptions undergirding modernity had caved in.

Charting New Age spirituality

Widespread disenchantment with modernity's shortcomings has stimulated the development of a perspective known as post-modernity or globalism. It is a different way of viewing the world and the way we can live. Modernity uses the "stories" of science to understand things. Postmodernity sees these as limited stories. In postmodernity the stories need to include the supernatural or at least be open to views that go beyond pure materialistic expla-nations. John Drane is convinced New Age spirituality is the religious expression of the postmodern mindset.[22] However, a chief feature of it is the notion that truth is shaped by social fac-tors—race, gender and culture. Therefore, spiritual truth is a matter of pragmatic experimentation and personal preferences, as summed up in the oft-used expression, "That's your truth—I have my own." Postmodernity also has a secular element to it, and it would be incorrect to assume that New Age spirituality and post-modernity are merely synonyms.[23]

Trying to define New Age spirituality has been compared to nailing jelly or bean curd to a wall.[24] This is because it has no central organizing body (like a church council or synod) and no confessional statement of belief (like the Nicene Creed). There is no founder or central leader in this spirituality. As these customary features of organized religion are absent, precise definitions are problematic.

Although a simple definition might seem elusive, we can still describe some key features. New Age spirituality is characterized by the notion that human beings can evolve spiritually. The seeker undertakes an interior spiritual journey to tap into those creative powers or energies within that link us to the divine source of the cosmos. A major focus is on holistic answers for mind, body, and spirit. For the individual seeker, spirituality impinges on all facets of living—business, career, diet, ecology, education, health, home and office design, parenting, and relationships. Each seeker explores various tools—be it astrology, channeling, rebirthing, or tarot—to achieve personal healing, spiritual evolution, and global transformation. Within this do-it-yourself impulse, there is also a corresponding yearning for a sense of mystery about the cosmos and a spiritual longing for authentic community.

Today's seekers accept many of the benefits of scientific discovery, but reject the naturalistic explanation of the cosmos. Many seekers find spiritual inspiration in pre-modern times. Seekers do not wish to revert to pre-modernity, but rather to blend the best elements of modernity with carefully selected morsels of pre-modern spiritual practice. So New Age spirituality attempts to re-sacralize a world that has been de-supernaturalized by modernity. According to Irving Hexham and Karla Poewe of the University of Calgary, this re-sacralization process is stimulating the creation of new cosmic myths—myths here being sacred stories that give meaning to a given group or culture. These myths not only highlight modernity's shortcomings but also offer New Age spirituality as the remedy. Advocates generally reject dualist thinking that separates mind from matter and humanity from God. Their alternative is to proclaim holism—that the whole of reality is in essence one seamless fabric. It promulgates a vision of a transformed cosmos.[25]

As New Age spirituality is in a state of constant flux, what we are about to outline will no doubt require modification as time goes by. We suggest that New Age spirituality presently entails several different strands or visions about life and the cosmos.

Monist holism

The monist vision emphasizes the oneness of reality. Some Christians have narrowly defined the New Age spirituality by this formula: all is one = monism; since all is one, all is divine = pantheism. Monism + pantheism = New Age spirituality. However, as we discuss in chapter 7, monism has several subtle nuances to it, and this perspective is not uniformly accepted within New Age spirituality.

Two key concepts in the monist vision are the hologram and spiritual evolution. The hologram is based on ideas formulated by David Bohm and Karl Pribram, also outlined in chapter 7. But to sum up, spiritual evolution is a positive process where we reconnect with the divine source of the cosmos or where we may progress into divinity ourselves. This is the vision presented in James Redfield's best-selling novel *The Celestine Prophecy*.

Unfortunately, some Christians have assumed that the concept of spiritual evolution is just an extension of Darwinian theory. Their hearty response has then involved rebutting Darwinian evolution as the first critical point of engagement with seekers. While some seekers may accept some form of biological evolution, their understanding of spiritual evolution derives from 18th-century romantic views of oriental religion and has no connection with Darwinian theory.[26] The question of who made the cosmos and how long ago this happened is a peripheral matter in the minds of most seekers.

Some advocates do espouse a form of pantheism (all is divine) where seekers discover their own inner divinity. God is viewed as an impersonal energy. Realizing that beyond the physical realm we are all divine is what transforms our consciousness. So some seekers will say that they are earnestly striving to return to the ultimate source from whence we came. The key to unlocking this divine consciousness will involve the various psychotechnologies we discuss chapter by chapter.

Others adopt a different monist outlook that is grounded in a popular, westernized form of neo-Buddhism. Here the vision does not entail discovering inner or cosmic divinity, but rather is a quest for the ineffable experience of nirvana's nothingness. Neo-Buddhist seekers tend to scoop up techniques from a smorgasbord of Buddhist traditions. As spiritual consumers, they happily combine elements of Sangharakshita's teachings in the Friends of the Western Buddhist Order with Thich Nhat Hanh's Zen teachings, Vipassana meditation, and aspects of the Dalai Lama's Tibetan Buddhist thought.[27] We are finding that more and more seekers are adopting the neo-Buddhist view of karma as an explanation for human suffering because they find the Christian view of a loving God permitting evil an absurdity. We have also observed that neo-Buddhism is now a strong spiritual option in the gay culture. It may well be that neo-Buddhism becomes one of the most important strands for the 21st century.

Still others are panentheists (all is in God), believing that there is a personal God, but the cosmos is part of God's being. In line with Matthew Fox's theology, these seekers chart their spiritual life as one that develops as God develops and changes. The world is affirmed as an "original blessing." Our observation is that seekers are more inclined to have a panentheist view of God, and some Christian apologists seem to have overlooked panentheism while stressing the significance of pantheism. (For more on this, see chapter 7.)

NEO-GNOSTIC HOLISM

Neo-gnostic spirituality is framed around the concept of *gnosis*, or knowledge. Spiritual knowledge is embedded symbolically within the human psyche. Holistic transformation occurs when mythic symbols, such as the universal hero and the tempter, are discovered in altered states of consciousness and dreams. Carl Jung is the seminal influence here. Also in this strand we would include the interest in spirit guides, angels, extraterrestrials, and the ancient Gnostic writings. Writers such as George Trevelyan differ on neo-gnostic holism because they see themselves in a direct lineage to ancient Gnosticism and operate with dualist ideas.[28]

NEO-PAGAN / WICCAN HOLISM

Here spirituality is framed around natural magick, as we will discuss in chapter 3. The neo-pagan/Wiccan holistic vision is about our oneness with nature and the presence of the goddess in the world.[29] Neo-paganism has overtaken a considerable section of what was New Age spirituality, probably because it offers a more structured and rigorous pathway, while still encouraging a do-it-yourself approach to ritual.

HERMETIC HOLISM

Hermeticism can refer to the teachings found in a body of ancient texts called the Hermetica. The Hermetica consists of various tracts and sermons with the chief character being Hermes Trismegistus (meaning thrice-great Hermes). He may represent the blending of the Greek deity Hermes with the Egyptian god of wisdom Thoth. His famous axiom concerns correspondences between the cosmos and the individual human ("as above, so below").

The term hermeticism may also be used in a broader sense to refer to the Western esoteric and magickal traditions of alchemy, astrology, Qabalah, and tarot. These arts are employed as tools for self-awareness and counseling. The cosmos contains symbolism that is revelatory about God and cosmic unity, and these are the tools used to decode the symbols and discover ultimate healing.[30] Esoteric groups such as Rosicrucianism and the Masonic orders are partly based on a hermetic philosophy.

Summary of Today's New Age Influencers

This chart can provide a helpful, general look at influences upon New Age worldviews:

- **Eastern mysticism**—since European colonialism, Western societies have increasingly come into direct contact with the spiritual traditions of Asia (Buddhism, Hinduism, Jain, Shinto, Sikh, and Taoism). Two of the most influential Hindu gurus in the West have been Swami Vivekananda (1863-1902) and Swami Muktananda Paramahansa (1908-82).

   Vivekananda was the first Hindu missionary to the modern Western world and founded the Vedanta Society in America. He addressed the World Parliament of Religions in 1893. He taught that, in essence, we are all divine and that the goal of life is to awaken this inner divinity.

   Muktananda brought Siddha Yoga to the West, which has gained over a quarter of a million adherents worldwide. In Siddha Yoga the emphasis is on the kundalini and a charismatic experience called the awakening. Baba Ram Dass and Werner Erhard sponsored Muktananda's first visit to the West in 1970. Muktananda influenced two American gurus in the Siddha tradition: Swami Rudrananda (Albert Rudolph) and Da Free John (Franklin Jones). Power of the mind teacher Michael Rowlands and Master Charles are former disciples of Muktananda. Siddha Yoga is now directed by Muktananda's nominated female successor, Gurumayi.

   Today's popular Western impressions of Buddhism owe their initial impetus to lay Buddhist gurus Daisetz Teitaro Suzuki (1870–1966) and Alan Watts (1915–73). Suzuki was a popular teacher of Zen Buddhism and, remarkably, both Swedenborg and theosophical thought influenced him. Alan Watts was an Episcopal priest who quit the church and became a Buddhist. His many books, such as *The Way of Zen* and *Beat Zen*, had a major impact on the counter-culture of the 1960s. Understandably in a multicultural global civilization, such traditions are now even more evident.[31]

- **Theosophy**—Theosophical traditions in Western thought can be traced back to the Renaissance. However, in modern parlance, it specifically refers to the Theosophical Society established in 1875 by Madame Blavatsky. Theosophy drew on the Buddhist, Hindu, and Western esoteric traditions to provide an amalgam of spiritual ideas. In many ways, theosophy was a forerunner to the New Age movement.

- **Counter-culture**—the late 1960s and early 1970s were exciting times of political and social upheaval where the baby-boomers experimented with alternative lifestyles, mind-altering drugs, and Eastern gurus. The counter-culture was the immediate cradle from which New Age spirituality emerged in the late 1980s as a mainstream social phenomenon.[32]

- **Occult**—the word "occult" means the secret, esoteric, or hidden things. Throughout human history there have been a variety of esoteric traditions where such practices as divination and shamanism have flourished. Since the 1970s various forms of occultism have been popular in the Western world.[33]

- **Human potential movement**—the elements of this, which we discuss at length in chapter 10, develop out of the work of Freud, Jung, Maslow, Erickson, and Perls. The basic belief is in attaining "peak experiences" through an array of power of the mind techniques. Courses progressively disclose how to become a metaphysical master as you script your own destiny and understand verbal and non-verbal forms of communication. Major power of the mind gurus include Master Charles, Andrew Cohen, Wayne Dyer, Werner Erhard, Eric Jensen, John Kehoe, Harry Palmer, Anthony Robbins, Michael Rowlands, Jose Silva, and Stuart Wilde.[34]

- **Hermeticism**—as mentioned earlier, the ancient hermetic literature and the hermetic traditions of alchemy, astrology, Qabalah, and tarot are sources of inspiration for New Age spirituality.[35]

- **Western consumerism**—spirituality has become a commodity with consumers purchasing transformation technology. New Age spirituality exhibitions have a strong commercial component as workshop facilitators and exhibitors promote their goods and services to the consuming public. New Age spirituality devotees have at times bought up raw materials—ideas and practices—found in ancient spiritual traditions to produce an entirely new package.

- **Postmodernity**—with the basic collapse of modernity as a viable worldview, the postmodern critique emphasizes how the individuals find their own sense of meaning: whatever works for you. For some people this leads to a secular outlook, while others feel personal meaning is available in spirituality. The New Age spirituality at present seems best suited to a postmodern mindset that is receptive to spiritual journeys.

Assessing apologetic responses

So far, we have considered the shape of New Age spirituality. We now want to explore how Christians have responded to it. This then sets the scene for explaining our incarnational approach.

As Hexham and Poewe propose, New Age spirituality can be understood as a distinct culture with its own cosmologies, spiritual myths and symbols, and a spiritual language that gives seekers an attractive vision of who they are and who they might become. As a culture in its own right, New Age spirituality constitutes a mission field. Once we start conceiving of it as a mission field, we must necessarily begin considering how we will present the unchanging good news of Jesus Christ.

Since the 1980s, Christians have been prolific in writing about New Age spirituality. However, only a few have paused to both survey and reflect on the cogency and quality of the material.[36] Apologetics is the discipline of giving reasons for faith and certain apologetic styles have predominated in responding to this spirituality.

END-TIMES CONSPIRACIES

Constance Cumbey and Texe Marrs responded to New Age spirituality by interpreting it as a gigantic conspiracy that poses a terrible threat to the church. The conspiracy model is unsound for a number of reasons. One concerns the source material cited by these authors. Too often they naively accept at face value the statements they quote and fail to consider their evidential worth.

Another concern is that conspiracy theories are a species of anti-Semitic thought.[37] Apologists such as Elliot Miller have astutely shown how Cumbey misinterprets New Age sources and makes absurd allegations.[38] Dave Hunt builds scenarios about end times prophecies that are based in conspiracy theories. The trouble with his model is it "cries wolf" about fulfilled prophecy. Douglas Cowan has demonstrated that Hunt's quotations are often inaccurate, cast the person quoted in the worst possible light, or are simply out of context.[39] This model is reactionary and fearful and, by misconstruing the search as a sinister conspiracy, the apologist fails to recognize that here is a culture that needs to be reached.

SPIRITUAL WARFARE

Frank Peretti's novels also rest at times on a conspiracy theory and, in this context, his remedy is fighting demons. But missiologists have pointed out that Peretti's view of the demonic is animistic—either good or bad spirits cause whatever happens to us. That is not consistent with the Bible. While not intentional, his novels may stimulate fear by demonizing New Age spirituality rather than focusing on presenting meaningful answers to seekers.[40]

James Lewis feels that there is an unhealthy fascination with the occult in Peretti's novels, to the point where the tactics of the good guys and bad guys mirror each other. Lewis notes how some prominent televangelists now hold spiritual combat crusades based on Peretti's books. He makes this provocative observation:

◆

Peretti's writings have encouraged charismatics and fundamentalists to adopt an attitude of greater hostility to the non-Christian world by providing quasi-theological justifications and dramatized prayer-exorcism tactics for attacking Satan's forces—the net effect, for readers who buy into Peretti's version of Christianity, is to bring

Christians closer in spirit to the very form of occult spir-
ituality they claim to despise: the New Age movement.[41]

◆

The great danger, then, is that Peretti's fictional tactics can be used as a substitute for evangelism. The seeker may simply be viewed as a mere pawn in a dramatic role-playing cosmic battle between the forces of good and evil. When spiritual combat becomes the sole priority, then evangelism, mission, and apologetics recede into the distance. Spiritual warfare is assuredly a biblical truth, but it must be kept in balance with other biblical teachings.

APOSTATE TESTIMONIES

Some former New Age spirituality pilgrims have shared their spiritual autobiographies in print. While their journeys need to be given a good hearing, we must also remember that people often reinterpret events. Like a "reformed smoker," they may recast their sojourns as utterly evil or demonic. Very few seem prepared to acknowledge how their spiritual quests positively opened them up to search for Christ.

HERESY-RATIONALIST APOLOGETIC

Some apologists contrast New Age beliefs with the Bible, holding up the cross of Christ in protest at it. Others, such as Elliot Miller and Douglas Groothuis, have astutely demonstrated obvious differences in belief between Christianity and New Age spirituality. The great benefit of this approach is in highlighting for the Christian what is biblical teaching and what is not scriptural. This model resembles the work of the early church apologists who defined and defended orthodox beliefs in the face of heresies.

Good mission should flow out of good teaching, but few apologists have extensive field experience in sharing with devotees and seekers. Consequently, they rarely offer any practical suggestions about how to understand the search and how to effectively share the Good News. What is often overlooked is that this spirituality is addressing serious questions to the church—to see it as a mirror in which we find ourselves reflected for what we have neglected to do as Christ's disciples.

A close reflection on this literature is that few seekers appear to have been introduced to Christ. The quality and cogency of apologetic literature varies, and regrettably, a minority of highly educated apologists indulge in the academic sin of plagiarism.[42] Douglas Cowan has suggested in his thesis that many writers, whether intentionally or not, have actually become propagandists to the church by manipulating and misquoting what New Age spirituality stands for. Cowan concludes that they act as gate-wardens fending off alien teachings whenever they impinge on the Christian believer. John Saliba remarks that most of these responses simply constitute a soliloquy or monologue inside the church. He observes that:

> It [the church] cannot engage New Agers in a fruitful exchange of ideas or in a constructive discussion on ideological standpoints, spiritual goals, and practical agendas—[it] fails to give real witness to the Christian message of the Good News, because its methods and message are more attuned to elicit fear and anxiety and to dwell on foreboding and pessimistic outlooks for the future. Moreover it unintentionally confirms negative impressions of, and elicits antagonistic feelings towards, Christianity.[43]

Incarnational mission

The concept of incarnational mission is grounded in both scripture and the history of Christian mission. Down the centuries, missionaries have sought to understand the cosmology, cuisine, culture, and customs of those people they wanted to reach with the gospel. Classically, missionaries have joined the tribe and communicated the gospel in culturally meaningful ways. Attempts to completely dismantle a culture and debunk its values have invariably created havoc. The gospel certainly stands above all cultures, but the disciples of Christ must live and practice their faith within culture. We see this worked out in the New Testament where the Gentiles were not obliged to adopt Hebrew customs such as circumcision and kosher cuisine (see Acts 15).

Jesus Christ said to the disciples, "As the Father has sent me, I am sending you" (John 20:21, NIV-UK). In that commission, Jesus indicates that just as God became flesh—incarnated as a human and taught within a particular culture—so we must also incarnate the gospel by living and sharing inside other cultures.

It is easy to cope with the idea of mission taking place outside the Western world where many peoples have neither bibles nor a church. To reconsider our Western cities as venues for mission probably sounds odd, especially when we have been trained in basic techniques of evangelism (Campus Crusade, Navigators, Evangelism Explosion, Christianity Explained, Alpha, Life Works, and The Y Course). These programs have all been blessed by God, and we have happily used them in ministry and seen people won to God's Kingdom.

However, we are persuaded that they are now only really effective with the God-fearers who inhabit the fringes of our congregations. Most non-Christians have no background of relatedness with the local church and are unlikely to respond positively to invitations to attend these discipleship courses. One reason for this is that these courses are highly cognitive, crammed with information, but with minimal opportunities for personal exploration and spiritual experiences to occur. The seekers' important questions remain un-addressed because such courses are structured to deal with the questions we think it is important for them to have answers to. It is analogous to a door-to-door salesperson promoting ice chests to owners of refrigerators—who needs the ice chest?

In today's global civilization, Christianity is declining in the West while simultaneously growing in Africa, Asia, and Latin America. Western Christians need to recall Paul's missionary model to become "all things to all people" (see 1 Cor. 9:16-22). As we now live side by side with Buddhists, Hindus, Muslims, and New Age spirituality seekers, older formulaic techniques for sharing must give way to incarnational mission, which is not only biblical but also pertinent to living in postmodernity.

A classic example of incarnational mission and apologetics is found in Acts 17. Paul went to Athens. He shared his faith in the synagogue with Jewish people who believed the Hebrew Scriptures. He established a dialogue with them about Jesus being the Messiah foretold in their Scriptures. Here they had a common background and understanding.

However, when Paul tried to transfer this dialogue to outside the synagogue, he encountered Greek people who had no background of knowledge or belief in the Hebrew Scriptures. Paul entered their world and culture. He sought some common ground with the Greek philosophers as an entry point to sharing his faith. He commended the Athenians for their religious search and, although their idols offended him, he did not start a campaign to smash their objects of devotion or demonize them. He built up more common ground on the basis of a creation theology, affirming the unity of humanity in creation and the supremacy of God over the creation. Paul chose to quote the Stoic philosophers (Epimenides, Aratus, and Cleanthes in Acts 17:28) in a favorable way, confirming what was true in their insights, yet building on them to God's revelation in Jesus. He spoke about the resurrection, righteousness, and judgment, which was consistent with his preaching everywhere else. However, he never quoted the Bible to his audience, simply because they did not know its contents. That day, some people came to faith, others wanted to know more, and some scoffed.

Sadly, some Christians have mistakenly claimed that Paul failed in Athens. Those who believe Paul failed tend to offer three criticisms.

- If Paul was a success in Athens, then why do we never hear more about this church in the New Testament. The fact that nothing more is said about Athens surely proves he was a failure.
- Paul's message contains too much Greek philosophy, and this is worldly wisdom.
- Paul was not Christ-centered in Athens, and he admits this in 1 Corinthians 2:1-3.

We believe that these sincerely held convictions are inconsistent with the biblical data for the following reasons.

- The fact that we never hear about Athens cannot be construed as proof that Paul was a failure. There are many places referred to in Acts where the apostles visited for which there is no corresponding epistle: Antioch, Berea, Derbe, Iconium, Lystra, Malta, Paphos, Rhodes, and Troas. The fact that some places did receive an apostolic letter is not a litmus test for success either. Not one of the seven churches of Revelation exists today, yet a church has existed in Athens for almost 2,000 years.
- Paul was invited by the philosophers to speak because he was already speaking about Jesus and the resurrection (Acts 17:18), and not because he was flirting with Greek philosophy. Paul was indeed Christ-centered because he shared about Jesus (Acts 17:18, 31).
- As to 1 Corinthians 2:1-3 indicating a change of heart in Paul, Don Carson points out that this argument is both illogical and involves an incorrect interpretation of the texts. The logical fallacy (technically known as *cum hoc, propter hoc*) mistakes correlation for causation. Carson remarks:

---◆---

An example of cum hoc, propter hoc *that occurs frequently in evangelical preaching runs as follows: Paul in his Athenian address (Acts 17:22-31) erred in trying to approach his hearers philosophically rather than biblically, and his own acknowledgement of his error turned up in 1 Corinthians, where he pointed out that, at Corinth, the next stop after Athens, he resolved to know nothing while he was with them except Jesus Christ and him crucified (1 Corinthians 2:2). This exegesis seriously misunderstands the address at the Areopagus and Luke's purpose in telling it; but it also connects pieces of information from two separate documents and without evidence affirms a causal connection: because Paul allegedly failed miserably in Athens, therefore he resolved to return to his earlier practice. In fact, there is a geographical and temporal correlation (Paul did travel from Athens to Corinth), but not a shred of evidence for causation.44*

---◆---

Paul's remarks to the Corinthians need to be read in the context of the epistle. After commending the Corinthians (see 1 Corinthians 1:7), Paul tackles a series of problems dividing the congregation. Some were into guru devotion, breaking into factions centered on a favorite apostle. Paul rebukes them for chasing human oratory and human wisdom. It is in the midst of theological anarchy that Paul reminds them that they need to be Christ-centered.

Finally, scholars such as E.M. Blaiklock, F.F. Bruce, J.D. Charles, David Hesselgrave, Alister McGrath, John Warwick Montgomery, and Ned Stonehouse all agree that Acts 17 is a handsome illustration of the incarnational mission model we should all be using today, particularly with those who are unfamiliar with the Bible.45

Incarnational Mission Work

Missionaries such as Patrick and Columba mirrored what Paul undertook in Athens. They interacted with the native pagan culture and religious symbols of the Irish and Celtic peoples. Their principal method for communication was hymnology and church art in a biblically illiterate world. In modern times, the most striking incarnational work with Muslims was pioneered by Samuel Zwemer and continues on with the likes of Phil Parshall. Narayan Vaman Tilak and Lakshmibai Tilak offered a good incarnational model for reaching high caste Hindus that today has finally been recognized as the way forward in India. Similarly, John Farquhar's model of Christ as the crown of Hinduism still has much to offer. The same can be said of Karl Ludvig Reichelt's approach to Chinese Buddhists. Don Richardson's *Peace Child* explains how he had to find redemptive analogies in the Sawi culture of Irian Jaya. Mark Mullins has similarly highlighted the incarnational work of indigenous Japanese churches.[46]

In the same way our plea is for incarnational mission to be swiftly taken up as the most effective way of impacting not only New Age spirituality seekers, but all of Western culture. This model takes note of the strengths of the apologetic models we have assessed, but at the same time leaves the fortress of the church and enters the seeker's world. We believe that some apologists may have inadvertently overlooked the application of incarnational mission principles with new spirituality devotees. What we are advocating is nothing new, because other evangelical apologists have already shown how it can be applied to mystic and occult spirituality.[47]

We believe our call is in the exact same spirit as that which was expressed at the Lausanne Committee for World Evangelization meeting at Pattaya, Thailand, in June 1980. The Lausanne Occasional Paper Christian Witness to the New Religions, which issued out of the Thailand conference, clearly linked evangelism to the new religions with the model of Paul's Areopagus speech and acknowledged the need to find common ground in mission. Walter Martin (1928-89), the US pioneer of the heresy rationalist model of counter-cult apologetics, nonetheless expressed similar sentiments about finding common ground with devotees using Paul's principle of "all things to all people" (see 1 Cor. 9:22) in his magnum opus *The Kingdom of the Cults*. Dr. Ronald Enroth, professor of sociology at Westmont College in Santa Barbara, and David Fetcho, the co-founder of the Spiritual Counterfeits Project, have also noted the role of incarnational mission to alternative spirituality.[48]

HOW WE STARTED AN INCARNATIONAL MINISTRY

"Why do you guys go to alternative spiritual exhibitions?" Christians and secular journalists often ask us this question. For us, these are gatherings where Jesus would obviously be touching seekers. We feel it is normal for Christians to be involved. Here are people hungry for a spirituality that takes them beyond the facts, figures, and deadlines of their nine-to-five daily grind.

We want to be among those who crave that authentic inner life and who will not settle for simplistic answers to their deep questions. These are people who need the Lord Jesus Christ. These eshibitions are the best placesto be for anyone into evangelism, mission, and apologetics.

In 1990, the two of us, independent of each other, visited a major crowd-drawing New Age festival that had just opened in our hometown. When we entered the venue we were staggered: this was culture shock. What a contrast between reading about this spirituality and being caught up in a huge crowd of seekers. Was this how Paul felt when he visited Athens (see Acts 17:16)? We spent the whole day soaking up the atmosphere, observing the activities and the kinds of people attending—their gender, age group, social class, and attire. We considered how the stands were decorated and operated and asked ourselves, "What is it that makes this exhibit attractive?" We spent time browsing the literature and watched public performances on the stage. Then we struck up conversations with exhibitors and patrons alike and sought opportunities to talk about Christ.

When the day was over, we were both exhausted and buffeted by mixed feelings. Several stands appalled and disturbed us in terms of what they offered as spiritual truth. We were pained to see so many people earnestly searching and sampling. We asked ourselves, "Where is the church? Why is there no Christian witness taking place?" We pondered, should we stand outside the venue handing out tracts in the hope of dissuading people? We realized how antagonistic that would seem and futile it would be. We quickly concluded that we ought to be inside the festival and our thoughts turned to how we could have a stand.

Philip wrote two articles about this challenge.[49] When Ross spotted one of them, he phoned, and we decided to team up. Ross then approached the organizers about the feasibility of joining the following year's festival. There was real excitement about our proposal of running a stand that featured healing in the form of the laying on of hands, prayer, and a video on Jesus. However, as the proposal began to unfold, clouds of concern enveloped the conversation. "Hey, who are you guys? What's this all about?" Ross said that we represented a group of people who empathized with those who, like us, are involved in a spiritual pilgrimage. We wanted to share our journey with Jesus. Surely as they felt that all pathways are valid, how could they exclude followers of Jesus? Their hesitation was now most apparent. "Let us think about this and call you back." And they did!

Once our application was accepted, we canvassed financial support and named our stand "The Community of Hope."[50] We then began to work on devising an appropriate display. We considered what sort of literature would be suitable and set a timetable for training volunteers to man the stand.

The 1991 festival was our baptism of fire. Despite many years of study, training, and experience in evangelism and apologetics, we still had much to learn. Although it was an exhilarating time, when we had a post-festival debrief, we recognized several things. First, our witnessing encounters quickly revealed how shallow our preconceptions were. We had taken a strong adversarial stance of "us" versus "them," and it had often inhibited effective communication. So, we appreciate what a struggle it can be to stop viewing this spirituality solely as a threat and switch to seeing it as an opportunity to make disciples. We also discovered the drawbacks to simply deconstructing and debunking a seeker's experiences. Most took umbrage at our being dismissive of their journey. We also found that some of our volunteers were temperamentally ill suited to this type of outreach.

Ever since that initial venture, we have been active in many more in various cities. Like Paul in Athens, we positively interact with the myths, symbols, and practices of the culture so that the message of Christ will make sense to them. When talking with seekers, we have found that Christian jargon can be a stumbling block. More effective communication occurs when we use words that the non-Christian understands, so we sometimes use the expression "soul-sorrow" when speaking of sin. We also refer to the Bible as the *Christian Sacred Writings* or *Hebrew-Christian scriptures*. The rest of this book shows how seekers can discover "the unknown God" by starting from where they are.

We never stop learning new ways of doing things and are continually reassessing what we do. We are persuaded that our ministry at the festivals is just one of many different and effective ways to make contact with today's seekers. It takes Christians beyond the walls of the church (where efforts to reach them often have mixed results) and places us directly in the marketplace as it was in the apostolic era. (You will find more practical advice about how to conduct your own ministries like ours in chapter 13.) Now, let us introduce you to today's New Age spirituality seekers.

Endnotes

Chapter 1

[1] Nevill Drury, *Exploring the Labyrinth: Making Sense of the New Spirituality*, Sydney: Allen & Unwin, 1999, p. 177.

[2] Walter Martin, *The New Age Cult*, Minneapolis: Bethany, 1989, p. 35.

[3] John A. Saliba, *Christian Responses to the New Age Movement*, London: Geoffrey Chapman, 1999, p. 231

[4] Phil Rickman, *Midwinter of the Spirit*, London: Macmillan, p. 39. The ellipses are in the original text.

[5] Jay Kinney, "Dissecting the New Age," *Gnosis*, 49, 1998, pp. 14-17.

[6] See Saliba, *Christian Responses to the New Age Movement*, p. viii.

[7] John Drane, *What is the New Age Still Saying to the Church?*, London: Marshall Pickering, 1999.

[8] See Zygmunt Bauman, *Intimations of Postmodernity*, Oxford: Basil Blackwell, 1992; and Paul Heelas, David Martin and Paul Morris (eds), *Religion, Modernity*.

[9] Theophilus Parsons, *Outlines of the Religion and Philosophy of Swedenborg*, Boston: Roberts Brothers, 1876; Signe Toksvig, *Emanuel Swedenborg: Scientist and Mystic*, London: Faber & Faber, 1948; and J.K. Van Baalen, *The Chaos of Cults*, 4th revised edition, Grand Rapids: Wm.B. Eerdmans, 1962.

[10] For introductions to Freemasonry, see David Stevenson, *The Origins of Freemasonry: Scotland's Century 1590-1710*, Cambridge: Cambridge University Press, 1988; and Alexander Piatigorsky, *Who's Afraid of Freemasons?* London: Harvill Press, 1997. On the satanic hoax, see Christopher McIntosh, *Eliphas Levi and the French Occult Revival*, London: Rider, 1972, pp. 207-218.

[11] Misunderstandings do occur in evangelical anti-Masonic literature, and readers need to be discerning.

[12] John Warwick Montgomery, *Cross and Crucible*, 2 volumes, The Hague: Martinus Nijhoff, 1973; Frances A. Yates, *The Rosicrucian Enlightenment*, London: Routledge & Kegan Paul, 1972; and J. Gordon Melton (ed.), *Rosicrucianism in America*, New York: Garland, 1990.

[13] Christopher McIntosh, *Eliphas Levi and the French Occult Revival*, London: Rider, 1972.

[14] R.A. Gilbert, *Revelations of the Golden Dawn: The Rise and Fall of a Magical Order*, London: Quantum, 1997.

[15] Eric J. Sharpe, *The Universal Gita: Western Images of the Bhagavadgita*—a bicentenary survey, La Salle, Illinois: Open Court, 1985, pp. 15-31.

[16] J. Stillson Judah, *The History and Philosophy of the Metaphysical Movements in America*, Philadelphia: Westminster Press, 1967.

[17] Sylvia Cranston, *HPB: The Extraordinary Life and Influence of Helena Blavatsky, Founder of the Modern Theosophical Movement*, New York: Jeremy P. Tarcher/Putnam, 1993; Robert Ellwood, *Theosophy: A Modern Expression of the Wisdom of the Ages*, Wheaton: Quest, 1986; and Jill Roe, *Beyond Belief: Theosophy*

in Australia 1879-1939, Kensington, New South Wales: New South Wales University Press, 1986.

[18] Greg Tillett, *The Elder Brother: A Biography of Charles Webster Leadbeater*, London: Routledge & Kegan Paul, 1982, p. 4.

[19] J. Gordon Melton, Jerome Clark and Aidan A. Kelly, *New Age Almanac*, Detroit: Visible Ink, 1991, pp. 9-12 and 315-17.

[20] J. Gordon Melton, Jerome Clark and Aidan A. Kelly, *New Age Almanac*, pp. 30-31.

[21] Richard Noll, *The Jung Cult*, London: Fontana, 1996; and Robert Ellwood, *The Politics of Myth: A Study of C.G. Jung, Mircea Eliade and Joseph Campbell*, Albany: State University of New York Press, 1999.

[22] John Drane, *What is the New Age Still Saying to the Church?*, London: Marshall Pickering, 1999, pp. 13-14.

[23] Paul Heelas, David Martin and Paul Morris (eds), *Religion, Modernity and Postmodernity*, Oxford and Malden, Massachusetts: Blackwell, 1998.

[24] Gordon Lewis, "*The Church and the New Spirituality*," Journal of the Evangelical Theological Society, 36, 4, 1993, p.434.

[25] Irving Hexham and Karla Poewe, *New Religions as Global Cultures*, Boulder: Westview, 1997; Wouter J. Hanegraaff, *New Age Religion and Western Culture*, Albany: State University of New York Press, 1998, pp. 119-120 and 520-521; and Paul Heelas, *The New Age Movement: The Celebration of the Self and the Sacralization of Modernity*, Oxford and Cambridge, Massachusetts: Blackwell, 1996.

[26] Wouter Hanegraaff, *New Age Religion and Western Culture*, pp.113-181.

[27] See Sangharakshita, *Vision and Transformation*, Birmingham: Windhorse, 1990; Thich Nhat Hanh, *Being Peace*, London: Rider, 1987; William Hart, *The Art of Living: Vipassana Meditation as Taught by S.N. Goenka*, San Francisco: Harper, 1987; and Dalai Lama, *The Power of Compassion*, London: Thorsons, 1995.

[28] John Drane, *What is the New Age Still Saying to the Church?*, London: Marshall Pickering, 1999, pp. 68-80.

[29] Hanegraaff, *New Age Religion and Western Culture*, pp. 77-89.

[30] Hanegraaff, *New Age Religion and Western Culture*, pp. 384-401.

[31] See Robert S. Ellwood, *Islands of the Dawn: The story of Alternative Spirituality in New Zealand*, Honolulu: University of Hawaii Press, 1993, pp. 19-26; Philip Jenkins, *Mystics and Messiahs: Cults and New Religions in American History*, New York: Oxford University Press, 2000, pp. 25-45; William Lawton, *Being Christian, Being Australian*, Sydney: Lancer, 1988, pp. 84-102; and Donald S. Lopez (ed.), *Curators of the Buddha*, Chicago and London: University of Chicago Press, 1995.

[32] Theodore Roszak, *The Making of a Counter Culture*, New York: Doubleday, 1968; and Os Guinness, *The Dust of Death*, Leicester: InterVarsity Press, 1973.

[33] John Warwick Montgomery, *Principalities and Powers*, Minneapolis: Bethany, 1973.

[34] Nevill Drury, *Exploring the Labyrinth*, Sydney: Allen & Unwin, 1999, pp. 11-27

and 102-124; and Carl Raschke, "The Human Potential Movement," *Theology Today*, 33, 3, 1976, pp. 253-262.

35 Roelof van den Broek and Wouter J. Hanegraaff, *Gnosis and Hermeticism: From Antiquity to Modern Times*, Albany: State University of New York Press, 1998.

36 Exceptions include Irving Hexham, "The Evangelical Response to the New Age" in James R. Lewis and J. Gordon Melton (eds), *Perspectives on the New Age*, Albany: State University of New York Press, 1992, pp. 152-163; John Drane, "Methods and Perspectives in Understanding the New Age," *Themelios*, 23, 2, 1998, pp. 22-34; John A. Saliba, *Christian Responses to the New Age Movement: A Critical Assessment*, London: Geoffrey Chapman, 1999; and Philip Johnson, "The Aquarian Age and Apologetics," *Lutheran Theological Journal*, 34, 2, 2000, pp. 51-60.

37 On the weaknesses in conspiracy theories, see Gregory S. Camp, *Selling Fear: Conspiracy Theories and End-Times Paranoia*, Grand Rapids: Baker, 1997; and Paul Coughlin, *Secrets, Plots and Hidden Agendas*, Downers Grove: InterVarsity Press, 1999.

38 Elliot Miller, *A Crash Course on the New Age Movement*, Grand Rapids: Baker, 1989, pp. 193-206; and SCP Staff, "The Final Threat: Cosmic Conspiracy and End Times Speculation" in Karen Hoyt and J. Isamu Yamamoto (eds), *The New Age Rage*, Old Tappan: Fleming Revell, 1987, pp. 185-201.

39 Douglas E. Cowan, "Bearing False Witness: Propaganda, Reality-Maintenance, and Christian Anticult Apologetics," Ph.D. thesis, University of Calgary, 1999/Ann Arbor: Bell & Howell Information & Learning, 1999, pp. 367-593. Cowan also deals with Cumbey and Marrs on pp. 344-357.

40 On Peretti's novels, see Irving Hexham, "The Evangelical Response to the New Age" in James R. Lewis and J. Gordon Melton (eds), *Perspectives on the New Age*, Albany: State University of New York Press, 1992, pp. 156-157; and A. Scott Moreau, "Religious Borrowing as a Two-Way Street: An Introduction to Animistic Tendencies in the Euro-North American Context" in Edward Rommen and Harold Netland (eds), *Christianity and the Religions*, Pasadena: William Carey Library, 1995, pp. 166-183.

41 James R. Lewis, "Works of Darkness: Occult Fascination in the Novels of Frank E. Peretti" in James R. Lewis (ed.), *Magickal Religion and Modern Witchcraft*, Albany: State University of New York Press, 1996, pp. 342, 348.

42 One small example, of several that could be cited from the same text, is John P. Newport, *The New Age Movement and the Biblical Worldview*, Grand Rapids: Wm.B. Eerdmans, 1998. Compare Newport on pp. 6-7 under the subheading "Reincarnation and Karma" with J. Gordon Melton, Jerome Clark and Aidan A. Kelly (eds), *New Age Almanac*, Detroit: Visible Ink, 1991, p. 89.

43 John A. Saliba, *Christian Responses to the New Age Movement: A Critical Assessment*, London: Geoffrey Chapman, 1999, pp. 77-78; and Philip Johnson, "The Aquarian Age and Apologetics," Lutheran Theological Journal, 34, 2, 2000, pp. 51-60.

44 D.A. Carson, *Exegetical Fallacies*, Grand Rapids: Baker, 1984, p. 134.

45 E.M. Blaiklock, "The Areopagus Address," *Faith and Thought*, 93, 3, 1964, pp.

175-191; F.F. Bruce, *Paul: Apostle of the Free Spirit,* revised edition, Exeter: Paternoster, 1980, pp. 235-247; J. Daryl Charles, "Engaging the (Neo) Pagan Mind: Paul's Encounter with Athenian Culture as a Model for Cultural Apologetics,"Trinity Journal 16NS, 1995, pp. 47-62; David J. Hesselgrave, *Communicating Christ Cross-Culturally,* 2nd edition, Grand Rapids: Zondervan, 1991, p. 40; Alister McGrath, *Bridge Building,* Leicester: InterVarsity Press, 1992, pp. 49, 231-233; John Warwick Montgomery, *Faith Founded on Fact,* Nashville: Thomas Nelson, 1978, pp.36-38; and Ned Stonehouse, *Paul Before the Areopagus and Other New Testament Addresses,* London: Tyndale, 1957, pp. 1-40.

[46] See David J. Hesselgrave and Edward Rommen, *Contextualization: Meanings, Methods and Models,* Grand Rapids: Baker, 1989; A. Scott Moreau (ed.), *Evangelical Dictionary of World Missions,* Grand Rapids: Baker, 2000; Mark R, Mullins, *Christianity Made in Japan,* Honolulu: University of Hawaii Press, 1998; Phil Parshall, *New Paths in Muslim Evangelism,* Grand Rapids: Baker, 1980; H.L. Richard, *Following Jesus in the Hindu Context,* Pasadena: William Carey Library, 1998; Don Richardson, *Peace Child,* Glendale: Regal, 1974; Eric J. Sharpe, *Not to Destroy But to Fulfil,* Lund, Sweden: Gleerup, 1965; and Eric J. Sharpe, *Karl Ludvig Reichelt: Missionary, Scholar and Pilgrim,* Hong Kong: Tao Fong Shan Ecumenical Centre, 1984.

[47] For example, consider the apologetic approach of John Warwick Montgomery in his apologia to the occult, *Principalities & Powers,* Minneapolis: Bethany, 1973.

[48] See Lausanne Occasional Papers: The Thailand Report on New Religious Movements at www.gospelcom.net/lcwe/LOP/lop11.htm; Walter Martin, *The Kingdom of the Cults,* revised edition, Minneapolis: Bethany, 1997, p. 453; Ronald Enroth (ed.), *Evangelising the Cults,* Milton Keynes: Word, 1990; pp. 19-20; and David Fetcho, "Disclosing the Unknown God: Evangelism to the New Religions," *Update,* 6, 4, 1982, pp. 7-16.

[49] Philip Johnson, "Now the (New Age) Carnival is Over," *Take A Closer Look,* 11, December 1990, p. 11, and "It's True for You, but not for Me," *Australian Presbyterian Living Today,* February 1991, p. 31.

[50] The Community of Hope is the frontline ministry of Global Apologetics & Mission Inc., which operates in several states of Australia. We can be contacted at PO Box 367, Hurstville, New South Wales, 1481, Australia, and at PO Box 54, Seville Vic, 3139, Australia.

Chapter 2
Angel Phenomena

---◆---

No one who has seen an angel ever mistakes it for a ghost. Angels are remarkable for their warmth and light, and all who see them speak in awe of their iridescent and refulgent light, of brilliant colors, or else of the unbearable whiteness of their being. You are flooded with laughter, happiness.[1]

It is not right to place too much emphasis on angels. Perhaps if we could keep angels in their right perspective, neither overemphasizing them, nor refusing to recognize their validity, we would be allowed to see them more often.[2]

For he will command his angels concerning you to guard you in all your ways (Ps. 91:11, NIV-UK).

---◆---

"As we lay hands on Helen, we ask that she might be released from her painful back complaint, that she might have strength in her spine and will know peace in her personal journey." After our prayers, Helen thanked us and joined her friends. Vanessa, who was in her early twenties, came over to our stand for a chat.

"I couldn't help but notice your slogan on the display board— 'On life's journey it's great to have friends in high places.' I love it. It's so colorful and those angels are really jazzy. You know I believe there are angels and that they can help us on the journey," she told us. "I joined in Denise Linn's workshop on angels this morning. It was awesome! Now I am determined to get closer to my guardian angel." Vanessa said how she had had several intuitive encounters where she was aware of an invisible presence accompanying her. "I feel so at ease in these moments, because I know that someone is out there looking after me."

I (Philip) immediately connected with Vanessa. "I have had three encounters with angels involving healing, guidance, and protection," I said. Vanessa smiled and begged me to recount them. I told Vanessa that the first occurred when I was a child.

I had developed ingrown warts on my heels, which made it difficult to walk. The local doctor had visited and advised that the only available treatment was to cut them out. The prospect of surgery can be terrifying for a child, and as the day drew near I was scared stiff. My parents, however, set a great example for me of prayer and faith. As I lay in bed, they encouraged me to ask God to do something about it.

Feeling somewhat shy, I insisted that they leave the room. I then asked in a very simple way for God to fix my feet. After praying, an angel appeared and touched my feet. I called out to my parents and told them that an angel had just touched my feet. Although they heard me, they did not come into the room. They thought that I was imagining things, but I persisted in saying my feet had been touched, and when they looked, the warts were gone!

Vanessa was rapt, and so I briefly described my two other encounters. I showed her a copy of our book *Riding the Rollercoaster* where my stories are retold.[3] Vanessa bought it, but there was so much more to talk about. We were fellow travelers with a common interest.

More angel stories

Angels are found in major religious traditions such as Zoroastrianism, Judaism, Christianity, and Islam. Through the ages, angelic intercessions have been celebrated in prayers, poetry, and art. Angels have been regularly depicted in three tarot cards: The Lovers,

Judgment, and Temperance. The 1990s saw an explosion of revived interest in them, so we started talking about how other people—celebrities and ordinary folk alike—have angel stories to share. Sir Ernest Shackleton, the Antarctic explorer, reputedly said that on one expedition an angel accompanied his team. Similarly, Francis Smythe, who attempted a solo ascent of Mount Everest in 1933, was aware of an invisible companion during the climb. However Smythe was unsure if this presence was real or a hallucination.[4]

Hope Macdonald in her book *When Angels Appear*, has collected 50 contemporary stories of encounters with angels.[5] She relates the story of three-year-old Lisa. Lisa was playing on the railroad tracks that abutted on to the backyard of her home. Lisa's mother was in the kitchen and, on looking out, saw that the back gate was open and Lisa was on the train line. She heard an approaching train and, panic-stricken, she ran from the house screaming. She saw a figure, clothed in white, lift Lisa off the track. This figure stood with Lisa as the train passed by, but disappeared just as her mother reached her side. Joan Wester Anderson in her best-selling book *Where Angels Walk* has collected similar stories of children being rescued.[6]

Another story comes from Ecuador, and it is one of the most dramatic of the 20th century. Five young men went as missionaries to the Huaorani people in the Auca territory. These men were all speared to death as a result of a misunderstanding between them and the Huaorani tribesmen. Later, Elisabeth Elliot, a widow of one of the men and the sister of another, went to live with the Huaorani. Many of the tribe came to accept the missionaries' aid and embraced faith in God.

Almost 50 years later, the full story has now come to light about what happened on the day the missionaries died. Steve Saint, a son of one of the men killed, has spoken to some of the tribesmen who were present at the slaying. They spoke of hearing singing as the men were dying, music like the sound of a choir, which at the time was unknown to these people. Figures were seen above the trees and others along the ridge. There was talk of lights moving around and shining, a sky full of "fire flies." The men said that, at the time, they felt scared because it was something supernatural. Steve Saint has mused about his father passing over to the other side in the presence of angels.[7]

Popular signposts

A few years ago, five of the ten American religious bestsellers for the year were books about angels. In 1994 a CNN/USA Today/Gallup poll ascertained that 72 percent of those surveyed believed in the existence of angels. The workshop Vanessa attended was packed and more than three-quarters of the participants claimed to have encountered angels. Shortly after a major New Age spirituality exhibition in another city, Philip also convened an angel workshop and many of the participants had angel stories to tell. Vanessa said she subscribed to the magazine *Angel Times* where there are regular contributions about angel encounters, angel art, books and CDs. We chatted about how popular magazines such as *Life* have devoted cover stories to the subject.[8]

Vanessa had enjoyed the two-hour prime-time special *Angels: The Mysterious Messengers* (broadcast in Australia and the USA), which was hosted by Patty Duke. We reminisced about the TV fantasy series *Touched by an Angel* and the movies *Michael*, starring John Travolta, and *City of Angels*, with Nicolas Cage and Meg Ryan. Neither of us felt that these series and films offered anything particularly spiritual. We had checked out the highly popular "angelnet" on the Internet, which has had more than seven million visitors since its inception. We also swapped notes about our respective favorite books about angels.

Skeptics about angels

Of course not everyone has welcomed the upsurge of interest in angels. There are the traditional rationalists and skeptics who dismiss out of hand any reports of spiritual phenomena. On the positive side, skeptics goad us on to discern, question, and thoroughly examine claims and spiritual manifestations. The skeptics have exposed con artists and religious hucksters. However, skepticism tends to be primarily concerned with debunking claims, and many skeptics seem to have a mindset that rigidly refuses to be open to any genuine spirituality.

Vanessa pointed out that even within New Age spirituality there are some teachers who regard angel phenomena with disdain. She had attended a workshop presented by Dick Sutphen. In his "Radical Spirituality" workshop she said that Sutphen challenged what he calls the "cosmic foo-foo" of angelic communications.[9] We responded by saying that Dick Sutphen's pathway is influenced more by Zen Buddhism and human potential concepts. In those traditions there is no room for metaphysical or spiritual beings such as angels. Zen masters love to use shock tactics to challenge devotees out of their "illusions about reality." As Sutphen has a reputation for being an anarchic teacher, it was not surprising to hear that he was applying this method in his workshop.

We came back to a basic legal principle on which our postmodern society rests. Before rendering a verdict, the jury or judge needs to examine the evidence. Eyewitness testimony must first be heard and then sifted for its truthfulness. So, we simply have to let people who claim they have seen angels tell their stories before we make any assessment. Only closed minds will presuppose from the outset that encounters with angels are impossible.

Seeking something spiritual

Vanessa felt that by exploring angel phenomena she could grow as a person and find spiritual nourishment. She shared how for two years she had been involved in an abusive relationship. The manipulation and lack of love she had experienced at the hands of her former partner left deep hurts and scars within. At death's door, she was longing for love. She said, "There were several times when I sensed someone invisible was there, and I heard a voice inside me say 'Get out quick!' and I soon did. The angels were looking after me just when I needed it most. Life can never be boring, and I know I'm not alone with the angels to guide me."

What Vanessa said reminded us of remarks made some years ago by the Danish scholar Johannes Aagaard:

———————————— ◆ ————————————

Humankind has three great problems: death, love, and boredom. Only religions that take all three seriously can make a go of it.[10]

———————————— ◆ ————————————

As far as Vanessa is concerned, the angels care for her, make life intuitively exciting, and bring her guidance. It was her abusive relationship that started her on a journey of reflection seeking spiritual meaning. For Vanessa, angels have become an open door to finding transformation.

We were appalled to hear how she had been subjected to abuse and exploitation. We acknowledged that her intuitive feelings about angels had obviously been a source of consolation and comfort in those painful experiences. We said that in our own times of desolation we draw comfort from the fact that we have friends in high places. Indeed, we feel that we relate to the ultimate friend. We indicated that angels are God's servants who may bring messages as a way of demonstrating how God cares for us.

Remembering the Sacred Writings

We then began to explore the Hebrew-Christian Sacred Writings where there are dozens of passages mentioning angels. The Hebrew word *malak* and the Greek word *angelos* both refer to a messenger or courier. In the majority of instances, these terms are used to refer to heavenly messengers. The Sacred Writings indicate what their nature, organization, and tasks are comprised of.

As to their nature, angels are created and ministering spirits (see Ps. 148:1-5, Heb. 1:14). Though they are spirits, they may appear in human form (such as in Luke 1-2, where Gabriel appears in human form). They are intelligent, have free will, and neither marry nor die (see 2 Sam. 14:20, Jude 6, Luke 20:34-36).

As to their organization, they have God as their head (see Ps. 148:1-5). They make up a heavenly court, comprising the Archangel Michael, an "ambassador" named Gabriel, guards—the cherubim, servants of God—the seraphim, and the heavenly hosts (see Jude 6, Luke 1:26, Ezek. 10, Isa. 6, Luke 2:13).

As to their tasks, they praise God, are God's messengers, and rejoice over our spiritual transformation (see Rev. 5:1-11, Matt. 1:20-21, Luke 15:10). They serve us, can bring strength to us, and protect us (see Heb. 1:14, Luke 22:43, Ps. 34:7, 2 Kings 6:8-17, Ps. 91:11-12). They are advocates for children, some would say as guardian angels (see Matt. 18:10). They are involved with the nations of earth, sometimes bring answers to prayer, and convey us to the other side (see Dan. 6; 10, Luke 16:22).

Edmund Spenser's famous poem *The Fairie Queene* wonderfully expresses some of these themes:[11]

How oft do they their silver bowers leave,
To come to succour us, that succour want!
How oft do they with golden pinions cleave
The flitting skies, like flying pursuivant,
Against foul fiends to aid us militant!
They for us fight, they watch and duly ward,
And their bright squadrons round about us plant,
And all for love, and nothing for reward—
O Why should heavenly God to men have such regard?
(II. viii. 2)

As angels are God's servants, we need to be wise. Here the old adage applies about not seeing the wood for the trees. That is, if we only look for angels, we will miss the far greater blessing of directly encountering God. To illustrate, we talked about how this difficulty plagued the ancient pilgrims known as the Gnostics.

Gnostic

The word "Gnostic" comes from the Greek word *gnosis*, meaning "knowledge." The Gnostics formed various religious movements, some of which were related to Christianity, some totally independent. They offered esoteric spiritual knowledge to those initiated into their ranks with secret rituals and code words. As a worldview, it was elitist. At the heart of their thought, reality was a duality of two realms: spirit and matter. They offset spirit over and against matter, where the spirit was paramount and the body or material world was disparaged as a prison. They became obsessed with celestial beings and offered a bewildering array of angelic catalogues. God was viewed as a remote being who could be best contacted through these intermediaries.[12]

In contrast to the Gnostics, the Sacred Writings confirm the appropriateness of staying within the God-given parameters of encountering angels. There is no need for secret initiations, rituals or code words when meeting angels. However, the angels do not seek our prayers or worship but point beyond themselves to the Creator (see Rev. 22:8-9). The Sacred Writings emphasize that God "is not far from each one of us" (Acts 17:27, NIV). God is a personal being who is present everywhere in the creation and active in sustaining our very life and breath. God seeks to get our attention and invites us into a divine relationship. So our focus should be on getting to know God personally, and in that context, angels may indeed participate in our journey.

Dark angels

In the angel workshop Vanessa had attended, the question was raised as to whether or not all angels are helpful and trustworthy. Across the religious spectrum we find that not all angels are good and positive. The tarot deck depicts the Devil on card 14. Tibetan Buddhist monks receive training in how to banish dark spirits or demons. In Islam, Muslims are familiar with the jinn—mischievous creatures made of smokeless flames that can appear as humans or animals. The Japanese new religious movement, Mahikari, has elaborate teachings about negative attaching spirits that need to be exorcized.[13]

The Sacred Writings affirm that there are fallen angels who can lead us astray. Their prince is Lucifer, the Devil (see Rev. 12:1-13, Eph. 6:12). Although traditional art has often depicted fallen angels as hideous looking, the reality is that they can be quite dazzling and attractive in appearance. This appearance can be a deceptive mask and the unwary may be easily hoodwinked by their charms. The Sacred Writings confirm that Christ has defeated these fallen angels.

At this juncture, Ross related to Vanessa how he has personally interacted with people who have been victims of such beings. He once spoke on a radio program about the dangers of astral traveling. Astral traveling involves entering a trance or sleep-like state where one's spirit is free to leave the body and journey into other dimensions. Ross unfolded some case studies that indicate dark angels at times accompanied people on their astral journeys. In those cases, he explained how dark angels took them to dimensions where they did not want to go, controlling their very movements and physically abusing them. The interesting reaction was the number of New Age seekers who rang the station to concur. They also warned of foreign spirits.

Here we have a sobering reminder of the dangers that can come from naively trusting any encounter we might have with an angelic being.[14]

Angels and the master, Jesus

"If there are good and bad angels," Vanessa mused, "how can I be sure that my angels won't trick me?" We suggested that the answer to this lies with a spiritual master and guide who is superior to angels. "I suppose you are referring to Jesus," Vanessa interjected as she gestured at our display board. The board depicted two angels peering over the shoulders of Jesus who was seated in a prayer posture.

We said that angels appeared throughout Jesus' life. The Sacred Writings record them being present to announce his conception and birth, at his temptations, during his agonizing last prayer before his death, as witnesses to his resurrection at the empty tomb, and on his return to heaven (see Luke 1-2; 4; 22:43; Matt. 28:2-6; Acts 1:10-11). The Sacred Writings stress that Jesus is the pre-eminent friend in high places. Angels are also our friends, but by no means as exalted. As the resurrected one, Jesus is superior to all beings. He has conquered the dark angels (see Col. 2:15; Mark 5:1-13, Acts 19:13-17). He has been declared to be divine (Rom. 1:4). Likewise, the angels must worship Jesus (see Heb. 1:6). In an earthly sense, he is also superior as he journeyed like us, knowing all the joys and sorrows humanity undergoes. What we must keep in focus is that Jesus is the master over all the angels. He is superior to them. If we trust him and his pathway of grace, then one of the many blessings he can bestow on us is the presence of angels in our lives.

We affirmed with Vanessa that trustworthy angels always direct us to Jesus. We illustrated this by relating the story of Gerry. We had met Gerry at a function where we were speaking, and the subject of angels came up. Gerry shared with us something of his own spiritual journey. Gerry was a disciplined seeker who was exploring personal growth and transformation via vision quests. The vision quest entails a meticulous approach to meditation and astral travels. Gerry's mentor instructed him to set aside a 40-day period for a deep vision quest. Part of the assignment was to meet up with an angel. During his astral travels, Gerry encountered a being who called himself Michael. Michael said he was an angel and he had urgent advice for Gerry. Gerry was urged to cease all further astral travels. Michael stated, "Follow Jesus." After returning to his body, Gerry began to pray and read the Sacred Writings. He found that what he had been seeking through the vision quests was fulfilled by following Jesus. He pondered with us, "Wasn't Michael one of God's true angels?"[15]

We agreed that whether you have an angelic encounter or not, the important point for the journey is that God cares for each of us. If the most significant being of all, the one who created the cosmos cares, then no matter what happens, we can be confident that our need for healing and transformation can be fulfilled by the Creator.

Endnotes

Chapter 2

[1] Sophy Burnham, *A Book of Angels*, New York: Ballantine, 1990, p. 17.

[2] Hope Price, *Angels: True Stories of How They Touch Our Lives*, London: Pan Macmillan, 1994, p. 188.

[3] Ross Clifford and Philip Johnson, *Riding the Rollercoaster: How the Risen Christ Empowers Life*, Sydney: Strand, 1998, pp. 74-75. Some portions of the fifth chapter have been incorporated into our dialogue with Vanessa.

[4] Sophy Burnham, *A Book of Angels*, pp. 41-42. Unfortunately Burnham does not give any references to verify these reports.

[5] Hope Macdonald, *When Angels Appear*, New York: HarperCollins, 1995.

[6] Joan Wester Anderson, *Where Angels Walk*, New York: Ballantine, 1993.

[7] Steve Saint, "Did They Have to Die?" *Christianity Today*, 16 September 1996, pp. 20-27.

[8] George Howe Colt, "In Search of Angels," *Life*, December 1995, pp. 65-72, 76, 78-79.

[9] Dick Sutphen, *Radical Spirituality: Metaphysical Awareness for a New Century*, Malibu: Valley of the Sun, 1995.

[10] Johannes Aagaard, "Conversion, Religious Change and the Challenge of New Religious Movements," *Cultic Studies Journal*, 8, 2, 1991, p. 93.

[11] See C.S. Lewis, *Spenser's Images of Life*, Cambridge: Cambridge University Press, 1967

[12] On the Gnostics, see B. Layton (ed.), *The Rediscovery of Gnosticism*, 2 volumes, Leiden: Brill, 1980-81; and Edwin Yamauchi, *Pre-Christian Gnosticism*, 2nd edition, Grand Rapids: Baker, 1983.

[13] See John Powers, *Introduction to Tibetan Buddhism*, Ithaca: Snow Lion, 1995; Ruqaiyyah Maqsood, *Islam*, London: Hodder & Stoughton, 1994; and Winston Davis, *Dojo: Magic and Exorcism in Modern Japan*, Stanford: Stanford University Press, 1980.

[14] See John Warwick Montgomery (ed.), *Demon Possession*, Minneapolis: Bethany, 1976.

[15] The occasion was a presentation at Butterworths Legal Publishers, Sydney on April 7, 1998.

Chapter 3
Wicca—Goddess Worship Revival

———————————◆———————————

I love the rich earthiness of the goddess religions. I love the way they speak directly to my female experience of the world, the way they honour life and fertility, change and growth. Yet all logic in me riles at the notion of a deity of either gender.[1]

I dig Jesus and so do many other witches. It's not his fault that Christianity is so confused today, and as a person he was a very special guy, wise and generous, selfless and loving. I think he'd be horrified to see what his teachings have come to today. In fact, I'd go so far as to say that if he was around today, with his values of tolerance, acceptance, respect for nature and fellow people, he'd be a witch![2]

God depicts himself to us, as it were, in the form of a woman and mother.[3]

———————————◆———————————

We met Hayley, Kimberlee, Lady Moonfire, and Laren on the Internet. As practitioners of Wiccan spirituality (the old English word for witchcraft), they had each initiated a dialogue with us. What stimulated it was an article by Philip about Wicca that was placed on the Internet. The response was overwhelmingly positive, and we soon found ourselves in fruitful dialogue with several Wiccans from around the globe.[4]

This spurred us to attend the Magick Happens festival in our hometown. This was an exhibition catering to Wiccan and neo-pagan interests. The venue was packed with mostly women spanning age groups from those in their fifties all the way down to teenagers.

Some exhibitors were promoting tools used in the Craft, such as candles, ceremonial swords, figurines, and ritual clothing. Magazines such as *The Green Egg, Spirit Earth*, and *Witchcraft* were on sale. There were books about casting spells, eco-feminism, the goddess pathway, empowerment through menstruation, and neo-pagan parenting. A few Wiccan priestesses gave private consultations for self-awareness and guidance using numerology, tarot, and the runes. There were fairy children shows, African dancing, storytelling, pagan songs, and folk music performed. Workshops covering Wiccan solitary rituals, crystal magick, and the Wiccan traditions were also well attended.

After the exhibition we reflected on what we had seen. Several things struck us. First, we had met so many warm, caring seekers who welcomed us and were happy to enter into a dialogue. These people did not fit the misleading stereotype of Devil worshippers. Some were highly educated, employed in government departments and major corporations. Others were living as the sole custodial parent of young children, struggling to eke out a meaningful life for themselves and those in their care. Second, here was a spiritual gathering attracting large numbers of women, especially teenagers. What was it they found so appealing? Undoubtedly they found there a spirituality that affirmed them as women and offered spiritual succor seemingly unavailable in the church. Third, this spirituality was addressing a number of important questions about god language, ecology, spiritual giftedness, healing, and spiritual fraternity. Our sense of current trends is that Wicca is fast becoming the preferred spiritual pathway for a lot of teenage females, particularly those fed up with their parents' hand-me-down faith.

Wicca versus satanism

One of our new friends is Judy. We first met at a New Age festival, then caught up with one another a few weeks later at

Magick Happens. As a sole parent, Judy has to juggle her commitments with her children, work, and Wiccan way of life.

We confirmed that Wicca is known as the "old religion." The word "Wicca" has come into common currency because the word "witchcraft" carries with it very pejorative images. We see these negative stereotypes in movies such as *The Craft*. Wiccans also tend to be circumspect about television series such as *Sabrina, the Teenage Witch* and *Charmed*. These shows, in their desire to be entertaining, unintentionally belittle the seriousness of Wicca.

Satanists who sometimes use the word "witch" also compound the problem. Wiccans completely disassociate themselves from satanism and black magic. Wiccans do not believe in the existence of Satan, nor do they worship Satan. Contrary to lurid rumors, they do not offer human or animal sacrifices to the Devil. Wicca does not need to define its spirituality using the church as a point of departure. After all, satanism is a direct perversion of Christian beliefs and values: satanism's *raison d'être* needs the church so it can exist as a reactionary opponent to it. If the church did not exist, then there would not be anything called satanism. Wiccan beliefs and practices are antithetical to satanism, so there cannot be any correlation between them.[5]

Judy was aware that some Christians link Wicca with satanism because of Aleister Crowley (1875-1947). We told Judy that even though we were appalled by Crowley's behavior, we saw no point in calling him a satanist. He was a late Victorian decadent. When Crowley accepted his mother's branding of him as the "Great Beast," he reveled in being the provocative, profligate rebel. Yes, his rituals were often ridiculous, obscene, and sometimes sadistic, but he did not worship Satan. As Crowley was neither a Wiccan nor a satanist, there is no point trying to insinuate otherwise or impugn Wiccans for his outrageous activities.[6]

Crowley and the Confusion

Wiccans acknowledge that Crowley was a powerful magickian, while satanists such as Anton LaVey (1930-97) looked to him as an inspirational figure. Crowley grew up in the fundamentalist Plymouth Brethren, but quickly rebelled against his upbringing. He was an outrageous non-conformist who sought to provoke, shock, and offend everyone with his bisexual behavior, occult writings, sadistic rituals, and drug abuse. He so enjoyed the bad characters in the Bible that his mother dubbed him the "Great Beast" after the anti-Christ figure in Revelation.

Crowley went through a series of memberships with various esoteric groups before he formed his own. He practiced sex magick, and developed his own tarot cards, relating them to the Qabalah. His magickal maxim was "Do what thou wilt shall be the whole of the Law." The maxim concerns the discipline and power of the will but is often misconstrued because the refrain that immediately follows it is usually omitted by critics: "Love is the Law, Love under Will."

Christians have classified Crowley as a satanist on several counts. One reason is due to his gleeful acceptance of the title "Great Beast." Another is that in his book *Magick in Theory and Practice*, Crowley discusses blood sacrifices and states that "a male child of perfect innocence and high intelligence is the most satisfactory and suitable victim.[7] He further stated that Frater Perdurabo (Crowley's pseudonym) made this sacrifice about 150 times a year between 1912 and 1928.[8] As for Crowley's remarks on human sacrifices, R.A. Gilbert points out that the meaning of these statements is clarified by reference to Crowley's diaries. Gilbert says that "he is not referring to human sacrifice," but, rather, is "referring to sex acts, most commonly to masturbation."[9]

Fiona Horne, the international pop star and journalist, rightly speaks for all Wiccans when she bluntly says:

◆

How many times do I have to tell you? Witches do not worship Satan! One of the earliest and most common misconceptions about witches is that we worship Satan. Whenever I am asked by individuals or the media if I am a "Devil-worshipper" I always say, "My parents have more to do with Satan than I do—they're Christian."[10]

◆

Judy was relieved to hear that at least some Christians are prepared to make that careful distinction. Understandably, contemporary practitioners like Judy are quite properly offended by the negative stereotypes. Of course some Wiccans have a sense of humor about this, such as when they confess that they have "come out of the broom closet." However, tongue-in-cheek remarks aside, Wiccans have genuine grounds for concern, especially when Christians vilify, harass, and persecute them.

Wicca as it really is

Judy indicated that Wicca embraces natural magick. The word "magick" is used to differentiate it from the conjuring of professional stage illusionists of the likes of David Copperfield. Wiccans have a reverence for the natural world and strive to attune themselves with it. A distinct feature of Wiccan belief is the concept of the mother goddess and her male consort the horned god (known as Cernunnos, Karnayna, or Pan). Some assuredly believe in and worship the mother goddess or invoke a variety of pre-Christian goddesses, such as Aphrodite, Astarte, Brigit, Ceres, Cybele, Demeter, Diana, Gaia, Hecate, Isis, Tiamat, Vesta, and Yemaya. Other male gods invoked include Horus, Janus, Mercury, Osiris, Poseidon, Thoth, and Vulcan. The belief that several deities exist is technically known as polytheism.

Some Wiccans are pantheists—the idea that God and the universe are one. Some are panentheists—the idea that the whole universe is in God, but God is not identical with the universe. Other Wiccans simply take the concept of a mother goddess as an archetypal mythic symbol of empowerment where practitioners discover their own sense of the goddess within them.[11] Here the gods and goddesses are understood to be merely projections of inner symbols. Quite a few claim that, in prehistoric Europe, the goddess was uniformly worshiped, and so Wicca represents a return to true primeval spirituality.[12]

Wiccans may operate as sole practitioners—sometimes known as "hedge witches"—working earth magick rituals from a sacred altar at home. Many, though, elect to join a coven. A coven often comprises members of both sexes, but generally the leader is female. Membership numbers vary between four and twenty-two devotees. Although many Wiccans are heterosexual, some covens have only female membership and some of those may be wholly lesbian. There are also gay Wiccan covens.[13]

A coven normally meets on the new and full moon, known as *esbats*, where magickal rituals and ceremonies are performed. They also gather together for major festivals, known as *sabbats*, which relate to the eight cycles of the Celtic tradition. Each *sabbat* represents a different phase in the annual cycle of life, death, and rebirth in the natural world. An elaborate myth or sacred story unfolds with each successive *sabbat*, so each one tells an episode in an eight-fold myth. Due to seasonal differences, the "wheel of the year" celebrations, as they are known, vary between the northern and southern hemispheres.[14] The northern hemisphere celebrations begin with Halloween, which is in mid-autumn, and flows through to the following autumn. Based on the Celtic calendar, the eight *sabbats* are set out below:

The coven is usually led by a high priestess, with a subordinate male priest. Ceremonial magick is governed by the Wiccans' golden rule: "That you harm none, do what you will." Ritual magick is directed to harmony within oneself and harmony with nature. The casting of spells is intended to promote healing, as well as protecting the earth from harm. They pronounce ritual blessings on rivers, stones, trees, flowers, and birds. Wiccans usually reject labels such as "white witch" and "black witch" because they insist magick happens when they attune themselves with the earth's elements. As these energies are good, Wiccans regard it as absurd to think about white or black magick. Wiccans honor both the creative and destructive forces in the cosmos. They also acknowledge that some seriously dysfunctional people can commit acts of malevolence, but malice is not in keeping with the prime directives of the Craft. Wiccans affirm that whatever one does—whether benign or malevolent—will return threefold on the doer.

Wiccan affirmations

Judy stressed to us that Wiccans do not subscribe to a common creed or confession of faith such as has developed within Christianity. However, Wiccans are happy to express some of their foundational principles in personal affirmations or vows like the following:

- I undertake this path of my own free will and for the good of myself and of humankind.
- I will follow the Wiccan law—"That you harm none, do what you will."
- I do not seek power over others but aim to increase my own knowledge, self-esteem, and happiness through the Craft.
- I cast no spell against another's wishes or best interests.
- I promise to keep the identity of my fellow practitioners secret and help to protect them from harm.
- I shall follow my coven's democratic rulings and laws to the best of my abilities.
- I will attempt to gain a true and deep understanding of the Craft.
- I respect all life as sacred and treat the earth and its inhabitants with love and care.
- I thank the goddess for this path and promise to uphold the best traditions of the Craft.

As these vows show, Wiccans strive to be people of integrity and peace, upholding the sanctity of life in the pursuit of spiritual nourishment.

Some covens include a strand of sex magick, where life partners have intercourse as a means to empowerment. It is not conducted in any orgiastic sense, but is concerned with utilizing the power generated for magickal purposes. A few practitioners work in the sex industry, affirming the role of the "sacred prostitute."[15]

With the strong emphasis on empowerment for women in Wicca, many practitioners celebrate rites of passage concerned with puberty, fertility, menstruation, menopause, and post-menopause. This is often symbolically linked to the phases of the moon. Their changing roles from virgin to mother to old woman (maiden, mother, and crone) are ascribed with great spiritual significance.[16] A feminine sense of nurture and care for others, and also for mother earth, comes through rituals, songs, and stories.[17]

Varieties of Wicca

As is the case with other organized religions, within Wicca there are various schools of thought. However, it is very misleading to see them as being akin to denominations or sects, because this presupposes some standard creed as a litmus test for orthodox belief.

Modern Wicca originates with the works of Gerald Gardner (1884-1964). He is often credited with "reviving" witchcraft around 1939. So Wiccan spirituality is a 20th-century creation. As Wicca encourages and celebrates diversity, not all practitioners follow Gardner, and it is continuing to evolve as a movement.[18] Other major figures include Raymond Buckland, Zsuzsanna Budapest, Janet and Stewart Farrar, Gavin and Yvonne Frost, and Alexander Sanders. Wiccans may pursue any number of pagan paths such as pre-Christian Celtic spirituality, the Norse traditions, Native American Indian spirituality, and ancient Egyptian and Sumerian thought.

Quite a few Wiccans combine their pathway with Taoism, because of its emphasis on harmony between opposite principles—bringing together positive/negative, light/dark, male/female. A well-known Taoist symbol is this: ☯.

Wiccans see themselves as pagans, but not all pagans are Wiccans. The word "pagan" comes from the Latin *paganus* and originally meant "village dweller."[19]

The Wiccan vision

Wiccans have a vision of reality that radically departs from the arid rationalism of modernity. They have a keen sense of spiritual realities permeating our world. This is evident in their awareness of the mother goddess being present throughout the whole natural world. From such awareness it follows that they see the natural world as sacred and imbued with spiritual powers. As the world is sacred and all life is valued as sacred, Wiccans understandably have deep concerns for the environment. Some Wiccans call themselves eco-feminists because they are admirably dedicated to protecting mother earth from further ecological devastation.[20]

Wiccans place the accent in their spirituality on a feminine, nurturing, intuitive approach. They perceive the modern world as having been dominated by an aggressive, patriarchal society that, in its worst excesses, has oppressed women and ravaged nature. The dominant spirituality of the Western world has been that of the Christian church, which is seen as being controlled by men preaching about a father figure God. Wiccans feel quite strongly that the Western world is spiritually unbalanced and so they seek to provide a corrective whereby both female and male principles—mother goddess and her consort—are held in a harmonious equation.

Tools and symbols of the Craft

Judy clarified for us what the tools and symbols of the Craft are and how they are used.[21]

- Ankh A—Cross that has a loop or circle at the top. It derives from Egypt as a sign of eternal life. It can also signify the duality of female and male or represent reincarnation.
- Athame—This is a black-handled double-sided knife used in rituals to cast or banish a Wiccan circle. It is also a tool for protection against inharmonious entities.
- Bells—A feminine symbolic tool used in ritual. The bell represents water, which is associated with healing, fertility, and friendship. Bells are used to invoke the goddess, ward off evil spirits, and signify either the beginning or ending of a spell.
- *Book of Shadows*—Wiccans keep this book of rituals and spells, preserved in the handwriting of the coven members.
- Broomstick—A symbol of sexual union: "The rod which penetrates the bush." The broomstick is used in ceremonies celebrating spiritual rebirth.
- Casting the circle—The circle is the sacred space created around an altar, either in a room or in a bush setting. It defines the area of ritual, holds within it the positive energy used for magick, and wards off negative forces.
- Drawing down the moon—This ceremony, which is performed by the male high priest, invokes the spirit of the goddess to enter the body of the high priestess.
- Familiar—An animal spirit guide, mascot, or totem of guidance.
- Four elements—The four classic essential elements of nature: earth, air, fire, and water. Earth gives the gifts of prosperity and stability. Air represents the spirit and intellect. Fire encourages creativity, passion, and strength. Water brings compassion, love, healing, and psychic awareness.
- Handfasting—A Wiccan marriage ceremony where life partners make special vows to one another.
- Invocation—To call in a higher force to request assistance or favor.
- Pentagram—A five-pointed star-like figure used in ceremonial blessings. Each point represents one of the four elements and the spirit.
- Philtre—A potion used to produce magickal effects.
- Runes—A Wiccan alphabet that derives from ancient Norse culture. The

runes, which may be reproduced on stones, are used as a tool for guidance and divination.

- Scrying—The practice of clairvoyance using a crystal, candle flame, or incense.
- Skyclad—An expression referring to ceremonies some Wiccans perform in the nude.
- Shape shifter—A shape shifter is a shaman, healer, visionary, and other world traveller.[22]

Saying "sorry"

Sadly, too many Christians bear false witness about Wiccans, particularly in published polemics. Four notorious cases include John Todd, Mike Warnke, Lauren Stratford, and Rebecca Brown. Back in the 1970s Todd (alias Lance Collins) claimed he was involved in an international conspiracy of witches to take over the world, alleging that witches already controlled Christian ministries. Over time, his story became more embellished. Although his inconsistent testimony was discredited, his negative caricature of witches remained firmly implanted in the minds of many Christians.[23]

Similar problems of credibility, combined with crippling autobiographical inconsistencies, undermined Mike Warnke's *The Satan Seller*, Lauren Stratford's *Satan's Underground*, and Rebecca Brown's *He Came To Set The Captives Free*.[24] R.A. Gilbert has also raised some preliminary concerns about Doreen Irvine who in *From Witchcraft to Christ* claimed she was crowned queen of black witches in the 1960s.[25]

A further bone of contention is what Wiccans dub "the burning times." Many believe that about nine million women were exterminated. Margot Adler has pointed out that the actual number of those who perished was only around 40,000.[26] Still, that was 40,000 casualties too many. We said to Judy that the Inquisition and Salem trials were a hideous violation of human dignity and utterly inexcusable. Witchcraft should not have been treated as a criminal activity. As a Christian human rights expert has said in connection with the witch trials:

---◆---

The proper function of human law is to regulate conduct so as to prevent injustice . . . it is not to regulate ideas or coerce opinions.[27]

---◆---

Witchcraft entailed ideas and beliefs more than it had to do with acts. The Craft did not constitute a threat to the body politic. So, the prohibition, persecution, and prosecution of Wiccans had no legal justification. The Christian prosecutors engaged in evil, the exact opposite of what Jesus taught his followers to do.

So, on both counts—false witness and the burning times—we felt compelled to say to Judy on behalf of all Christians, "we're sorry for what has been done to you and your folk in the name of Jesus." This visibly moved Judy and she responded, "I think that pagans have also been guilty of doing the same kinds of things to Christians."

Wicca challenges Christianity

We came to a point of mutual challenge. We indicated to Judy that we felt Wicca had a lot of things to say to the church, but we also felt that we had things to offer back to Wiccans. These are the issues we explored and challenged one another about.

THE CONCEPT OF DEITY

Wiccans perceive the Christian concept of God as a patriarchal one. The universal Christian confession is that God is triune. Within the unity of the one eternal God, there are three persons—Father, Son, and Holy Spirit. Each person shares in the same nature and attributes. They form a loving, harmonious unity in relationship with each other.

The Sacred Writings employ a variety of images, similes, and metaphors when speaking of God. The language is often anthropomorphic, but in context does not portray a God with male genitals. The image of God as father is meant in the sense of a nurturing parent. In fact, there are both paternal and maternal images presented in the Sacred Writings. For example, God is likened to a mother who nurses and comforts us, as a midwife and as a seamstress (see Isa. 66:12-13, Ps. 22:9, Luke 12:27-28). God's wisdom is personified as a woman (see Prov. 8 and 9). The nurturing and tender support God gives is portrayed in bird-like imagery, such as that of a female eagle (see Deut. 32:11, Ps. 91:4). Jesus also likens his concern to that of a mother hen gathering her chicks (see Matt. 23:37).

In the Sacred Writings, one of God's names is *El Shaddai*. This name derives from the Hebrew word *shad*, meaning "breast." We quoted the father of the Protestant Reformation, Martin Luther, who, in his commentary on Genesis, saw maternal images evoked by this divine name. Luther wrote: "God depicts Himself to us, as it were, in the form of a woman and mother."[28] Other early Christians who did not hesitate to speak about the motherhood of God include John Chrysostom, Gregory of Nyssa, Venerable Bede, Thomas Aquinas, Bonaventure, Bernard of Clairvaux, Hildegard of Bingen, and Anselm.

Christians do not embrace an androgynous God. As God is a spirit, deity is beyond gender, but within God's being we see both masculine and feminine characteristics. The creation narrative avers that in the image of God both male and female are created. This means for us that complete harmony is found within the very being of God and does not require us to posit two separate deities—one female and one male. We said to Judy that Wiccans goad Christians into remembering the symbolic and figurative nature of language used about God in the Sacred Writings.[29]

We wondered if some Wiccans have overreacted to patriarchal images in exchange for a matriarchal deity. On a historical level, we felt that it is a very moot point that prehistoric European cultures were universally worshipping the goddess. The position taken by Marija Gimbutas on this point is by no means accepted by religious studies scholarship.[30] Cross-cultural historical records show that the goddess "is still primarily the product of patriarchal cultures and, therefore, more a projection of the feminine by men than by women."[31]

AN IMMANENT SPIRIT

Another aspect of Wiccan thought concerns the immanence of the goddess or spirit in the natural world. Once again, Wicca challenges Christians to give full expression to what the Sacred Writings present. In classic Christian thought, God is said to be both transcendent and immanent. By "transcendent" is meant that God is a being who is separate from the creation and is sovereign over it. By "immanent" is meant that God's being is present everywhere within the creation. Another way of using these terms is to think of transcendence as referring to ultimate things and immanence as referring to intimate things.

We indicated to Judy that Christians have been very strong in emphasizing God's ultimacy, but we've been slipshod in saying much about God's intimacy. We pointed out that the Sacred Writings firmly uphold God's presence within the creation. The Spirit was not only involved in the act of earth's creation, but continues to maintain, sustain and renew the creation (see Gen. 1:2; Ps. 36:10; 54:4; 104; 139:7; Acts 17:28; Heb. 1:3). The apostle Paul instructed, "God . . . is not far from each one of us" (Acts 17:27, NIV). As Wiccans affirm the intimacy of the divine, we are likewise compelled to refocus on these truths, which are to be found in the Sacred Writings. Our awareness of God's presence around us must surely revolutionize the way we live each moment in grace and gratitude.

CREATION STEWARDSHIP

A further area of challenge is with respect to caring for the earth. Wiccans have a deep appreciation for the beauty and sacredness of the earth. Wiccans and neo-pagans alike revel in the earth just as it is. We acknowledged that many Christians have mistakenly presumed that the earth is to be exploited. They think the earth has a "use-by-date." They are, however, out of step with the Sacred Writings because God has no plans to discard the earth. A new heaven and new earth is envisaged (see Isa. 65; 2 Peter 3:13; Rev. 21).

The creation narratives make it clear that God placed the primordial humans in an unspoiled garden with the privilege of tending it. They were intended to be stewards answerable to God for the care of the earth. When the Sacred Writings talk about the "dominion" given to humans, this did not connote a carte blanche for rapacious, greedy exploitation and destruction of the earth. Rather, it is referring to the high responsibility conferred on them by God to act as stewards.

The Sacred Writings also disclose that the creation is not a wound-up clock abandoned by God to its own devices. As we have seen, the Spirit of God is intimately involved in maintaining and sustaining everything with life and breath. Moses wrote that the earth belongs to the Lord, while the followers of Christ identify Jesus as the Creator (see Exod. 9:29; John 1:3; Col. 1:16; Heb. 1:3). Paul the apostle offers a glowing portrait of the creation being made by, through, and for Christ (see Col. 1:16-17). So, the creation is imbued with inestimable value, which Christians can celebrate.

The value placed on the creation is reiterated several times in the Scriptures. After the great flood, a covenant was made between God, Noah's family, the animals, and all of creation (see Gen. 9:8-17). The divine law given to Moses set forth ecological principles for agriculture. The land was to be tilled for six years, with a seventh year as sabbath rest. Produce was also to be set aside for the poor and the refugee. This was to be observed in seven cycles of seven-year periods, culminating in the fiftieth year of jubilee where unpaid debts were to be forgiven (see Exod. 23:10-12; Lev. 25; Deut. 15:1-11).

We said that the Christian writer Francis Schaeffer (1912-84) tackled ecology in his 1970 book *Pollution and the Death of Man*.[32] Sadly, many Christians ignored his fervent pleas until the late 1980s when it became trendy for middle-class people. We indicated, however, that Christian thinkers have contributed some sophisticated work.[33] So, if some Christians regard the earth as something to be exploited and discarded, then their value system is misaligned with the Sacred Writings.

ANIMALS AND THE RENEWED WORLD

Judy told us how Wiccan spirituality affirms the sacredness of animals. Some even find a role for animals as spirit guides in astral travels.[34] We responded by affirming that animals are valuable as part of God's good creation. As Jesus taught, God watches over the animals, but they are on a different scale of importance to that of humans (see Matt. 10:29-31). Whereas humans are capable of making moral decisions for good or evil, animals are not. Instead animals have a Creator-consciousness where they praise the Creator just by their mere existence (see Ps. 148).

In the Wisdom books of the Sacred Writings, animals are sometimes used as object lessons on the practicalities of life and the spiritual journey (see Prov. 30:24-31; Job 39; 40:15-24, 41). Animals also had a place in the coming of Christ. They were assuredly witnesses to Jesus' birth because he was born in a stable and placed in a feeding trough afterwards. Jesus used animal illustrations in his teachings, and he chose a donkey to ride on for his triumphal entry into Jerusalem (see Matt. 8:20; Luke 13:34; Luke 18:25; John 12:14-15). At Jesus' baptism, the divine Spirit descended on him in the form of a dove (see Luke 3:22). Animals, however, are not seen as spirit guides.

As we talked about the coming renewed heaven and earth, we indicated how the animals and whole cosmos are swept up in this magnificent vision (see Isa. 65; 2 Peter 3:13; Rev. 21). Isaiah envisioned a time when the wolf and lamb would lie down together side-by-side in harmony (see Isa. 11:6-8; 65:25). Paul the apostle saw the whole cosmos yearning for our transformation and that, through Jesus' cross and resurrection, all creation would be restored to harmony (see Rom. 8:19-22).

SACRED SITES AND MAGICK

Judy said that Wiccans feel very strongly about sacred sites where they perceive there to be spiritual power. And again, we acknowledged that followers have encountered God at sacred places, such as Moses at the burning bush on Mount Sinai, Isaiah in the temple, and when Jesus was transfigured (see Exod. 3; 19; Isa. 6; Matt. 17). However, we stressed to Judy that God may be encountered anywhere and that sacredness is not limited to any geographical locale. The world is made holy by God's presence and this is reiterated in the Lord's prayer: "hallowed be thy name, on earth as it is in heaven." The coming of Christ sanctifies the creation. Here we feel, though, that people are yearning to have their connection with God and the creation brought together. So there is a message for the church to include much more creation celebrations as part of our praise to the Creator.

Judy's benevolent use of magick is aimed at healing and harmony. Our concern is that malevolent spirits do abound and great harm may befall the most sincere practitioner. Terry Pratchett portrays that concern in his neo-pagan *Discworld* fantasy stories. For us, spiritual power rests in the paradox of our weakness being made perfect by the Spirit of Christ. The risen Christ energizes us within so that we may serve others and tend the good creation.

SEXUALITY AND SPIRITUALITY

Wiccan spirituality speaks to the church regarding the issue of women. We are not surprised that many women are leaving Western churches and looking for a spiritual life that affirms them. Here the church has not been in tune with the Spirit of Jesus. Jesus set himself against the mysoginist attitudes of his day and upheld the dignity and equality of women. He offered spiritual empowerment to women to live in a society where they were

denigrated. He accepted and healed single mothers and prosti-
tutes (see Mark 7:24-30; Luke 7:36-50; John 4; 8:3-11). Jesus
counted among his closest supporters a number of women,
including Mary Magdalene, Joanna, Susanna, Mary, and Martha
(see Luke 8:2-3, John 11).

The Sacred Writings disclose that it was the women who provided an unbroken chain of eyewitness testimony to the
execution, burial, and resurrection of Jesus. In the first century,
the testimony of women was disregarded, so clearly the values
espoused in the early church went against the culture's grain.
This is further evidenced by the sacred principle that every
female and male believer is considered a priest before God (see 2
Peter 1:4-10).

Paul the apostle valued women among his colleagues in ministry, as can be seen from the women listed in his salutations to
the church at Rome (see Rom. 16). He also taught that, in Christ,
there is neither male nor female (see Gal. 3:28). In ancient Israel,
Miriam and Huldah were prophetesses, Deborah was both a
prophetess and judge over Israel, and Ruth's faith was a paramount example to all (see Exod. 15:20; 2 Kings 22:14; Judg. 4-5;
and the entire book of Ruth).

Mary, the mother of Jesus, exercised great faith. Her example
is often downplayed by Protestants because of perceived excesses
in Catholic and Orthodox traditions, but such downplaying of her
role and example creates another kind of imbalance.[35] Elsewhere
the Sacred Writings clearly document women exercising spiritual
gifts and ministry (see Acts 2:17; 9:36; 18:26; 21:9).

We said that some church groups have become polarized in
debates concerning questions of power and authority, so they will
often fail to address the basic issue of women in ministry.[36] We
emphasized that the church must, likewise, repent of the misog-
yny and abuse that takes place in its ranks. We said that Eve was
not the stereotype of a dumb woman. She holds the first recorded
theological discussion in the Sacred Writings. The serpent's
attempt to deceive her occurs because she was spiritually intuitive

and intelligent. Both male and female were held accountable for humanity's descent from original spiritual harmony.

We also discussed the Wiccan approach to sex magick. We said that, at times, Christians have been so terrified of sex that they have espoused celibacy as the ultimate virtue while simultaneously denigrating the human body. The repression of sex inevitably erupts into abuse or promiscuity. All of this is at odds with the Sacred Writings. Sex is celebrated as a good gift from God to be enjoyed within marriage. The Song of Songs is devoted to the joy of sex. Christians who denigrate the human body have more in common with Gnosticism than with the life-affirming path of Christ. However, we do not find that sex magick is upheld in the Sacred Writings.

The wheel of the year myth

We then talked about the Wiccan sacred calendar and introduced Judy to the unpublished work of our colleague John Smulo. John has found intriguing links between the wheel of the year myths and the historical Christ. As we noted earlier, each sabbat tells an episode in an eight-fold myth. Samhain in the Celtic myth is a creation story where the virgin goddess conceives the child of promise. At Yule, the Christmas season, the wheel declares that the child is born.

We saw two challenges. First, this cyclical myth celebrates the seasons, departed ancestors, and acknowledges the beginning of life and the end of its cycle in death. We feel that celebrating our connection with the seasons and reflecting on the inherited wisdom of our forebears is something that many Christians lack. This is a challenge to us.

The other challenge was for Judy to reflect on this cyclical myth. It takes on flesh in the virginal conception and birth of the historical Christ. Judy was intrigued that what is so symbolically foreshadowed in the Wiccan wheel might be fulfilled in Christ.

Admiring Jesus

A lot of Wiccans like Judy admire Jesus. For example, Fiona Horne's provocative and challenging sentiments are cited at the beginning of this chapter. Anatha Wolfkeepe is a Wiccan who advocates pagan Christianity. The Gnostic writings and books such as *The Holy Blood and the Holy Grail* have influenced her understanding of Jesus:

In the early days of Christianity, Jesus Christ was readily accepted by many members of the Old Religion as a manifestation of their own eternal God. With His apostles, He was the leader of a coven of 13. In His parables of agricultural and pastoral imagery, Jesus expressed the language of the Fertility Mysteries, and in His miracles he proved himself to be a magickal healer and a powerful Spirit of Plenty, turning water into wine and causing the sea to "be fruitful and multiply." His sacrificial death was foreshadowed, announced, and willingly accepted and was in every detail identical to the most ancient patterns of the old nature religion.[37]

Other Wiccans and pagans defer to Timothy Freke and Peter Gandy's book *The Jesus Mysteries* in which they claim that Jesus did not exist but was a mythical figure whose teachings the apostles created by directly borrowing from the mystery religions. Still others find reading the Christian Sacred Writings a real struggle. Fiona Horne encapsulates this by saying:

Read the Bible if you're drawn to it and see what you think. I found it contradictory, disempowering, confusing and depressing— but you might find it otherwise! . . . I have to say that I don't relate to Jesus as he's described in the Bible as well as I do to his

presentation in alternative writings about him, like the book Jesus the Man *by Barbara Thiering.*[38]

We applauded Judy's admiration for Jesus and encouraged her to discover more about him. We suggested fresh ways of reading the Sacred Writings, such as trying some of our meditative exercises (set out in chapter 12). We were also candid about the difficulties we had with the Gnostic sources, Freke and Gandy, and other radical reinterpretations of Jesus (as we explain in chapter 11).

The fulfilment of Wicca

As our time with Judy came to a close, we felt that there was an issue still be faced. Judy indicated, quite honestly, that her life suffers from all kinds of pressures and she does not have all the answers. Fiona Horne echoes this:

For what it's worth, I'm as screwed up as anyone else. I'm often plagued by self-doubt and fears, I'm rarely satisfied with anything I do, and sometimes I feel like the life I've built since Def FX broke up is a house of cards that could blow down any minute. But the one redeeming quality I'll grant myself is that I never give up—I refuse to . . . Witchcraft helps—often a lot—but it demands you acknowledge the dark. Witchcraft encourages you to accept total responsibility for your life: you can't hide from yourself, you can't cop out.[39]

We indicated that we, too, have doubts, struggles, trials, and unanswered questions in our journey. Judy appreciated our openness. We said that, for us, Jesus had a specific mission, to make people right again with God. Jesus fulfills what we spiritually yearn for. We indicated that, through the resurrected Jesus, we find personal acceptance and forgiveness, authentic values to live by, the promise of a renewed world, and the comforting power of his Spirit here and now. We felt that Judy's aspiration to become the best person she can be together with the positive elements of her spirituality find their fullness in the person of Jesus. We invited Judy to explore the grace and resurrection power we celebrate in Jesus.

Endnotes

Chapter 3

[1] Samantha Trenoweth, *The Future of God*, Sydney: Millennium Books, 1995, p. x.

[2] Fiona Horne, *Witch: A Personal Journey*, Sydney: Random House, 1998, p. 8.

[3] Martin Luther, *Luther's Works: Lectures on Genesis*, volume 7, WA 43, 541, St Louis: Concordia, 1965, p. 325.

[4] The article "The Way of Wicca" is at www.shootthemessenger.com.au/u_jun_99/1_wicca.htm. A longer version entitled "Wiccans and Christians: Some Mutual Challenges" is at www.jesus.com.au. Portions of them are reproduced here in this chapter.

[5] On the differences between satanism and Wicca, see Nevill Drury, *The History of Magick in the Modern Age*, London: Constable, 2000, pp. 189-210; Lynne Hume, *Witchcraft and Paganism in Australia*, Melbourne: Melbourne University Press, 1997, pp. 214-218; and Bob and Gretchen Passantino, *Satanism*, Grand Rapids: Zondervan, 1995, pp. 45-48.

[6] On Crowley, see John Symonds, *The Great Beast*, London: Mayflower, 1973; and Susan Roberts, *The Magicians of the Golden Dawn*, Chicago: Contemporary Books, 1978.

[7] Aleister Crowley, *Magick in Theory and Practice*, Edison, New Jersey: Castle Books, 1991, p 95.

[8] See Crowley's fourth footnote in *Magick in Theory and Practice*, p. 95.

[9] R.A. Gilbert, *Casting the First Stone*, Dorset: Element, 1993, p. 143.

[10] Fiona Horne, *Witch: A Personal Journey*, Sydney: Random House, 1998, p. 199.

[11] See Vivianne Crowley, *Wicca: The Old Religion in the New Age*, London: Aquarian, 1989, pp. 162-182; and Jennifer Barker Woolger and Roger J. Woolger, *The Goddess Within*, London: Rider, 1990.

[12] Marija Gimbutas, *The Goddesses and Gods of Old Europe*, revised edition, Berkeley: University of California Press, 1982.

[13] Arthur Evans, *Witchcraft and the Gay Counterculture*, Boston: Fag Rag Books, 1978; and Martin A. Davies, "Witch Gender," *Witchcraft*, 10, pp. 30-33, available from FPC Magazines, Locked Bag 1028, Alexandria, New South Wales, 1435, Australia.

[14] See *Starhawk, The Spiral Dance*, revised edition, San Francisco: HarperCollins San Francisco, 1989, pp. 178-196; and Matthew and Julia Phillips, *The Witches of Oz*, Berks: Capall Bann, 1994, pp. 65-89.

[15] Kenneth Ray Stubbs (ed.), *Women of the Light: The New Sacred Prostitute*, Larkspur: Secret Garden, 1994.

[16] Kisma K. Stepanich, *Sister Moon Lodge: The Power and Mystery of Menstruation*, St Paul: Llewellyn, 1992.

[17] Ceisiwr Serith, *The Pagan Family: Handing the Old Ways Down*, St Paul: Llewellyn, 1994.

[18] Graham Harvey, *Contemporary Paganism: Listening People, Speaking Earth*, New York: University of New York Press, 1997, pp. 50-52; and Aidan Kelly, *Crafting the Art of Magic: A History of Modern Witchcraft*, 1939-1964, Book 1, St Paul: Llewellyn, 1991.

[19] See Margot Adler, *Drawing Down the Moon,* revised edition, Boston: Beacon, 1986, p. 9.

[20] Charlene Spretnak, *States of Grace,* San Francisco: HarperCollins San Francisco, 1991; and Starhawk, *Dreaming the Dark,* revised edition, Boston: Beacon, 1988.

[21] For a helpful summary, see "A Dictionary of Witchcraft," in *An Introduction to Witchcraft,* a compilation edition of *Witchcraft* magazine, issues 1 and 2, pp. 10-13.

[22] Michele Jamal, *Shape Shifters: Shaman Women in Contemporary Society,* London: Arkana, 1987.

[23] Darryl E. Hicks and David A. Lewis, *The Todd Phenomenon,* Harrison: New Leaf, 1979; and Ed Plowman, "The Legend(s) of John Todd," *Christianity Today,* 2 February 1979, pp. 38-40, 42.

[24] See Mike Hertenstein and Jon Trott, *Selling Satan: The Evangelical Media and the Mike Warnke Scandal,* Chicago: Cornerstone, 1993; Gretchen Passantino, Robert Passantino and Mike Hertenstein, 'Satan's Sideshow: The True Lauren Stratford Story', Cornerstone, 18, 1990, pp. 23-28; and G. Richard Fisher, Paul R. Blizard and M. Kurt Goedelman, "Drugs, Demons and Delusions," *The Quarterly Journal,* 9, 4, Personal Freedom Outreach, 1989, pp. 1, 8-15.

[25] Doreen Irvine, *From Witchcraft to Christ,* Cambridge: Concordia, 1973. Also, see her two sequels, *Set Free to Serve Christ,* Cambridge: Concordia, 1979; and *Spiritual Warfare,* Devon: Nova Publishing, 1992. On Gilbert's concerns, see his *Casting the First Stone,* Dorset: Element, 1993, pp. 44-45, 144-145, 154.

[26] Margot Adler, "A Time for Truth" at http://beliefnet.com/story/40/story_4007_1.html.

[27] John Warwick Montgomery, "Witch Trial Theory and Practice" in *The Law Above the Law,* Minneapolis: Bethany, 1975, p. 77.

[28] Martin Luther, *Luther's Works: Lectures on Genesis,* volume 7, WA 43, 541, St Louis: Concordia, 1965, p. 325.

[29] For contrasting views, see Aida Besancon Spencer, Donna F.G. Hailson, Catherine Clark Kroeger and William David Spencer, *The Goddess Revival,* Grand Rapids: Baker, 1995, pp. 110-129, and Roland Mushat Frye, "Language for God and Feminist Language: A Literary and Rhetorical Analysis," Interpretation, 43, 1989, pp. 45-57.

[30] Graham Harvey, *Contemporary Paganism,* pp. 72-75, 179-181.

[31] Larry D. Shinn, "The Goddess: Theological Sign or Religious Symbol?" *Numen,* 31, 1984, p. 183; Mary Jo Weaver, "Who Is the Goddess and Where Does She Get Us?" *Journal of Feminist Studies in Religion,* 5, 1, 1989, pp. 49-64; and Sally Binford, "Are Goddesses and Matriarchies Merely Figments of Feminist Imagination?" in Charlene Spretnak (ed.), *The Politics of Women's Spirituality,* Garden City: Doubleday, 1982, pp. 541-549.

[32] Francis A. Schaeffer, *Pollution and the Death of Man: The Christian View of Ecology,* Wheaton: Tyndale, 1970.

[33] Ian Bradley, *God is Green,* London: Darton, Longman & Todd, 1990; Calvin B. DeWitt (ed.), *The Environment and the Christian,* Grand Rapids: Baker, 1991; Rosemary Radford Ruether, *Gaia and God: An Ecofeminist Theology of Earth Healing,* San Francisco: HarperSan Francisco, 1992; and Keith Suter, *Global Agenda: Economics, the Environment and the Nation-State,* Sutherland, New South Wales: Albatross, 1995.

[34] Timothy Roderick, *The Once Unknown Familiar: Shamanic Paths to Unleash Your Animal Powers*, St Paul: Llewellyn, 1994.

[35] See Bob Moran, *A Closer Look at Catholicism: A Guide for Protestants*, Dallas: Word, 1986, pp. 220-230; and Elliot Miller and Kenneth R. Samples, *The Cult of the Virgin*, Grand Rapids: Baker, 1992.

[36] Ann Brown, *Apology to Women*, Leicester: InterVarsity Press, 1991; Bonnidell Clouse and Robert G. Clouse (eds), *Women in Ministry*, Downers Grove: InterVarsity Press, 1989; and Ruth A. Tucker and Walter Liefeld, *Daughters of the Church*, Grand Rapids: Zondervan, 1987.

[37] Anatha Wolfkeepe, "Jesus is one of us," *Witchcraft*, 12, 1999, p. 42.

[38] Fiona Horne, *Life's a Witch!*, Sydney: Random House, 2000, pp. 2-3.

[39] Fiona Horne, *Witch: A Magickal Year*, Sydney: Random House, 1999, p. 204.

Chapter 4
Myths and Wisdom

---◆---

At the beginning as well as at the end of the religious history of man, we find the same yearning for Paradise. If we take into account the fact that the yearning for Paradise is equally discernible in the general religious attitude of early man, we have the right to assume that the mystical memory of a blessedness with history haunts man from the moment he becomes aware of his situation in the cosmos.[1]

I began to read American Indian myths, and it wasn't long before I found the same motifs in the American Indian stories that I was being taught by the nuns at school.[2]

For wisdom is more precious than rubies, and nothing you desire can compare with her (Prov. 8:11, NIV).

---◆---

Wayne was a very open person who had lived in Taiwan studying both Buddhist and Taoist scriptures. He had also read widely, exploring Jungian psychoanalysis and modern scholarship on myth. He was now dedicating the remainder of his life to the pursuit of wisdom and plumbing the power of myths to heal and guide.

We believe myths cannot be dismissed as religious fiction, but rather are stories that give meaning to life—it is a simplistic understanding that relegates "myth" to "falsehood" or even "lie." Some myths are created at a particular point in time and place—they are related to historical events; others are not and can come to the surface from within our own being. Joseph Campbell (1904-87) once said, "All the gods, all the heavens, all the worlds are within us . . . Myth is a manifestation in symbolic images, in metaphorical images, of the energies of the organs of the body in conflict with each other."[3]

Wayne was attracted to our "Man behind the millennium" poster—it had struck a chord in him. This was a six-by-four-foot blow-up of the new millennium edition cover for the famous *Jesus* video. The poster comprised a close-up shot of the actor who portrayed Jesus, with a horizon shot of the sun rising underneath. Mr. Young Goh from the Jesus' Gift to the Nation/Campus Crusade ministry graciously loaned us this poster and supplied us with videos for free distribution from our booth. Wayne said, "Powerful stories of life's cycle—from my birth, growth, death, resurrection, and salvation—are found in common form in all cultures and religions." We heartily agreed. We went on to consider other common images, such as evil, creation, and Paradise.

"Our postmodern world is engaged in myth-making," Wayne asserted. "Movies like *Star Wars* and *The Matrix* draw on the world's myths and folklore." We then chatted about the movie-maker George Miller, who made *Babe* and the *Mad Max* movies. He maintains that the cinema has replaced the church as the place where people gather to hear significant stories to live by. Miller suggests that today's movie-makers are fulfilling the role played by priests and tribal elders in pre-modern times.[4]

Wayne's interest in Jungian psychoanalysis had led him over many years to consider the symbolism found in myths. Jung had been personally fascinated with occultism, Gnosticism, and the visionary teachings of Emanuel Swedenborg. Jung also delved into ancient occult texts such as the *I Ching*. There he had uncovered striking symbolic patterns between it and the images found in his patient's dreams. These symbols, which are scattered throughout human civilization, express the longing for healing, wholeness, and integration. For us all, this was a strong pointer to the psychic unity or oneness of humanity.

Spiritual Unity in Myth

One illustration of our spiritual unity that we discussed was the Sleeping Beauty myth. In this story, there is a common body of powerful symbolic images that highlight our need for healing.

There is, for example, the image of the old woman who brings a curse on an innocent young maiden. The curse involves a prophecy that, when she turns sixteen, she will fall into a deep sleep, and no one inside her kingdom will be able to save her. Be that as it may, another prophecy declares that a handsome prince who shall come from a faraway land will rescue her. The prince duly enters the kingdom after succeeding in great trials of courage, finds the young heroine, and liberates her with a kiss. She is restored, and the whole kingdom is healed as the curse is lifted.

Wayne went on to highlight the Sleeping Beauty motifs in various spiritual paths: the temptress who brings evil, the helpless victims who suffer, the error of lostness, the champion who brings deliverance, and Paradise restored.

As we were near the festive season, our thoughts readily turned to Father Christmas. With childlike enthusiasm, we talked about the common tales of Saint Nicholas, Père Noel, and Santa Claus.

Wayne's stress, therefore, was that we should explore and embrace the rich mythology of human experience. He invited us to find spiritual reality within these myths. We affirmed that if we open ourselves to the power of myth we can find truth, healing, and meaning in life. So, we agreed to look at some different myths, both ancient and modern.

The cosmic tree, floods, and mountains

The tree is a popular religious symbol. There is the promise of renewal found in the Christmas tree. The Druids saw the tree as a model of sacrifice. It gives food, air, wood, and shelter. They called it Hu-Hesus. Some Druid devotees find in this name a sign pointing to the sacrificial death of Jesus on a tree.

Also significant are the works of the Romanian phenomenologist Mircea Eliade (1907-86). Eliade found that the cosmic tree appears in many myths about Paradise. So it seems reasonable that its enactment can be found in the Tree of Life in the Garden of Eden.

Eliade likewise wrote of the Uitoto cannibals who experienced the whole of life as a dance. Their rituals continually reminded them of the pristine primordial paradise. They believed that partaking of human flesh connected them with the first human assassination that took place in this Utopia. Again myth would seem to point to the account of Cain and Abel, which speaks of such a primordial assassination as one brother slew another.[5]

Another widespread myth concerns floods. In some 200 different cultures there are flood myths. The predominant themes usually involve divine forewarning of a family, the building of a boat, livestock being taken on board and, when the flood hits, their preservation. Here we were reminded of what happened to Noah in the Sacred Writings.[6]

A similar motif is that of the cosmic mountain, where humans ascend to meet with the gods. The Christian's thoughts are naturally drawn to Moses on Mount Sinai.

All of us agreed that the works of Campbell, Jung and Eliade on myths offer a signpost to our basic unity—or, as Jung termed it, the "archetypes of the collective unconscious." We ourselves stressed that the Sacred Writings indicate that all humanity comes from the same stock, so we really should not be surprised to discover that we have common dreams, needs, and aspirations. As the Sacred Writings say, "From one person God made all nations who live on earth" (Acts 17:26, CEV).

Ross raised a growing concern that scholars have about Jung. Their apprehension is that people such as Jung have fallen for the fallacy of absolutizing myth. For example, the fact that Jung's patients had common mythological symbols in their dreams does not mean one can read this into the history of every religion.

A good illustration of this is the pole myth that appears in many communities. There is a pole that links the world to the heavens, and sometimes this pole is broken and needs to be restored. A few have sought to impose this myth on the Australian Aboriginal religion when it is not there.

New religious myths

Wayne felt that many new religious movements present myths to live by. Two scholars at the University of Calgary—Karla Poewe and Irving Hexham—have articulated this very thesis. Poewe is an anthropologist and Hexham a professor of religious studies. They suggest that today's new religious movements form miniature global cultures that offer distinct cosmologies and mythologies. They see alternative spiritualities as drawing on a common fund of ancient myths that are then recombined with modern ideas.[7]

Unquestionably, the interest in extraterrestrials provides fertile ground for significant myths to be recast. Such myths reflect universal human longings for a better way of living and for somebody greater than us to show us the way. Wayne himself astutely observed, "Many UFO stories seem to be about us being saved by those from other galaxies."

UFOs and extraterrestrials

When the Cold War started, unexplained aerial phenomena became widely discussed. Some spoke about alien abductions. Early science-fiction movies, such as *The Invasion of the Body-Snatchers*, often portrayed aliens as a threat. Others suggested that UFOs represented suppressed technology because, in the 1950s, aircraft makers experimented with anti-gravity craft. Even though the experiments failed, some believed that was only a cover-up, part of a global conspiracy to create a world government—a bit like an *X-Files* plot!

In groups such as the Raelians, contact with aliens is intimately connected with spiritual revelations.[8] The aliens' messages often emphasize recurrent themes, such as reincarnation, spiritual evolution, and the theosophical traditions of the ascended masters (Buddha, Jesus, and St. Germain).

Erich von Daniken maintained that prehistoric cultures had been visited by extraterrestrials in *Chariots of the Gods*. He argued that alien technology helped in the building of the pyramids. He saw alien encounters depicted in early religious art, and so the gods and goddesses were simply extraterrestrials. However, many would agree now that Von Daniken was a reductionist whose proposed evidence was very poor.[9]

While we agreed that new religions genuinely offer their followers myths to live by, we also pointed out that some have had grim reputations—as was the case with Jim Jones's People's Temple, David Koresh's Branch Davidians, and Heaven's Gate. Nevertheless, it would be a mistake to dismiss all groups as if they were just a variation on a theme. To understand them, we first need to let them speak for themselves and identify what myths they espouse before passing judgment.

Some detractors and ex-members counter these groups with myths about brainwashing or mind control.[10] At its crudest level, devotees are portrayed as dupes of behavioral and thought control. This is not to deny that some ex-devotees have had hurtful experiences. Some groups can be abusive and manipulative.[11] However, this myth-making can foster a "victim mentality" that diminishes personal accountability for decisions made as a member. Wayne observed that some disenchanted former devotees essentially swap sides but continue in similar thought patterns. The dedicated devotee who once sought to rescue the world in the group, now, as a former member, seeks to rescue the world from the group.[12]

The horned creature myths

Wayne then wanted to talk about a different but rather common tale in religious experience that relates to the personification of evil. Wayne said that, in his study of Taoism, he had become acquainted with the Chinese folk beliefs about ancestral and dark spirits.

Ross said that the figure of a trickster or tempter can be found in Icelandic myths, Celtic paganism, and Islam. Wayne spoke about how Gautama Buddha encountered the Mara when he was on the verge of enlightenment. He asked, "Is the idea of the Devil important for you guys?" We indicated that the Devil has a place in our understanding of the world. He then told us that one of his favorite movies is Al Pacino's *The Devil's Advocate*. "You know, that story confronted me with the ego's vanity," he remarked. We thoroughly agreed with him that vanity is something we have to deal with too.

However, Wayne saw the Devil only in symbolic terms, relating it to Jung's concept of the "shadow" in each of us. That there is a dark side woven into the fabric of our being is something that transformation writer M. Scott Peck has affirmed in *People of the Lie* and *Further Along the Road Less Traveled*.[13] We indicated that, for growth and transformation to occur, we have to own up to our personal "shadow" within.

We put it to Wayne that the Devil is not limited to symbolism. We raised with Wayne some seminal writings by the historian Jeffrey Russell. Russell argues that the only way to make sense of our universal experience of cosmic evil is to acknowledge the existence of a cosmic being who has poisoned human affairs. Russell surmises:

If the Devil does exist, what is he? If the concept has any meaning at all, he is the traditional Prince of Darkness, a mighty person with intelligence and will whose energies are bent on the destruction of the cosmos and the misery of its creatures. He is

the personification of radical evil, and he can never be irrelevant because humans have always sought to confront that evil. That search, that need, is a sign that meaning is there, however obscurely it seems to be hidden from the intellect . . . It is easier to go the Devil's way with hatred and violence and indifference. But the Devil's way not only is morally wrong; it is stupid. It will never work; it has never worked. Violence always provokes violence; hatred everywhere provokes hatred. Daily, we are reminded that we have not yet learned this. The Devil stands like a blind man in the sun, seeing only darkness where he stands among the brilliant green fields of God's creation. We have thought the Devil's way long enough. It is time for a new way of thinking.[14]

As a cosmic adversary, the Devil has been represented in the medieval European images of the great figure of Satan and has been present since time immemorial. One of the earliest Christian images is of Christ ransoming us from these spiritual bondages: "For he [God] has rescued us from the dominion of darkness and brought us into the kingdom of the Son he loves" (Col. 1:13, NIV).

Atlantis, Lemuria, and Paradise

Wayne was also interested in the Atlantis myth. The original story of Atlantis, of course, is found in the writings of Plato. The modern interest in the Atlantis story comes from the writings of I.T. Donnelly and has been further popularized by Shirley Maclaine. Donnelly saw it as a super-civilization of advanced technology and occult knowledge that gave birth simultaneously to the Egyptian and New World cultures.

Another potent lost continent saga concerns Lemuria (also called Mu). Some claim it sank into the Pacific, having once linked Japan with America and Oceania. Other occultists believe it connected Africa and India to Australia.

Atlantis and Mu Roots

Poewe and Hexham have shown that there is no evidence to suggest that Egypt and the New World had a common parentage. They had different languages, racial groups, technical developments, crops, medical insights, domestic animals, and cultures. Poewe and Hexham speak of these claims about Atlantis as being historically false. [15]

Charles Leadbeater, the influential theosophist, believed that a remnant of Lemuria was to be found among the indigenous tribes in Australia. If this were true, then the Aborigines would be the ancestors of our modern civilization. Occultists who believe in Lemuria imply that the secret spiritual practices of this lost continent are not fully expressed in the continuing Aboriginal traditions. One possible exception would be the spell of the tribal shaman pointing the bone. Despite this loss of Lemurian practices, they encourage us to learn from the Aborigines' attachment to the land.

Early European explorers groped for lost paradises in the uncharted parts of the world. Tales about lost continents such as Ponce De Leon's fountain of youth, the mythical kingdom of Prester John, as well as Sir Thomas More's Utopia inspired these quests. Those who followed in the wake of Columbus went west to the Americas in search of Paradise.

Many more believed that there was a great southern continent that was special to the heart of God and our human journey. Thus, the Spanish explorer Pedro de Quiros set out to find "the Great Southern Land of the Holy Spirit." The hopes of the Spanish, Portuguese, and Dutch of finding this virgin paradise of the Southern Hemisphere were put to rest by James Cook. In modern times, the common utopian myth inspired Marxists to build a new world uncorrupted by human evils. Their golden age of a classless society soured under the repression of the Iron Curtain.

The nourishment of myth

Since the Enlightenment, Western society has lacked the kind of unifying framework that traditional cultures have enjoyed. Wayne pointed to the indigenous peoples that have lived by their myths or "dreamtime." These stories have provided a context for meaning and a way of living in the world, whereas in our highly urbanized, technological society we have been lacking such a unifying fabric. The swing into postmodernity represents the first steps towards redressing these imbalances.

Alvin Toffler, in his *Future Shock*, describes our dilemma through the eyes of a young woman:

When you live in a neighborhood, you watch a series of changes take place. One day a new mailman delivers the mail. A few weeks later the girl at the check-out counter at the supermarket disappears and a new one takes her place. Next thing you know, the mechanic at the gas station is replaced. Meanwhile, a neighbor moves out next door and a new family moves in. These changes are taking place all the time, but they are gradual. When you move, you break all these ties at once and you have to start all over again. You have to find a new pediatrician, a new dentist, a new car mechanic who won't cheat you, and you quit all your organizations and start over again. It is the simultaneous rupture of a whole range of existing relationships that makes relocation psychologically taxing for many.[16]

John Naisbitt, in *Megatrends*, likewise strikes out at our anxieties by noting:

Helped by the news media, especially television, we seem to be a society of events, just moving from one incident—sometimes even

crisis—to the next, rarely pausing (or caring) to notice the process going on underneath.[17]

———————————— ◆ ————————————

The sense of disturbance in our mobilized technological society calls for the unifying framework of myth—folk tales that can be passed down from generation to generation. One "yarn" or folk tale that has broad application is the story of the prodigal son. We paraphrased it for Wayne this way.

A father has two sons and the younger asks for his freedom. The father gives him his share of the inheritance and the son goes and squanders it all in a foreign state. He ends up lost and alone, finding shelter in a pigsty. He plucks up courage and returns to his father, expecting at best to be received as a servant. His father, who has never lost his love for his son, sees him from afar and races to embrace him. The son who is lost has returned and is received joyously into the family. Sadly, the elder brother finds it difficult to accept the one his father has forgiven (see Luke 15:14-32).

In this story, we see the universal experience of mobility, lostness, greed, abandonment, and rejection. It speaks of our ache for healing, understanding, and unconditional love. Such tales of transformation to be found in the Sacred Writings offer truth to the individual, family, and community.

The power of fairy stories

Wayne loved *Lord of the Rings*, so we took time to consider the burgeoning field of fantasy novels. Three 20th-century authors who helped to spearhead this were C.S. Lewis, J.R.R. Tolkien, and Charles Williams. Lewis is remembered as the creator of the now classic fantasy novels The Chronicles of Narnia. Sir Anthony Hopkins poignantly portrayed Lewis's late-in-life marriage to Joy Davidman in the film *Shadowlands*. Tolkien, who wrote *Lord of the Rings*, was a colleague of Lewis at Oxford University. Together they formed an informal reading group called "The Inklings" and mutually encouraged each other as novelists.[18]

Charles Williams was a playwright, poet, and novelist, and worked at Oxford University Press in London. He joined The Inklings during the Second World War. Between 1930 and 1945, Williams wrote seven supernatural thriller novels, their themes of spirituality, magick, and the tarot resonating with today's New Age spirituality seekers.[19] Williams, Lewis, and Tolkien shared similar ideas about the power of myth to impact us spiritually.

Tolkien made some striking observations concerning our encounter with folk tales and myths. The climactic event or rescue that occurs in these stories Tolkien called the "eucatastrophe" —a joyful happening:

The gospels contain . . . a story of a larger kind which embraces all the essence of fairy stories . . . The birth of Christ is the eucatastrophe of man's history. The resurrection is the eucatastrophe of the story of the incarnation. This story begins and ends in joy. It has pre-eminently the "inner consistency of reality." There is no tale ever told that men would rather find was true, and none which so many skeptical men have accepted as true on its own merits. For the art of it has the supremely convincing tone of primary art, that is of creation. To reject it leads either to sadness or to wrath.[20]

We came with Wayne to a mutual understanding that common myths are at the heart of spiritual experience. The master Jesus put flesh on the myth.

Pursuing wisdom

Wayne was at a stage in life where inner reflection and walking in wisdom are paramount. We agreed with him that the journey of life involves growth and reflection, and living in wisdom is important. To deny it is to fall into dysfunctional living. The hunger for pithy, wise sayings to live by is reflected in popular pocket books such as *Life's Little Instruction Book*.[21]

We discussed how the wisdom books of the Sacred Writings—Proverbs, Ecclesiastes, and Job—help us to live. These texts set forth pithy, yet deep insights on everyday matters of life—rest, work, play, relationships, love, grief, and faith. We said that we do not view wisdom as being mere knowledge or understanding. For us, wisdom is a relational concept because it is connected with God. At a basic level, wisdom may concentrate on our conduct of life's practicalities. At its highest level, wisdom focuses us on a direct, personal relationship with God. Further, we said that the Sacred Writings offer us an unfolding view of wisdom. It begins with practical guidance for life and climaxes in the master, Jesus, whom the apostle Paul designated "the wisdom of God" (1 Cor. 1:24, NIV).

The fulfillment of myth

Wayne said it was essential for him to explore mythic symbols inside himself, and the key to this was Jungian analysis. Jung had goaded Wayne into knowledge (*gnosis*) of the heart via myths and motifs found experientially within. Wayne said that through this *gnosis* he saw a dualism within that needs to be reconciled.

We affirmed that Jung had been a seminal thinker. Many, like Wayne, undoubtedly feel a great debt of gratitude to Jung for his insights into human psychology. However, we wonder if Jung's approach to the interior journey alone is sufficient for transformation. Jung's interest in ancient Gnosticism and occultism had powerfully shaped the development of his psychoanalytic theory. Early on he also flirted with ideas akin to anti-Semitism.[22] Jung's inner gnosis differs at many key points from the holistic life-affirming way of Jesus. Although we feel that Jung's ideas can act as a catalyst for inner reflection, there is a much better door that opens us up to divine grace and spiritual transformation.

So, while affirming with Wayne that religion contains common myths that are available to be embraced in Christianity, we felt the need to stress one vital point. We explained that myths such as Sleeping Beauty and Utopia have an actual objective base. They are not just good internal realities, but are historical encounters. The champion (master Jesus) actually did come into our dimension to rescue the princess (us) by a kiss (the cross) and restore Paradise (heal our lost, soul-sorrow lives). This brings a unique light to the Sacred Writings.

All these myths testify to our universal longing to return to the "lost" Paradise where we have peace, harmony, and unity with one another and God. In *The Aquarian Guide to the New Age* we can sense the longing for a mythical past in the description of Atlantis:

Running halfway along the entire length of the island was a fertile coastal plain. Some miles away, in the center of the island, was a low mountain, possibly little more than a hill, on which developed the island's most ancient city. This city was surrounded by three moats, traditionally built by the god Poseidon. There was abundant vegetation and animal life, much of which seems to have been tropical in nature. There was mining for a now unknown ore, orichalcum, described as "more precious than anything but gold."[23]

In Christ, the myth has become reality and awaits its consummation:

Then I saw a new heaven and a new earth; for the first heaven and the first earth had passed away, and the sea was no more . . . And I heard a loud voice from the throne saying, "See, the home of God is among mortals. He will dwell with them; they will be his peoples, and God himself will be with them; he will wipe every tear from their eyes. Death will be no more; mourning and crying and pain will be no more, for the first things have passed away" (Rev. 21:1-4, NRSVB).

Endnotes

Chapter 4

1 Mircea Eliade, "The Yearning for Paradise in Primitive Tradition," in Henry Murray (ed.), *Myth and Mythmaking*, New York: George Braziller, 1960, p. 73.

2 Joseph Campbell with Bill Moyers, *The Power of Myth*, New York: Doubleday, 1988, p. 10.

3 Joseph Campbell, *The Power of Myth*, p. 39.

4 George Miller, "The Apocalypse and the Pig: or the Hazards of Storytelling," *The Sydney Papers*, 8, 4, 1996, pp. 39-49.

5 Mircea Eliade, *Myths, Dreams and Mysteries*, New York: Harper, 1975, pp. 43-47.

6 Lloyd R. Bailey, *Noah: The Person and the Story in History and Tradition*, Columbia: University of South Carolina Press, 1989; and John Warwick Montgomery, *The Quest for Noah's Ark*, 2nd edition, Minneapolis: Bethany, 1974.

7 Irving Hexham and Karla Poewe, *New Religions as Global Cultures*, Boulder: Westview, 1997.

8 James R. Lewis (ed.), *The Gods Have Landed: New Religions From Other Worlds*, Albany: State University of New York Press, 1995, pp. 105-135.

9 Erich von Daniken, *Chariots of the Gods*, London: Corgi, 1971; E.W. Castle and B.B. Thiering (eds), *Some Trust in Chariots*, Perth and Sydney: Westbooks, 1972; and Richard R. Lingemann, "Erich von Daniken's Genesis," *New York Times Book Review*, 31 March, 1974, p. 6.

10 Raphael Aron, *Cults Too Good To Be True*, Sydney: HarperCollins, 1999; Flo Conway and Jim Siegelman, *Snapping: America's Epidemic of Sudden Personality Change*, revised edition, New York: Stillpoint, 1995; and Steven Hassan, *Combatting Cult Mind Control*, revised edition, Rochester: Park Street, 1990.

11 Ronald M. Enroth, *Churches that Abuse*, Grand Rapids: Zondervan, 1992; and J. Gordon Melton, *Encyclopedic Handbook of Cults in America*, revised edition, New York and London: Garland, 1992, pp. 361-393.

12 On the weaknesses with brainwashing and mind control theories, see David G. Bromley and James T. Richardson (eds), *The Brainwashing/Deprogramming Controversy*, New York and Toronto: Edwin Mellen, 1983; Lorne L. Dawson, *Comprehending Cults*, Toronto and Oxford: Oxford University Press, 1998, pp. 102-127; Walter R. Martin, *The Kingdom of the Cults*, revised edition, Minneapolis: Bethany, 1997, pp. 49-78; and Larry D. Shinn, "Who Gets to Define Religion? The Conversion/Brainwashing Controversy," *Religious Studies Review*, 10, 3, 1993, pp. 195-207.

13 M. Scott Peck, *People of the Lie*, New York: Simon & Schuster, 1983; and *Further Along the Road Less Traveled*, New York: Simon & Schuster, 1993.

14 Jeffrey Russell, *The Prince of Darkness: Radical Evil and the Power of Good in History*, London: Thames & Hudson, 1989, pp. 276-277.

15 Irving Hexham and Karla Poewe, "The Evidence for Atlantis," *Christian Research Journal*, 12, 3, 1989, pp. 16-19.

16 Alvin Toffler, *Future Shock*, New York: Random House, 1970, p. 100.

17 John Naisbitt, *Megatrends*, New York: Warner, 1982, p. 2.

18 Humphrey Carpenter, *The Inklings*, London: George Allen & Unwin, 1978.

19 His novels include *Shadows of Ecstasy, Many Dimensions, War in Heaven, The Greater Trumps, The Place of the Lion, Descent into Hell* and *All Hallow's Eve.*

20 J.R.R. Tolkien, "On Fairy-Stories," in C.S. Lewis (ed.), *Essays Presented to Charles Williams,* Grand Rapids: Wm.B. Eerdmans, 1981, pp. 83-84.

21 H. Jackson Brown, *Life's Little Instruction Book,* Melbourne: Bookman, 1991.

22 Richard Noll, *The Jung Cult,* London: Fontana, 1996; and Robert Ellwood, *The Politics of Myth: A Study of C.G. Jung, Mircea Eliade, and Joseph Campbell,* Albany: State University of New York Press, 1999.

23 Eileen Campbell and J.H. Brennan, *The Aquarian Guide to the New Age,* London: Aquarian, 1990, p. 38.

Chapter 5
The Zodiac Revisited

Astrology gained such credit among men of all peoples of the world that it was the only branch of occult science which the church dared not formally condemn.[1]

Astrology is basically about self-awareness . . . It's about who you are and why you are here.[2]

During the time of King Herod, Magi from the east came to Jerusalem and asked, "Where is the one who has been born king of the Jews? We saw his star in the east and have come to worship him" (Matt. 2:1-2, NIV).

Matt is an astrologer whose stand was situated next to ours at a festival. After a career in the British navy and in advertising, Matt became a professional astrologer. We knew he was a colossus among his peers, with 25 years of experience as a practitioner. He proved to be one of the most interesting people we met at the festival.

Matt remarked, "It's great to see you Christians here. So often I find Christians very hostile to the sorts of pathways being explored at this festival. My own pathway to personal recovery and global harmony is astrology." We asked Matt, "What kind of astrology do you use?" He responded that his interest is in "judicial astrology"—the conviction that the planets and stars at the time of birth set forth your personality traits and the direction of your life.

Ross reached for the local newspaper and read out his horoscope. The star guide forecasted that he was going to enter into strong new relationships. "Is this the kind of astrology you're into?"

Matt laughed, "No, it's much more sophisticated than that. The pop stuff is not all that accurate—it's just for fun. Astrology, to be precise, must be calculated on the exact minute and place of your birth to discover what planet is ruling in the constellation you were born under. Also, the location of the Sun and other planets at that time is vital."

"So, do you hold to the ancient concept of the zodiac?" Philip interjected.

"Yes," Matt replied, and he explained in some detail how it worked.

Zodiac in a Nutshell

Stretched across the night sky is an imaginary band called the zodiac. The band or zodiac forms an arc across the sky that the Sun appears to take between sunrise and sunset. Now along that same arc 12 constellations appear to follow the Sun's movement. As you look at the night sky, you discover month by month what constellation is rising on the Earth's horizon and where the Sun, Moon, and planets are in relationship to it. This data helps astrologers to accurately determine which heavenly bodies were influencing you at the time of your birth. Each of the constellations has a sign, such as Aries, and the planets pass across the band some time during the 12-month cycle. Other influential factors on a person's horoscope include asteroids, comets, and eclipses.

The most important element is the Sun sign, which represents the Sun's position on the zodiac at the time of your birth. The Sun sign signifies personality traits. Then comes the rising sign, which reveals your character and talents. Each horoscope is subdivided into twelve houses. Each house influences a different dimension of life, such as personality, finance, health, relationships, career, and philosophy. Matt stressed to us that the horoscope is essentially a guide to both problems and opportunities.

There are two other systems of astrology, namely Chinese and Hindu. In these systems, much more emphasis is placed on fortune-telling, whereas in his modern Western approach astrology is more focused on therapy and counseling.

Our new friend Matt challenged us to assimilate into our path the benefits that judicial astrology brings. He has an unshakeable confidence in astrology as a guide to life. He looks to the zodiac as a means of helping himself and others recover from past hurts. For him, this is the way to find strength to lead a more productive life in relationships, business, and health.

Matt concluded, "Do you realize that astrology is in the Sacred Writings—that Christians have constantly dabbled in it?"

The Magi astrologers

We began to explore with Matt the path taken by one of the most famous groups of astrologers: the Magi. Long before the birth of Jesus, Babylon was the multicultural center of the fertile crescent. It boasted many prophets, priests, and sages who forecast the future.

In their midst flourished the Magi, a class of wise ones who devoted their lives to the study and interpretation of the stars. They were noted for lining up the births of significant people with cosmic signs. British scholar Richard France reports, "Astrological interest in Babylon and other parts of the East is well attested . . . The belief that the birth of great men was heralded by special stars is also widely attested."[3]

We reminded Matt that Nebuchadnezzar was Babylon's most famous king, and he customarily consulted the Magi. At a crucial point in his reign, Nebuchadnezzar had a mysterious dream, but its interpretation eluded the wise ones. It was at this time that a spiritually gifted Jew named Daniel joined the Magi.

Daniel was a Jewish exile whose reputation for prophetic gifts and understanding of dreams was widely regarded. He counseled Nebuchadnezzar about the limitations of the stars for personal guidance:

---◆---

No wise men, enchanter, magician or diviner can explain to the king the mystery that the king has asked about, but there is a God in heaven who reveals mysteries. He has shown King Nebuchadnezzar what will happen in days to come (Dan. 2:27-28, NIV).

---◆---

As Daniel unfolded the truths the king sought, he was appointed the chief of the astrologers (see Dan. 2:48).

The star of Jacob

Under Daniel's influence, the Magi came into contact with the Jewish Sacred Writings. These books recorded ancient predictions about Israel. One of these, known as the oracle of Balaam, forecast the coming of a spiritual master whose presence would be known by a heavenly sign: "the oracle of one whose eye sees clearly, the oracle of one who hears . . . and whose eyes are opened . . . A star will come out of Jacob; a scepter will rise out of Israel" (Num. 24:15-17, NIV).

Matt was not familiar with this oracle. Ross explained that it was a prophecy made by the pagan prophet Balaam.[4] The prophecy was about a mighty one, a descendant of Jacob, the tribal elder of Israel. This mighty one would arise in a far-off time, and a star would signify his presence. Balaam's allusion to the scepter indicated that he would be a king. That Balaam's oracle was well known and widely circulated in various, but corrupted forms is seen in the writings of the Roman historian Tacitus.[5]

Several centuries were to elapse before the Magi could positively identify "Jacob's star." Many feel that the star was the 6 B.C.

configuration between Jupiter (known in astrology as the king's planet), Saturn (the shield of Palestine), and Mars in the constellation of Pisces. The wise men traveled from Babylon to Jerusalem to find the Palestinian king whose birth was indicated by this sign.

The Magi were probably guided by more than just Balaam's oracle. As mentioned, Daniel predicted the future. He declared that the coming of the Messiah would occur before the destruction of the rebuilt temple in Jerusalem (see Dan. 9). The Magi would have been aware of the political disquiet in Palestine at the time of Jesus' birth. History reveals that the Romans destroyed the temple in A.D. 70.

So, the intriguing picture is of the Magi astrologers looking to the stars to connect them with the one foreshadowed by Balaam and Daniel. Their wish came true, and their door to transformation was opened. The Sacred Writings tell their story, and when they located the Christ-child, they worshiped him:

◆

When they saw the star, they were overjoyed. On coming to the house, they saw the child with his mother Mary, and they bowed down and worshiped him. Then they opened their treasures and presented him with gifts of gold and of incense and of myrrh.(Matt. 2:10-11, NIV).[6]

◆

The Mazzaroth

Matt enjoyed the story of the Magi. He believes that the Sacred Writings also support the use of the stars for casting horoscopes that bring personal guidance for our lives today. One commonly cited passage referred to by astrologers is found in the book of Genesis: "And God said, 'Let there be lights in the firmament of the heavens to divide the day from the night; and let them be for signs'" (Gen. 1:14, KJV).

The inference here is that the stars as signs have a spiritual message that can be decoded. Our friend Matt placed great weight on this, saying that even the Bible has judicial astrology. While we can appreciate this view, it is not supported by the text. The stars are evidence here of there being a Creator of our universe and its structures. As King David sang, "The heavens are telling the glory of God; and the firmament proclaims his handiwork" (Ps. 19:1, NRSVB).

Matt also claimed support from a lesser-known passage in the book of Job, where it reads:

Can you bind the chains of the Pleiades, or loose the cords of Orion? Can you lead forth the Mazzaroth in their season, or can you guide the Bear with its children? Do you know the ordinances of the heavens? Can you establish their rule on the earth? (Job 38:31-33, NRSVB).

The term *mazzaroth* is an ancient word for the zodiac, and the references to the constellations of Pleiades, Orion, and the Bear are believed to reinforce the idea that judicial astrology is looked on favorably here. The difficulty with this is that these words are only confirming that there is a zodiac (a band from which we see the position of the stars in the night sky) and constellations—concepts held by both astrologers and astronomers. It is not a passage that speaks of casting horoscopes, but describes in a poetic way the intricacies of the observable heavens. It is a passage that both the believer in astrology and the skeptic could affirm.

In fact, the context of the verse warns Job not to lose his faith in God in the hard times, as he is the one who controls all things. Indeed, the Sacred Writings draw attention to the dangers of pursuing personal guidance from the stars as opposed to positively connecting with their Creator. As we have recognized,

Daniel, the chief of the Magi, spoke against relying on the stars in this way. Isaiah the sage declared:

◆

Stand fast in your enchantments and your many sorceries, with which you have labored from your youth; perhaps you may be able to succeed, perhaps you may inspire terror. You are wearied with your many consultations; let those who study the heavens stand up and save you, those who gaze at the stars and at each new moon predict what shall befall you. See, they are like stubble, the fire consumes them; they cannot deliver themselves from the power of the flame (Isa. 47:12-14, NRSVB).

◆

Synagogues and zodiac mosaics

The next area we explored concerned the discovery of zodiac mosaics in several Jewish synagogues excavated in Asia Minor. Matt's basic point was that, despite the apparent denunciation of astrology in the Sacred Writings, the chosen people obviously found astrology important enough to incorporate the zodiac signs on the floors of their synagogues. We agreed that he had raised a good point, but suggested that there was more here than met the eye.

We said that the only synagogues excavated with these mosaics date from the Byzantine era (from the early fourth century until the mid-seventh century A.D.). This places the artwork several centuries after the close of the Jewish canon of the Sacred Writings.

The Byzantine Factor

Admittedly before the Byzantine period there is evidence to suggest that the Qumran sect that composed the Dead Sea Scrolls was open to astrology. However, they were a separatist sect not aligned with mainstream Jewish religious practices at the time of Jesus' ministry. The real encroachment of astrology on the Jewish faith occurs during the Byzantine era. The Jewish Talmud records a range of rabbinic views on astrology—from mild acceptance to utter rejection—but does not offer a conclusive answer.

Another point is that Jewish religious observances were dated by the lunar calendar, whereas classic astrology operates on a solar calendar. As the solar monthly astrological signs do not correlate to the Jewish lunar calendar, it is difficult to see how the star signs could fit in with their core spiritual beliefs and observances. So, the significance of the zodiacal signs for the Jews must be sought in something other than an outright acceptance of astrology.

In the ancient world, astrology was invariably associated with the power of one's gods and goddesses. Lester Ness, who is an expert on astrology in Judaism, points out that what the Jews did was to give a distinctive Judaic interpretation to the zodiac signs:

◆

The planets were God's angels and the rules of astrology were YHWH's [God's] rules. Jews also adopted astrological symbolism and gave it their own interpretation. It was not possible to portray God directly. This was forbidden by the Second Commandment. But it was possible to portray Him indirectly, by portraying his assistants, the angels of astrology. It is important, too, that the zodiac is always shown together with images of salvation, such as Daniel or Isaac, and with symbols of Jewish religion, such as the menorah or the Ark.[7]

◆

So, in this later Jewish context, the symbolism of the zodiac was employed in artwork as a reminder of the Creator's supremacy and associated with the salvation he brings to his people through the prophets and sacred instruments. Today, many contemporary synagogues' ceilings are decorated with stars, high-lighting our connection with the Creator and the cosmos.

The popularity of astrology

At this juncture Matt raised with us the exploding popularity of judicial astrology. He told us that he was personally aware of a growing number of Christians who are enchanted with the stars. We indicated that this fascination was not supported by the early church, which was the repository of the master's and his disciples' teachings. An early respected witness to this is the second-century treatise *The Teaching of the Twelve Apostles*, commonly known as The Didache. In its instruction on "the way of life," it unfolds this principle:

Be not an observer of omens, since it leadeth the way to idolatry; neither an enchanter, nor an astrologer, nor a purifier, nor be willing to look at these things; for out of all these idolatry is engendered.[8]

This principle was difficult for Matt to accept as he had firmly based his own road to recovery on the zodiac. He reiterated to us the undeniable trend among modern Christians to dabble in astrology in their search for meaning and self-discovery. We agreed with Matt that, sadly, the church has often not addressed their drive for meaning and direction. We decided to delve more deeply.

"Outing" Christian astrologers

Our probing brought us to the early Protestants of the 16th and 17th centuries, many of whom were both active astronomers and astrologers. This is a fact that many Christians are not aware of. As one historian of the occult, John Warwick Montgomery, reports:

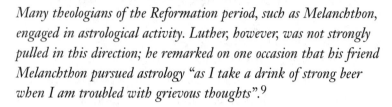

Many theologians of the Reformation period, such as Melanchthon, engaged in astrological activity. Luther, however, was not strongly pulled in this direction; he remarked on one occasion that his friend Melanchthon pursued astrology "as I take a drink of strong beer when I am troubled with grievous thoughts".[9]

Two of the early Protestant fathers of modern astronomy, Tycho Brahe and Johann Kepler, were also vigorous astrologers who cast their own personal horoscopes and forecast weather patterns by means of astrology. Oliver Cromwell is reputed to have consulted the famous English astrologer, William Lilly.[10] It is worth noting that, on the whole, these astronomer-astrologers were prominent supporters of Copernicus.

Copernicus

It may be remembered that Copernicus was the one who found that the Sun was at the center of the solar system. Kepler, who formulated the laws of planetary motion, in a real sense later confirmed his discovery. Kepler's approach to astrology involved rejecting the old Ptolemaic view that the Earth was at the center of the solar system. He sought to correct errors he found in astrology on the basis of the Copernican discovery that the Sun was at the center and all planets revolved around it.

We paused to consider what motivated them. Our discovery was that they were drawn to the heavens because they resonated with the work of an eternal architectural mind. Kepler aptly expressed that they were not into astrology for the sake of it, but it focused their lives on the one beyond the stars. Kepler wrote, "I thank thee, O Lord, our Creator, that thou hast permitted me to look at the beauty in thy work of creation; I exult in the works of thy hands."[11]

In fairness to these 16th- and 17th-century Christian leaders, it should be said that they found their surest guide to existence in dependence on Jesus and the Sacred Writings. Even when they toyed with horoscopes, they were never trapped into accepting that the stars ruled and life was fatalistic.

Further, while they had some leanings towards judicial astrology, their primary labors were directed at developing the more precise science of astronomical and meteorological calculations concerning the motions of the planets, stars, and comets. They flourished in an era when the boundaries between astrology and astronomy were blurred. Their overall outlook is seen in the teaching of Kepler's friend, Johann Valentin Andreae (1586-1654):

---◆---

It is an uncertain thing to make everything dependent on the first moment of existence and birth . . . The most fortunate horoscope is that of adoption into the ranks of sons of God, whose Father, when consulted by prayer, rarely is silent upon anything; when besought rarely refuses anything, so far is it from him to expose them to wanderings of the stars. The wanderer on the Earth realizes this; and in the shadow of God he fears no storms of the sky.[12]

---◆---

Links between Christianity and the zodiac

A novel, but lesser-known, attempt to integrate the zodiac with Christianity was made by two 19th-century writers, Joseph Seiss and Ethelbert Bullinger. These thinkers believed that the message of Jesus could be correlated with the signs of the zodiac. They saw in the constellations a cosmic witness to the coming of Christ.[13]

The "Cosmic Witness"

"Virgo the virgin" is maintained to be a foreshadowing of the birth of Christ. It is claimed that the name of one of the stars in this constellation means literally "the seed." Therefore, the two central characters of the Christmas story—maiden and child—are present and this predates the prophecy of Isaiah: "The virgin will be with child and will give birth to a son, and will call him Immanuel" (Isa. 7:14, NIV).

All the zodiac signs represent a cosmic dance that progressively discloses the lamb who brings healing to this world. The lamb waltzes his way through each constellation, signifying at every juncture what he will do to provide for our needs. Beginning with Aries, the sacrificial ram, and ending with Pisces, the fish (the symbol of the early Christians), each sign bears cosmic witness to our hearts about the lamb who is master over all the zodiac.

While this position is stimulating, some, such as ex-astrologer Charles Strohmer, suggest that it is speculative and have little sympathy for it.[14] While acknowledging some of Strohmer's valid concerns, we still feel that his antipathy resembles the reactions of a reformed smoker at a smokers' convention. Seiss and Bullinger, whatever their eccentricities, did make a fundamentally important point: the role of the stars is to lead people to God in Christ. They even took seriously nature's link with the human journey. Perhaps if humankind had not lost its link with Paradise, the stars would more clearly reveal God's blueprint for the world.

C.S. Lewis's living cosmos

Matt put it to us that astrology is filling a spiritual void in people's lives. We concurred with him. We are sure that one reason New Age seekers find it so appealing is that it gives a feeling of hope that we are in a living universe. One of the legacies of modernity is that the cosmos has been regarded as an object of study. While we can applaud the wondrous discoveries made through the telescope, we have become detached from the cosmos. We are passive observers, not active participants.

Another outcome is the sense that we are cosmic orphans. The French biologist Jacques Monod once aphorized, "Man finally knows that he is alone in the indifferent immensity of the universe."[15] Monod's remark epitomizes the modernity mindset in its antipathy toward spiritual and supernatural explanations of life. It is hardly surprising that this mindset is now regarded by many as bankrupt. No wonder there is a revolt against this moribund view and a resurgent interest in astrology. It is not necessarily a flight into irrationality, but, rather, reflects a hunger to restore something spiritual that was denied or suppressed by the agenda of Enlightenment thought.[16]

We suggested to Matt that postmodern yearnings for a living cosmos resonate with the novels of C.S. Lewis. Apart from his famous children's books, The Chronicles of Narnia, Lewis also wrote a science-fiction trilogy—*Out of the Silent Planet, Voyage to Venus*, and *That Hideous Strength*.[17]

In both his science-fiction trilogy and The Chronicles of Narnia, Lewis offers an alternative vision of the universe. Instead of outer space and the planets being cold, dead and bereft of meaning, Lewis portrays a cosmos that shimmers with love, meaning and vitality. Lewis does not simply introduce us to beings that live on Mars and Venus or in the mythical land of Narnia, he celebrates the cosmos as being alive. In the Narnian tale *The Magician's Nephew*, Aslan creates the cosmos by singing everything into existence. In Lewis's vision, the stars may be made of gases, but they signify something more. They reflect the beauty, order, and harmony of God's being. So, the stars do not propel our destiny, they are part of a seamless reality.

Through Lewis's stories we glimpse something that many ancient peoples affirmed: all existence is interdependent and resonates with the power and presence of the Creator God. The whole cosmos is connected because God created everything. This vision of vitality and connectedness is consistent with the Sacred

Writings, where the stars and cosmos sing praises to the Creator (see Ps. 148:1-6; Ps. 8; Job 38:4-7; Rom. 8:19-23). Like us, the stars are made of much more than mere matter.

Astrology as a science

Matt asserted that astrology is a science. We knew that, since the Renaissance, astrology has been classified, along with alchemy and the Qabalah, as one of the hermetic sciences. The hermetic sciences offer an esoteric vision of reality. The structures of nature are regarded as containing concealed symbols that can be deciphered and interpreted to furnish spiritual meaning.[18]

Matt was keen for us to consider the work of the late Michel Gauquelin, a scientist from the University of Paris who researched astrology for over thirty years. He told us how Gauquelin tested the influence of Mars on 2,088 sports champions at the time of their birth. Gauquelin's statistical results, which were published in the early 1960s, were significantly in favor of a correlation. He proposed that there could be an emerging new science, which he dubbed "cosmobiology."

However, Matt clearly intended more than just this. He also meant that astrology is scientific in two other senses. First, it is scientific due to the precise measurements made in the star charts. Second, it is a scientific tool for revealing the genetic and psychological make-up of people.

The precise measurements of the stars

Astrology is based on the view that the Earth is at the center of the solar system. However, as indicated before, we are now children of the Copernican revolution. We also know of three important cycles— the daily and yearly cycles of the Earth and the procession of the equinoxes. With the procession of the equinoxes, the constellations of the zodiac move backwards in relation to the Earth's cycles. Every 2,000 years, the zodiac signs change so that the constellation now in vogue is actually Capricorn not Aquarius. This means that, with respect to the signs of the constellations, astrologers are wrong in projecting their forecasts on the basis of the planets' interactions with a fixed Earth. Also, we know of the existence of more planets (Uranus, Neptune, Pluto) than the ancient astrologers were aware of. Surely these extra planets raise questions as to the precision of traditional astrology as a science.

Modern astrologers have tended to dismiss these problems by saying that the new discoveries simply make their science more exact and that even if we don't fully understand why astrology works, we do know that it does work.

However, Matt was unaware of the subsequent controversy about the Mars effect. In the 1980s, a committee of French scientists in co-operation with Gauquelin applied his Mars test to 1,000 sports champions. The statistical results were very poor. Gauquelin's original research was called into doubt and a bitter dispute ensued between him and his colleagues. Sadly, Gauquelin's loss of reputation led him to destroy his own files, and, after a nervous breakdown, he committed suicide on May 20, 1991. In 1996, after reanalysing the data, the French scientists published their report.[19]

Apart from this extraordinary debate, we also drew Matt's attention to Gauquelin's later writings, where he indicated that he was not convinced about astrology. Gauquelin did further detailed tests on astrologers, where he asked them to match up people's characteristics with their horoscopes. The results were dismal. Gauquelin concluded:

It is now quite certain that the signs in the sky which presided over our births have no power whatever to decide our fates, to affect our hereditary characteristics or play any part however humble in the

totality of effects, random and otherwise, which form the fabric of our lives and mould our impulses to action.[20]

As for one's psychological make-up, there are surely more complex influences on it than the planets.

The genetic and psychological make-up of people

Astrologers claim that the positions of the planets at the precise moment of your birth give you a natal chart that shows you your genetic make-up. Matt illustrated this by saying that the stars hold the key to understanding crime. He said that he had studied many cases where the horoscopes of both the victim and the criminal contain their roles. There is no need for punishment here. Astrology can help you understand yourself and enable you to rewrite your script.

There is no disputing that we as people are subject to genetic influences. That heart disease and genetically inherited proneness to illnesses can have a profound effect on a family's medical history is a documented fact. There is also the curious link between the presence of a full or new moon and an upsurge in lunacy, where the fluid on the brain appears to be affected. The connection between the moon and the monthly cycle of a menstruating woman is also known. However, to assert that all matters of health are correlated to the planets is at best conjecture.

Genetic scripting was explored by the French astronomer Paul Couderc who tested the oft-made claim that musical ability relates to the position of the sun at the time of birth. After looking at over 2,000 horoscopes of musicians, he concluded:

> *The position of the Sun has absolutely no musical significance. The musicians are born throughout the entire year on a chance basis. No sign of the zodiac or fraction of a sign favors or does not favor them. We conclude: the assets of scientific astrology are equal to zero, as is the case with commercialized astrology. This is perhaps unfortunate, but it is a fact.*[21]

Astrology works!

Another common response to the question "Why should we be
involved in judicial astrology?" (apart from "no" on biblical and
scientific grounds), is "It works." After the festival, Philip spent
five hours in further dialogue with Matt at the astrological college
where he trains people to be professional astrologers. He had
taken the initiative to prepare Philip's natal chart, even though
Philip had not requested it. Matt was keen to let astrology speak
for itself.

Philip was born at the start of the astrological year (Aries) at
1:00 a.m. Matt remarked that, in twenty-five years of astrological
work, he had never seen a natal chart where the Sun was at zero
degrees. He explained that, from the Sun and planetary configurations, he could pinpoint, year by year, when significant personal
events had occurred. For example, the chart disclosed a significant configuration when Philip was two years old. However,
when Philip indicated that nothing important occurred, Matt was
surprised.

Matt was further puzzled when, later on, a real significant year
came and there was no matching configuration for that period in
the chart. Matt then asked if the time for Philip's birth was correct. He said that each tick of the clock is important with respect
to the angles of the Sun and planets. Matt indicated that the
anomaly in the chart was probably due to an inaccurate recording
of the time of birth. After rechecking his calculations, he
announced that the chart's configurations when aligned with
Philip's true chronology indicated the correct time of birth was
12:40 a.m. Unfortunately for Matt, this is not so. Philip's mother
was meticulous in keeping accurate baby records, including the
times when each of her children was born. So the chart's configurations could not be aligned with the major personal events in
Philip's life.

In contrast to Philip's experiences, Ross has found that his
own star sign profiles have generally been correct with respect
to his personality. For many years, Ross has been fascinated
with Iceland. He has repeatedly encountered statements in

horoscopes for his star sign of Aquarius, stressing an interest in travel to Iceland.

On another occasion, we did witness an intriguing encounter between a leading astrologer, Barry and a Christian. We were teaching a course on alternative spirituality at a Bible college. We felt that the students should not be confined to mere ivory tower instruction, but should have some practical, first-hand exposure to devotees of other pathways. So, we made arrangements for Barry to address the class about why he became an astrologer. Barry remarked:

I became interested in astrology at the end of 1989 after my second marriage broke up and I went through a pretty dark phase. I did various self-awareness programs and also decided to study astrology. I started to look for some answers in life. The more I learned about astrology, the more I learned about myself. One of the things you learn is that if you are out of harmony with the universe, you are out of harmony with yourself. I've totally changed in the past couple of years. Even my first wife says I've changed. I'm not on an airy-fairy trip, but there is more to life than left-brain logic. You have to get in touch with your right-brain, intuitive self. I'm experiencing peace and harmony . . . I wouldn't waste my time on astrology if it was a sham. I know it works.[22]

After his presentation, the students had an opportunity to question and challenge Barry. One student challenged him by arguing that astrology was unscientific, unreliable, and irrational. Barry offered to demonstratse to the student that astrology works. He said that he did not have at hand all the technical apparatus for drawing up a complete chart, but that he had enough manuals with him to draw a fairly accurate profile. The student stated his time, date, and place of birth. Within a few minutes, Barry was ready to respond. Barry described the student's family background, what his interests in school were, the sorts of jobs he had had, what sort of women he had been attracted to and described the characteristics of his wife. In each of these respects Barry's profile was right on, so the student's skepticism was severely shaken.

So, it has been our experience that, at times, astrology can appear to be correct, but, at other times, it is completely wrong. We believe one reason for this is that, in the areas of personal guidance, astrology has biblical and scientific limitations. As well, a general psychological profile is likely to ring true in some cases. Charles Strohmer has this sobering thought:

As much as a person can be, I was into astrology for almost eight years. And I stayed with it because it "worked." I thought that this was good enough reason to stick with something. In July 1976, I found out that this was not reason enough. This may seem obvious, but not until then did I grasp that just because something "works," it is not necessarily synonymous with what is right and true. That a thing works does not mean that it should be used. Some things when they work explode and maim . . . Mars doesn't rule Aries; Venus doesn't rule Libra; Jupiter doesn't rule Sagittarius; Mercury doesn't rule Gemini. But God the Lord does have rule over all things. Pray to hear the impassioned plea that crackles in his voice.[23]

A final chat

Our exploration of astrology with Matt showed us that it does indeed appear in the Sacred Writings. When it is mentioned, though, the stress is not on personal guidance from the stars. Rather, the scrolls ask why one should seek guidance from the "rocks" of the universe when one can go to the source of the universe. The Magi discovered that the true role of the stars in the

Sacred Writings is to lead us to God in Christ. They found the path to transformation in him. This is precisely the same "therapy" Christian astrologers referred to above relied on.

As our final chat with Matt at the festival concluded, he asked Ross to supply him with the details of his exact time of birth so that he could draft his chart. This was embarrassing because, for personal reasons, Ross would never have access to this information. So Matt then could not help out with this "scientific" tool in mapping out a process for recovery. The sense of rejection that Ross experienced was intense. When it was pointed out to Matt that he could not touch the lives of many in need, he appeared to feel the pain. He had been a good friend.

In contrast to the evident limitations of Matt's astrology, there comes the universal and unlimited call of the master:

Come to me, all you who are weary and burdened, and I will give you rest. Take my yoke upon you and learn from me, for I am gentle and humble in heart, and you will find rest for your souls. (Matt. 11:28-29, NIV).

Endnotes

Chapter 5

1 Emile Grillot De Givry, *Illustrated Anthology of Witchcraft, Magic and Alchemy*, New York: Dover, 1971, pp. 221, 226.

2 Barry Eaton, interviewed by Lenore Nicklin, "Struck by the Stars," *The Bulletin*, 29 September 1992, p. 45.

3 "Scripture, Tradition and History in the Infancy Narratives of Matthew," in R.T. France and D. Wenham (eds), *Gospel Perspectives*, volume 2, Sheffield: JSOT Press, 1981, p. 257.

4 See J.A. Hackett, *The Balaam Text from Deir Alla*, Chico: Scholars Press, 1984.

5 Tacitus, *The Histories*, Book 5, 13.

6 See Edwin M. Yamauchi, *Persia and the Bible*, Grand Rapids: Baker, 1990, pp. 467-491.

7 Lester Ness, 'Astrology', *Archaeology in the Biblical World*, 2, 1, 1992, p. 51.

8 "The Teaching of the Twelve Apostles," chapter 3: 4, in A. Roberts and J. Donaldson (eds), *Ante-Nicene Fathers*, volume 7, Grand Rapids: Wm.B. Eerdmans, 1979, p. 378.

9 John Warwick Montgomery, *Principalities and Powers*, Minneapolis: Bethany, 1973, p. 65.

10 Derek Palmer, *Familiar To All: William Lilly and Astrology in the Seventeenth Century*, London: Jonathan Cape, 1975, pp. 201-202.

11 Johann Kepler, *Harmony of the World*, 1609, as cited by John Warwick Montgomery, *In Defense of Martin Luther*, Milwaukee: Northwestern Publishing House, 1970, p. 99.

12 Johann Valentin Andreae, *Christianopolis*, chapter 48, 1619, as translated in John Warwick Montgomery, *Cross and Crucible*, volume 1, The Hague: Martinus Nijhoff, 1973, p. 200.

13 Psalm 19:1-4 read in the light of Romans 10:17-18—see Joseph A. Seiss, *The Gospel in the Stars*, reprinted edition, Grand Rapids: Kregel Publications, 1972; and Ethelbert Bullinger, *The Witness of the Stars*, reprinted edition, Grand Rapids: Kregel Publications, 1967.

14 Charles Strohmer, "Is There a Christian Zodiac, A Gospel in the Stars?", *Christian Research Journal*, 22, 4, 2000, pp. 22-25, 40-44.

15 Jacques Monod, interviewed in *Newsweek*, 26 April 1971, p. 99.

16 For a contrasting view, see K.R. Birkett, "Starry Eyed: the Lure of Irrationalism," *Kategoria*, 4, 1997, pp. 11-28.

17 See C.S. Lewis, *Out of the Silent Planet*, London: Pan, 1979; *Voyage to Venus*, London: Pan, 1978; and *That Hideous Strength*, London: Pan, 1979.

18 On hermeticism, see R. van den Broek and W.J. Hanegraaff (eds), *Gnosis and Hermeticism: From Antiquity to Modern Times*, Albany: State University of New York Press, 1998.

19 Claude Benski (ed.), *The Mars Effect: A French Test of 1000 Sports Champions*, Buffalo: Prometheus, 1996.

20 Michel Gauquelin, *The Scientific Basis of Astrology: Myth or Reality*, New York:

Stein & Day, 1973, p. 145; and Michel Gauquelin, *Dreams and Illusions of Astrology*, Buffalo: Prometheus, 1979.

[21] Paul Couderc, *L'Astrologie*, Paris: Presses Universitaires de France, 1961, as translated by John Warwick Montgomery, *Principalities and Powers*, Minneapolis: Bethany, 1973, p. 114.

[22.] Barry Eaton, 'Struck by the stars', *The Bulletin*, 29 September 1992, p. 45. Although these summary remarks are from this interview, they are consistent with Barry's presentation at the college.

[23.] Charles Strohmer, *What Your Horoscope Doesn't Tell You*, Wheaton: Tyndale, 1988, pp. 11, 109.

Chapter 6
Psychotechnologies and Complementary Therapies

---◆---

The tarot is not magic or superstition, and its authority is not based in some occult or mysterious force. Rather, the power of the tarot comes from your own consciousness, from the thoughts and feelings that influence you and are important to you. The archetypal images of the tarot reflect the universal experience of humanity throughout the ages.[1]

Health and disease don't just happen. They are active processes issuing from inner harmony or disharmony, profoundly affected by our states of consciousness, our ability or inability to flow with experience. This recognition carries with it implicit responsibility and opportunity. If we are participating, however unconsciously, in the process of disease, we can choose health instead.[2]

Is any one of you sick? He should call the elders of the church to pray over him and anoint him with oil in the name of the Lord. And the prayer offered in faith will make the sick person well; the Lord will raise him up (James 5:14-15, NIV).

---◆---

Joanne, Vicki, and Elena were frequent visitors to our stand. They were initially attracted to our "Face in the snow" display and its accompanying slogan, "Life is a puzzle. He can make sense of it." The "Face in the snow" is based on a photographic negative that was taken of some burnt coals found in the snow.

After the negative was developed, the photographer believed he could discern the face of Jesus in the coals. Of course, none of us knows precisely what Jesus looked like. It was a talking point, as patrons were fascinated because it requires patient focusing of the eyes to see the "face." Some could spot it immediately, while others had to revisit the stand three or four times before they could see it.

Joanne and her friends were in their mid-thirties, and they had come to the festival to explore a wide range of psychotechnologies in their pursuit for inner healing. So we had a number of conversations with each of them about the most popular tools. We all found ourselves enjoying these discussions and were mutually challenged in our respective pathways.

Understanding psychotechnological tools

At this juncture, it might be useful to identify and describe some of these techniques and then explore whether or not they are in harmony with those found in the Sacred Writings.

ALCHEMY

Joanne had read some books about alchemy, which is one of the oldest hermetic sciences and was the forerunner of chemistry and metallurgy. It was associated with early metallurgy because the ores came from the "earth's womb." Popularly alchemy became associated with the attempt to turn lead into gold with the aid of a hidden, perfect substance. Alchemy then developed into a parallel spiritual quest for self-purification and immortality. Alchemists believed that they could find a substance that would confer immortality. It was known by various titles—the elixir of life, fountain of youth, and philosopher's stone.

Essential Alchemy

The ideas of the mythical figure Hermes Trismegistus (thrice-great Hermes) influenced alchemists. He is credited with the insight

"As above, so below." This means there are correspondences between cosmic reality and our world. If we are adept, we can master a part of the world, and so mastery can be attained over all things. So the alchemist seeks inner purity and eternal life. Chemical experiments are symbolic of the inner spiritual changes they are undergoing. Their secret texts on changing metals such as lead into gold are concerned about the inner spiritual realities.

Alchemy flourished during the Renaissance and Reformation eras in Europe and also in colonial America, but was submerged by modern chemistry. Brazilian storyteller Paulo Coelho captures the quest in his novel *The Alchemist*, coinciding with its re-emergence today as a tool for transformation.[3]

AURAS

Vicki showed us her aura photo. The psychic told her that all life forms have an "etheric" body, or energy shadow, surrounding their physical form and this is the aura. The aura is likened to the halo often drawn in artistic depictions of saints. The aura may be seen by means of a high-voltage, high-frequency electronic photographic technique, known as Kirlian photography.

Photographing an Aura

A Kirlian photo, it is said, shows flares of energy radiating around the body. The colors of an aura, it is claimed, can reveal your emotional and spiritual well-being.[4] Some students of the occult believe that our auras may survive for a short time after the death of the physical body and that this accounts for ghosts.[5]

CHANNELING

Elena was open to channeling. It involves opening up to a disembodied entity who may speak through us with a spiritual message. This entity could be a departed soul, an ascended master, such as Buddha, an entity from another galaxy, or perhaps, a group entity. Sometimes the channeller needs to enter a trance state in order to receive the message. Others surrender their body and some show little physiological or emotional change.

Variations on Channeling

Another way seekers try to receive messages from beyond is by using a Ouija board, where the message is slowly spelled out by a pointer in answer to questions, or by conducting a séance. Some of the best-known channeled entities include "Seth" (Jane Roberts), "Lazaris" (Jack Pursel), "Mafu" (Penny Torres) and "Ramtha" (J.Z. Knight).[6]

CLAIRVOYANCE AND PROPHECY

Clairvoyance is a gift that some highly attuned and sensitive people have by means of which they may foresee the future. Vicki said clairvoyants could have intimate knowledge of a person merely by touching an article belonging to them.

Prophecy

Prophecy is an inspired vision of events to come. The Hebrew prophets were involved in both foretelling future events and forthtelling, or reminding the Hebrew community not to neglect God's moral standards for social justice. Nostradamus (1503-66) is remembered for his cryptic prophecies. Edgar Cayce (1877-1945) the "sleeping prophet" gave predictions while in a trance. Jeane Dixon achieved notoriety for her prediction concerning the death of President Kennedy.[7]

A COURSE IN MIRACLES

Elena had read *A Course in Miracles*, which is a weighty tome divided into three parts: textbook, workbook, and teacher's manual.[8] It holds forth a pathway to transformation that requires dedication and discipline, as it takes a year to complete the Course's exercises.

The Course, which was first published in 1975, is a channeled work received by Helen Schucman between 1965 and 1973.[9] Although not explicitly stated by Schucman, she implies that the source of the message she wrote down is Jesus. *The Course* attempts to explain the illusory nature of our ego. According to it we mistake the material world for true reality. The ego is transient, while our true identity is found in God. We are one with God in our very being, for God is an impersonal mind. *The Course* also seeks to clear away our misconceptions about guilt. We have two choices in life—love or fear. *The Course's* exercises are designed to assist the seeker in integrating the channeled insights and finding transformation by choosing love, not fear.

Following the Course

The Course is a seminal work, having sold over a million copies and spawning a number of books inspired by its message. The spin-off books include Gerald Jampolsky's *Love is Letting Go of Fear*, Kenneth Wapnick's *The Meaning of Forgiveness*, and Marianne Williamson's *A Return to Love*.[10]

ENNEAGRAM

Joanne told us that the enneagram is a system of classifying and understanding human nature on the basis of a symbolic device (drawn as a circle containing nine equidistant points on the circumference) alleged to have been developed thousands of years ago. The Russian gnostic-sufi-mystic George Gurdjieff and the psychic Oscar Ichazo shaped the current form of the enneagram.

There are nine personality types categorized into three basic groups, or triads:
- the feeling triad embraces the helper, motivator, and artist
- the doing triad embraces the thinker, generalist, and loyalist
- the relating triad embraces the leader, peacemaker, and reformer

As you ponder on which group you fit into, you discover what personality type you are. Then you will have an enhanced self-understanding, improved relations with others, and be attuned spiritually.[11]

FENG SHUI AND GEOMANCY

Joanne was interested in feng shui. It is the ancient Chinese folk religious practice of placing objects in such a way as to promote good fortune in people's lives. This is achieved by arranging the environmental settings of home and office to create a harmonious space and atmosphere. Feng shui literally means "wind and water". The basic theory is that the way a building, room, window, street, mountain, or hill face the water and wind has a profound effect on human well-being.

Taoism and Feng Shui

Two Taoist concepts are important here: chi and yin and yang. To the Taoist, chi—cosmic energy or breath—flows throughout the natural world. If the flow is blocked, problems will occur. Yin and yang are two equal, opposite yet complementary forces (types of chi) found in everything that exists and which need to be kept in balance. These elemental forces are just two aspects of one reality, just like the north and south poles. Yin represents the dark, negative principles, while yang represents the light, positive principles. So, harmony with the natural order produces health, wealth, and happiness.

A feng shui master will test the surrounding environment using a nine-ringed compass, known as *lo pan*. Each ring contains symbols reflecting heaven and earth, yin and yang, stars and hexagrams. The master uses these symbols to interact with an individual's horoscope. In taking bearings from the compass, the master will consider five basic categories of the landscape. A master may also delve into the heavenly elements or spirits that interact with the world. Then recommendations will be made about design or remedies prescribed to correct faults that affect the flow of chi.[12]

Geomancy is similar to, but not identical to, feng shui. Geomancy is the Western esoteric craft of "earth magic." In geomantic theory, there are lines of energy—ley lines—that traverse the planet. Various sacred sites, such as Stonehenge, the pyramids, and Ayers Rock, or Uluru, to use its Aboriginal name, are believed to exist on very powerful ley lines.

Geomancy and the Ley of the Land

Geomantists study how the earth influences plants, animals, and people where ley lines are identified. They believe that there is a universal life force flowing throughout the cosmos. Geomantists seek to maximize the life force flowing in any given locality.[13]

American architect Walter Burley Griffin (1876-1937) employed the principles of geomancy and feng shui in his work. Griffin was personally influenced by the teachings of Swedenborg and was also active in the Theosophical Society. His use of geomancy and feng shui was particularly evident in his designs for the Australian capital city of Canberra.[14]

THE HOLY GRAIL

The quest for the Holy Grail was an important sacred myth in medieval Europe and in later English literature. The Holy Grail is, of course, said to be the chalice used by Jesus at the Last

Supper before his crucifixion. Elena claimed that Joseph of Arimathea, one of the men who buried Jesus, carried it from Palestine to Glastonbury in England. Often connected with King Arthur and Avalon, the Grail is a potent motif due to its connection with the conquest of death by Jesus.

The Holy Grail Mythology

The Holy Grail appears in the tarot deck as the Ace of Cups. It has been a symbol of power, healing, and fertility in Celtic spirituality. The grail myth has also been associated with the annual Glastonbury festival.[15] Glastonbury is traditionally linked to the Arthurian story of the Grail so neo-pagans feel an obvious affinity between the myth and the festival site. Grail myths have also featured in reinterpretations of Jesus' life, such as *The Holy Blood and the Holy Grail*.[16]

NUMEROLOGY

Numerology is a system of magick and divination that maintains the universe has been constructed according to numerical patterns. Vicki said that, allied to this, is the concept that all things contain spiritual vibrations and these vibrations can be expressed mathematically. Your personality, business, relationships, and future may be ascertained by means of numerology. This is done by reducing to numbers one's name, birthday, and birthplace.

Ancient Roots

The father of numerology is the Greek mathematician Pythagoras who created a mystical spirituality based on numbers and aspects of Greek philosophy.[17]

THE QABALAH

The Qabalah (also spelled as Cabala, Kabala, and Kabbalah) is a form of mysticism that began in Judaism. The word means "tradition," and it began as a supplement to orthodox beliefs among the Talmudists and Karaites. Later on it developed into an abstract mysticism concerned with God's attributes as well as with healing and magickal techniques. Vicki noted that Qabalists believe the cosmos can be represented symbolically using numbers and letters.

The Qabalah Tree of Life

Two major concepts are the *sephiroth* (emanation) doctrine and occult techniques for reading scripture. The *sephiroth* concerns ten emanations of God's attributes found in the cosmos. These emanations also represent ten principles of life and ten areas of personal attainment that are illustrated via a diagram called the tree of life. The diagram consists of ten circles connected by twenty-two branches in an ascending and descending structure. At the top is God, and below the tree is humanity. Some Qabalists say there is an eleventh *sephiroth* called *Daath*, which represents secret sexual knowledge and is concealed behind the tree.[18]

Qabalistic readings of scripture rely on various methods. One is by using acrostics—linking the initial or final letters of words in phrases to create a new word imbued with esoteric meaning. Another method, known as *gematria*, creates equivalences between words and numbers. As the Hebrew alphabetical letters were also used as numbers, Qabalists claim that it is possible to find divinely inspired numerical patterns embedded in scripture. From these patterns, secrets about God and the cosmos can be deduced.

A few Christian authors such as E.W. Bullinger, Ivan Panin, and F.C. Payne have used *gematria* in an attempt to prove the divine inspiration of the Bible. Michael Drosnin's *The Bible Code* also used this technique to argue that the assassination of Israel's premier Yitzak Rabin was prophetically secreted in the Bible.

QI-GONG AND T'AI CHI

Qi-gong (also known as chi kung), which literally means "work on chi," is a Chinese discipline concerned with breath, posture, motion, and sound. Elena said it originates in Taoism. Breath exercises are coordinated with movement and vibration to enhance one's chi.

Qi-gong is also concerned with healing and spiritual development involving meditative exercises combined with martial arts practices. Falun Dafa, the sect banned in the late 1990s in communist China, uses qi-gong as part of its core activities.

T'ai chi is a Chinese martial art that combines slow, fluid exercises with Taoist thought about the harmony of chi in the cosmos.[19]

REBIRTHING

Joanne and Elena had tried rebirthing, which involves regressing back to the womb, then going through one's birth or past life in order to confront past traumas, rejection fears, and inhibitions. The process often involves a tremendous catharsis of pent-up emotions, and sometimes the person releases great anger by punching into mattresses or pillows. The rebirther may use hypnosis or instruct the participant to use deep breathing exercises to enable regression.[20]

SACRED SEX

Elena talked to us about linking sexuality with spirituality by means of a discipline called *tantra*. Tantra is based in yoga. A couple will use various sexual postures to awaken spiritual energy. By means of the maithuna ritual, the couple seeks the suppression of thought, breath, and bodily fluid to achieve spiritual enlightenment. The male is said to be Shiva, and the female is said to be Shakti.

The couple seeks to unlock the kundalini, or sacred serpent, that is coiled at the base of the spine. By various magickal techniques in a sexual union, the couple can uncoil the serpent within. The serpent rises through various chakras—which are centers of power in the body—until it reaches the crown of the head, where the third eye is opened to see the spiritual realm. The couple is transformed into a god and goddess and liberation from the cycle of birth, death, and rebirth may be achieved by sacred sex.

Connection with Love

One famous exponent of tantra was Bhagwan Shree Rajneesh (Osho), who founded the Orange People. Annie Sprinkle, who was featured in the Australian-made documentary, *Sacred Sex*, says:

> Basically when I'm in a state of sexual ecstasy, that's when I feel a connection with the love, [I feel] all the love of the universe and bliss and the oneness of everything, pure divine love, with god and goddess and spirit. Nothing compares to it. To a night where you spend eight to ten hours slowly building and building the excitement and arousal, touching and breathing and baths and sensuality, and you get higher and higher, and higher, and higher and nothing, nothing . . . those are the most blissful moments I know. Nothing compares to that.[21]

SOUL TRAVEL

Vicki has tried soul travel. She said one can project his or her soul or etheric body into the spirit realm and roam free. There was some talk of astral travel to other continents, planets, and galaxies.

Soul travel normally takes place in deep meditation, trance, or sleep. One group that teaches soul-travel is Eckankar. It was also popularized by Lobsang Rampa, an Irish plumber, portrayed as a Tibetan Buddhist lama.[22]

TAROT CARDS

Joanne and her friends were into tarot readings. The cards are among the most popular tools for guidance and self-awareness.

A tarot deck consists of 78 cards divided into two parts—the major *arcana* of 22 trumps and the minor *arcana* of 56 cards. The word "arcane" means "secret." The major *arcana* cards are considered to be the most powerful as they display major spiritual symbols. The minor *arcana* are further classified into four suits—wands, swords, pentacles, and cups. These suits represent the four elements of fire (wands), air (swords), earth (pentacles) and water (cups). They stand for our lives' links with nature.

The cards' primary function is connected with questions of guidance and self-awareness of one's own personality, relationships, and career. A typical reading begins with the client and reader having a conversation about the client's life, work, and relationships. The reader asks the client to shuffle the deck. After shuffling, a certain number of cards will be dealt and arranged on the table in a particular configuration (circle or Celtic cross, say). The reader will then interpret the card's symbols as they relate to the client's recent past, work experiences, family relationships, and immediate prospects. This may also involve the reader's intuitions based on non-verbal cues and the body language of the client.[23] We have spoken with a number of readers who tell us that a session with a client is akin to the priest's confessional.

Tarot Origins and Sources

Many believe that the cards originated in ancient Egypt and were a pictorial book of spiritual wisdom. However, the evidence does not support this. The cards can be traced to Northern Italy in the 1400s, where they were used exclusively to play a card game known as Triumphs. In France after the 1770s, Antoine Court de Gebelin and

Jean-Baptiste Alliette (alias Etteilla) published separate works claiming the cards were designed for fortune-telling purposes. It was after their books were released that the cards were first used for predictive readings in the 19th century. De Gebelin is the originator of the claim that the cards came from Egypt. Eliphas Levi (1810-75) later connected the tarot with the Qabalah.[24]

Several sources influenced tarot imagery—the Bible, late medieval Catholic thought, and European Renaissance culture.[25] Joseph Campbell traced the cards' imagery to Dante's writings.[26] New Age writer Corinne Heline has linked the tarot directly to the Bible.[27] Timothy Betts has provocatively proposed that the earliest tarot images can be traced to illustrations found in late medieval manuscripts of the book of Revelation. He argues that the original purpose of the tarot was to pictorially represent the second coming of Christ and the anticipated new millennium.[28] Serious practitioners now link the cards to Jungian archetypes that reflect universal human needs for spiritual renewal.[29]

YOGA

Elena attends weekly yoga classes and said that it is an ancient Hindu philosophy and spiritual discipline. It aims to assist us in breaking free from the cycle of birth, death, and rebirth. The word *yoga* means "to yoke" or "be in union with." For the traditional Hindu, this union is with the god Shiva or the god Brahman.

Yoga Variety

- Hatha yoga is the best-known form because it deals with the various bodily postures people use today as a means of exercise. The postures, however, are not primarily concerned with health or fitness. They are intended to relax the body from all distractions so that the devotee may be enabled to meditate on a spiritual path.

- Siddha yoga is concerned with using various "siddhis," or powers, such as levitation. In this form of yoga, the seven major energy centers in the human body, called *chakras*, are used. By means of various meditative techniques, the practitioner can awaken these energy centers to encounter the spiritual world of the gods and goddesses. Swami Muktananda Paramahansa (1908-82), who was known as "the guru's guru," brought siddha yoga to the West in 1970. Muktananda offered a charismatic experience known as the awakening, which was associated with spontaneous bodily movements (kriyas), breathing rhythms, dancing, crying, laughter, animal noises, and utterances in tongues.
- Tantra yoga is a more radical path to liberation, which often involves the use of occult powers and sexual rituals (see sacred sex above).
- Raja yoga, or "royal yoga," emphasizes the use of body postures, deep meditative trances and mantras to achieve spiritual harmony.
  - Bhakti yoga is a devotional path where one is attached to a particular guru (or teacher) and follows a spiritual discipline combining body postures, meditative exercises, chanting, and contemplation of the writings of Hindu sages. The Hare Krishna movement is a well-known example of bhakti yoga. The essence of yoga is summed up in the philosophical writings of Patanjali, who wrote of yoga as the ultimate path to enlightenment.[30]

The value of these tools

We let Joanne, Vicki and Elena know that the Sacred Writings wholeheartedly uphold the use of spiritual practices for personal and group transformation. This is what we found in our reflections on the tools we have outlined above in the light of the Sacred Writings.

ALCHEMY

The Sacred Writings convey several images of transformation also found in the alchemist's yearning for purification. A number of early Protestant pioneers, such as Johann Valentin Andreae (1586-1654), saw the fulfillment of the alchemist's quest for the philosopher's stone in drinking from the eternal wells of salvation provided by Jesus. We suggested to Joanne and her friends that they could let the alchemist's symbols be a step towards embracing the fullness of Christ.[31]

AURAS

We compared Vicki's aura photo with each of ours. We were encouraged when the psychic found that we were in tune. In Ross's case the dominant white rays in the photo around his ears indicated that he was channeling truth from the highest source! When Philip's wife, Ruth, had her aura photographed, the psychic interpreted all the colors positively. However the psychic's insights into Ruth's personality were wide of the mark. Whatever anyone makes of the aura, it is not a good tool for guidance. Rather, the Sacred Writings redirect us to entrust ourselves to God.

Aura Arguments

How can we account for the aura? One possibility is that auras may be a plausible source for the halo phenomenon and ghosts. However, it might be too simplistic to limit our definition of ghosts as auras alone, as they may be a mind projection, an evil spirit, or a messenger from God. One of the most unusual cases concerns the popular translator of Sacred Writings, J.B. Phillips. At a time of personal desolation, he had an encounter with the late C.S. Lewis:

> A few days after [Lewis's] death, while I was watching television, he "appeared" sitting in a chair within a few feet of me, and spoke a few words that were particularly relevant to the difficult circumstances through which I was passing.[32]

Another view has been put forward by two skeptics, Arleen Watkins and William Bickel. They claim that the Kirlian image of the aura is really just the corona discharge of a gas in the

ambient air and is unrelated to human physiology.[33] William
Tiller of Stanford University suggests that it merely reflects
the changing chemistry of the skin. New Age writer Nevill
Drury concludes, "The present status of Kirlian photography is
controversial."[34]

CHANNELING

The sole instance in the Sacred Writings where there is an
actual illustration of channeling is King Saul's visit to the medium
of Endor (1 Sam. 28). There, at Saul's request, the deceased
prophet Samuel is contacted, and he delivers a message of judgment to Saul for using this method of guidance. Saul could have
used trustworthy methods that didn't require entering the
uncharted spirit world. We stressed with Elena that not every
spirit is to be trusted. For this reason, as well as losing a reliance
on God, the Sacred Writings forbid our consulting foreign entities and using tools such as Ouija boards (1 John 4:1-4, Deut.
18:10-11).

CLAIRVOYANCE AND PROPHECY

One possible explanation for clairvoyance is that some people,
like Vicki, may be able to live beyond the moment in their consciousness. This may explain ESP and is certainly reflected in
prophetic utterances. In the case of a clairvoyant, the concern is
when the paranormal is perverted for self-aggrandizement and
the vessel seeks to pass on teachings that are not connected to the
Creator's wisdom.

In the area of prophecy, the Sacred Writings confirm that a
prophet may receive insights into the future, and the Writings
offer criteria for testing the prophet's credentials. The most

important credential is the premise that the prophecy comes directly from and is spoken on behalf of the Creator—any other source is not to be trusted. Beyond that, there are two key tests of a prophet: one test is if a prophet foretells and the prediction does not happen, then the Sacred Writings instruct that the prophet is deceived and should not be listened to (there are even provisions for severe punishment of false prophets); the second test is, should the prophecy come true, and the prophet invites you to embrace teachings outside the Creator's guidelines, then you should not follow that prophet (see Deut. 13:1-5, 18:5-22). Prophets such as Nostradamus, Edgar Cayce and Jeane Dixon have a mixed record of successes and failures, and they give no indication of speaking on behalf of the Creator.[35] In contrast to this, the prophets who speak from and for the Creator in the Sacred Writings have an impeccable track record.[36]

A COURSE IN MIRACLES

Although *A Course in Miracles* is at times an inspiring piece of literature, we related to Elena its four drawbacks.

- It is a recent channeled work, and unlike the historical records in the Sacred Writings, there is no verification that it truly carries the words of Christ. If it does not, then it is the message of a deluded spirit guide.
- It is inconsistent with what we know Jesus said. A good instance of this is seen where, in the Course, "Jesus" tells us: "The Holy Spirit dispels [guilt] simply through the calm recognition that it has never been."[37] In John 16:8 Jesus taught, "When he [the Holy Spirit] comes, he will convict the world of guilt in regard to sin and righteousness and judgment." If Jesus is a great guru, we cannot live with two inconsistent statements like these.
- It is not in touch with life. Evil and suffering and wrongdoing are simply not overcome by positive thought. The world is more complex.
- Some postmodern pilgrims have found that the Course is

detrimental to their spiritual journey. Genise, a former teacher of the Course, gives this insight:

During this time, I counselled and rebirthed many people. They thought I was a very wise person, because I could tell them about the Course. It sounded so profound, but I knew in my own heart that the Course was not helping me get over my hurt. I still felt resentful and unforgiving. For me, the Course was guilt-producing, rather than guilt-releasing.[38]

ENNEAGRAM

The enneagram offers a model of nine human personality types. Joanne chuckled when we said it is good and fun to know what our personality type is like. She did not know many men who understood personality types. We emphasized that we need to keep in mind that we are not limited to the "boxes" some practitioners place us in.

The enneagram has proven popular in New Age and secular circles. It has also been modified in a Catholic context.[39] Some Catholics propose that the only human being who perfectly embraced all nine categories of the enneagram was Jesus. Can any of us lay claim to that?

Mitch Pacwa, a former practitioner, argues that the enneagram's spiritual foundations are flawed and can open people up to negative spiritual forces.[40] Another Catholic writer, Richard Rohr, while more sympathetic in his appraisal, still does find problems with the way the enneagram has been used in New Age and secular circles to manipulate people. He also urges spiritual discernment, but finds weaknesses with Pacwa's critique.[41] For those troubled by the enneagram, an alternative personality test is the highly regarded Myers-Briggs Type Indicator, based on sixteen personality types.

FENG SHUI AND GEOMANCY

We told Joanne that there are both positive and negative sides to feng shui and geomancy. On the positive side, feng shui can serve as a catalyst to refocus ourselves on some forgotten truths. The emphasis on cosmic harmony should remind us that God's Spirit energizes the whole cosmos. To find harmony, we need to turn to our Creator, who is the source of all harmony. We can also reflect on the presence of God's Spirit throughout the whole earth. The Sacred Writings declare that God "is not far from each one of us" (Acts 17:27, NIV).

As we have seen, "feng shui" means "wind and water." The creation narrative begin with how God's Spirit hovered over the chaotic waters and brought about order and design. The Hebrew word used was *ruach*, which can be translated according to context as spirit, wind, or breath. We have forgotten that God gives us the breath of life, which should goad us into thanksgiving (see Gen. 1:2, 2:7). The geomantic "universal life force" happens to be the person of God's Spirit and not an impersonal energy. Jesus also associated spiritual renewal by the Spirit with the imagery of both wind and water (see John 3:5-8).

Aside from these spiritual reminders, we ought to be mindful of how we design and use our domestic and commercial places. Are our homes, offices, and cities places where we are aware of God's presence and experience harmony? Our use of space should prompt us to design our surroundings in ways that acknowledge God's presence and keep us linked with the creation. If our minds are darkened we will forget about the Creator and even erect physical barriers to shut out all truth.

On the negative side, we feel that feng shui and geomancy can draw people into a limited understanding of reality where magickal forces or alien spirits hold sway. The Sacred Writings instruct us to be discerning about seeking magickal powers and relying on lesser spiritual forces. There are negative forces and energies, and spiritual entrapment by dark powers is an unpleasant and undeniable reality. The Sacred Writings direct us to depend on and enquire after God (see Isa. 8:19-20).

The Holy Grail

Charles Williams's novel *War in Heaven* was a murder story that involved black magick and the discovery of the Holy Grail in an old English church. One of the chief characters realizes that, although the Grail was the chalice used at the Last Supper, it is only an artifact and no substitute for the person of Christ.[42]

Even though the Grail legends are fascinating, we suggested to Elena that finding out why Jesus instructed us to drink from his cup is to take the highest path of all.

Numerology

We responded to Vicki by saying that the basic difficulty with numerology rests with its fundamental assumptions about the universe being constructed according to numerical patterns. The arithmetical erudition of numerologists may be superb, but such skills give no assurance that their interpretations are true. Numerical patterns are not proof of any cause-and-effect relationships in the cosmos.

The Qabalah

We struggle with the Qabalah, particularly with respect to both the *sephiroth* concept and the *gematria* as an interpretative tool. Montgomery observes:

The sephiroth doctrine is an attempt to explain the nature of a God who is both immanent and transcendent to the degree that he cannot have contact with man and remain God. This latter view of God is not justified by either the Jewish or Christian Scriptures; it was the product of rationalism at Alexandria.[43]

We drew Vicki's attention to the Sacred Writings where we do find numbers that are used in both conventional and symbolic ways.[44] However, the symbolic use of numbers is governed by the plain context of the passage and does not support the Qabalist's basic assumption that there are messages encoded beneath the text's surface. The big problem is that the initial premise of encoded messages is not open to question and, apart from using Qabalistic techniques, is never independently demonstrated. So, the *gematria* produces results that have already been presupposed. Furthermore, when Qabalists apply the *gematria* to the Sacred Writings or other texts, they often reach wildly contradictory conclusions. This is because the whole enterprise is so speculative. It can prove addictive for those impressed by arithmetical skills.

Finite Numbers

Oswald Allis has hilariously shown how easy it is to find hidden messages in 1776, the year of American Independence. Allis points out that, once numbers are given a mystical value, we can engage in endless conjecture. He concludes:

> The attempt to find mysterious numerical patterns and values in sentences, words, and phrases which have a plain and obvious meaning is sublime or trite or trivial; whether it is found in the Bible, or in a masterpiece of secular literature, or in the commonplaces of ordinary life, is, to say the least, a tremendous waste of time and effort; and, what is far more important, resting as it does on principles that are demonstrably false, it may lead to serious and disastrous consequences.[45]

QI-GONG AND T'AI CHI

We affirm the value of bodily exercise for optimum physical fitness and appreciate the lessons one can glean from rigorous discipline. The martial arts have become appealing as a result of the Bruce Lee and Jackie Chan movies. Their abilities are impressive. It must be remembered that these fighting techniques are based on principles of mechanics and from observations of the attacking and defense mechanisms of animals. In and of themselves these techniques are neither magickal nor mystical.

We suggested to Elena that some reflection is important before embarking on a martial arts course. One such area to think about is the metaphysical premises that may be taught in conjunction with the physical regimen. For example, Da Liu indicates that the goal of t'ai chi classically entailed "the attainment of physical immortality."[46]

Question the Arts

Are you attracted to a particular discipline because you want to gain physical fitness and learn the art of self-defense? Learning self-defense techniques and becoming physically fit are legitimate goals. Has your teacher indicated that Taoist or Zen Buddhist principles are an essential component of your training? Have you been taken on a spiritual trek to a place you never intended to go? Some instructors accept and others disavow the Taoist and Zen Buddhist metaphysics, and so consumers need to shop around. Another concern relates to motivations. Are you only concerned with fitness and learning self-defense, or do you seek to intimidate others and misuse what you have been taught?

The way of Jesus challenges selfish motivations and certainly affirms the importance of intervening to protect the helpless. Self-defense skills sadly seem to be needed where urban violence is a daily reality, yet Jesus also instructed that we should seek to be at peace with all people and to treat even our enemies with kindness. The martial arts are an area where keen discernment and discretion need to be employed.

Rebirthing

We acknowledged that Joanne and Elena had found the experience of rebirthing very helpful to their emotional well-being. In fact, it has been our personal experience that we have suppressed hurtful events that have only been unlocked many years later. The Sacred Writings understand the value of catharsis. An enthralling case study is the famous encounter of Jesus with the woman at the well in John 4. Jesus identified the troubles in her life and offered to heal her past. She declared to her neighbors, "Come, see a man who told me everything I ever did. Could this be the Christ?" (John 4:29, NIV).

Like us, many pilgrims have found the Christ of catharsis heals. In him, there is a real rebirth. He frees us from human dependency techniques, such as hyperventilation, found in rebirthing. This is not to deny the essential role and therapeutic value of counseling skills used by those professionally trained in recovery.

Sacred Sex

This concept is found in the Sacred Writings, but it is describing the relationship between a man and a woman committed to each other for life in marriage. Therefore, there is no sacred context for group sex or voyeurism.

Elena was amazed to find that one of the most erotic love poems has been preserved within the Sacred Writings. Spouses would enjoy a time of meditating on it together:

Under the apple tree I roused you; there your mother conceived you, there she who was in labor gave you birth. Place me like a seal over your heart, like a seal on your arm; for love is as strong as death, its jealousy unyielding as the grave. It burns like blazing fire, like a mighty flame . . . I am a wall and my breasts are like towers. Thus I have become in his eyes like one bringing

contentment . . . Come away, my lover, and be like a gazelle or like a young stag on the spice-laden mountains (Song of Songs 8:5-6, 10, 14, NIV).

—————————◆—————————

A good element of tantric sacred sex is the emphasis on learning about each other through touch and exploration. In particular, there is a recognition that men need to develop an intimacy that involves more than just sexual intercourse.

In contrast to the tantric, in the Sacred Writings, sex brings us to praise God for his goodness, not to self-deification. The ultimate difficulty with tantric sacred sex is its primary goal of self-worship and cosmic oneness. It is inconsistent with Jesus' view of life.

SOUL TRAVEL

Soul travel is not directly mentioned in the Sacred Writings. Eckankar teachers maintain that Paul's visit to the third heaven, recorded in 2 Corinthians 12, is an account of soul travel. Their suggestion is conjecture, as even Paul cannot specify how his experience took place. He may even have remained in his body and was simply quickened by the Spirit of God.

John the apostle's entering into the throne room in the book of Revelation is in the same category as Paul's vision. While not denying that a miracle is occurring in these people's lives, there is no suggestion that this is soul travel. It is interesting to note that the apostles' teachings following their experiences did not speak of soul travel.

We spoke with Vicki about some cases we have investigated that show trauma can accompany the regular pursuit of soul journeys. Anna was in her twenties when she related her story to us. She initially found soul travel exciting, but, after a while, it became very disturbing. She wanted to give it up, but it had become a compulsion to do it every time she went to bed. She began to meet people in her excursions that she would be introduced to in the flesh weeks later. The most frightening experience she had was one evening when a spirit guide led her out of her body. She then watched a dark spirit creature abuse her body. We encouraged Anna to find release through prayer in the name of Jesus. Happily, she later reported that her soul travels ended after she sought serious prayer counsel. Soul travel is a hazardous door to open and so is best left shut.

TAROT CARDS

These days there are hundreds of different tarot decks, using a wide range of motifs—Aboriginal, Celtic, feminist, Wiccan, and even ones based on *Lord of the Rings*.[47] As we noted before, the earliest decks originated in Renaissance Europe and reflect biblical influences.

The most famous and widely used deck in modern times is the Rider-Waite deck. A.E. Waite drew his inspiration from the Bible. We chatted with Joanne and her friends about Waite's major *arcana* cards. The Lovers card symbolizes Adam and Eve before God in Paradise. The Devil card shows them after the Fall in chains. The Judgment card shows people being resurrected from their tombs as the archangel blows the trumpet. The Fool—the most mysterious and potent card of all—shows Jesus as the divine prince in our realm whom we fail to recognize.[48]

The poet T.S. Eliot in "The Waste Land" and Charles Williams in *The Greater Trumps* have drawn on the tarot's symbolism to illustrate our spiritual desolation and the way forward in the salvation story of Christ.[49] In our book *Beyond Prediction*, we give a detailed explanation of the tarot symbols and how they relate to Christ.[50]

Sadly, many who use the cards miss the spiritual truths displayed on them and rely upon the tarot for guidance. The Sacred Writings instruct that the highest path for guidance is found in a direct relationship with God and warn against divination (see Deut. 18:10-11).

YOGA

In the Sacred Writings we do find examples of devotional postures and we explore this a bit more in chapter 12. Jesus' path, though, was not centered on body postures. His primary spiritual discipline consisted of self-denial, and he calls us to follow in his steps. In contrast to yogic union in an impersonal energy, the way of Jesus is to bring us into an encounter with a personal, living God.

After discussing these different kinds of psychotechnologies with Joanne, Vicki, and Elena, we then looked at the fascinating and vital subject of holistic healing and complementary medicine.

Holistic healing and complementary medicine

The last decades of the 20th century saw a pronounced trend to supplement or even, in some cases, move away from orthodox medical practice with its emphasis on surgery and synthetic drugs. Nowadays, holistic approaches to medicine—also known as complementary medicine—have achieved mainstream status. Some major teaching hospitals now have complementary therapy centers attached to their cancer care units. Degrees and diplomas in complementary medicine can now be studied in the medical faculties of several mainstream universities.

Joanne and her friends said that the focus in holism is on health and well-being in mind, body, and spirit. A key factor is not merely using therapies or techniques to cure illnesses, but offering frameworks for promoting health and fitness via diet, relaxation, exercise, mental outlook, and spiritual development. Holistic healers often employ "natural" therapies, such as herbs, massage, and meditation. Some treatments concentrate on body-work, others on the mind, and still others involve the use of energy. Some healers are committed to New Age spirituality, while others are not.[51] The therapies we talked about are detailed in appendix III.

THE VALUE OF HOLISTIC HEALING AND COMPLEMENTARY MEDICINE

We affirmed Joanne and her friends' views that holistic healing and complementary medicine offers some correctives to gaps in mainstream approaches to medicine. The tremendous emphasis on treating the whole person—not just an isolated complaint or infection—is a good and highly attractive contrast to the "conveyor belt" approach of processing patients that exists in some clinics and hospitals.

We noted with Joanne a fundamental axiom of the Sacred Writings, that the Creator is "the LORD, who heals you" (Exod. 15:26, NIV). The Sacred Writings focus a lot on God's miraculous interventions, prayers, and sometimes laying on of hands. We see instances where miraculous healings occurred in the lives of both believers and non-believers (see Gen. 20:17; 2 Kings 5; 2 Chron. 30:20; Luke 17:12-17; John 9:1-11). However, the Sacred Writings do not confine the concept of healing to miracles. The entire ministry of Jesus was one of holistic healing in body, mind and spirit.[52]

Many years ago, S.I. McMillen, a medical practitioner, showed how the Sacred Writings also set forth sound principles relating to diet, hygiene, physical, mental, emotional, and spiritual well-being.[53]

There are some issues, however, that we must be mindful of when exploring complementary therapies. Ross said that a very basic issue, which applies in other spheres of life too, is the problem of consumer fraud. Unfortunately, there is a small percentage of self-appointed healers whose credentials and remedies may be very suspect. It is a sad commentary on human nature that con artists seek to exploit others at personal points of vulnerability. So, we urged Joanne and her friends to be discerning, to ask questions, and check the integrity of both the healer and the healer's remedies. As our health and well-being are vital concerns, it is wise to do some careful research. Sometimes enquiries of official agencies that monitor consumer fraud can help.[54]

Other significant matters for reflection concern the philosophy or metaphysics of the healer and the healing techniques employed.[55] Some New Age healers subscribe to ideas that are in conflict with the Sacred Writings. One viewpoint that some practitioners affirm is that illness is purely of our own creation. This view of illness and healing has its base in mind powers and is discussed in a later chapter. There is no denying that much illness is psychosomatic and related to our own mental well-being and how we see the world. However, sickness cannot be confined in this way. For example, bacteria are innocently passed one to another; people accidentally fall; there is the matter of genetic inheritance of certain conditions; and no matter how much we may wish otherwise, there is plain old age.

Ross emphasized that a consequence of viewing illness as being self-inflicted is that it can create in us a false sense of security. It may also lead to despair that our illness is because of our own lack of faith. The astonishing end product of this is found in certain metaphysical groups that claim all illness is an illusion and the symptoms should be denied. One of the foremost advocates of this was Mary Baker Eddy, the founder of Christian Science.[56]

Another divergence from the Sacred Writings is where some healers rely on foreign spirits to assist in diagnosis and therapy. Some may also claim that their elixirs, oils, or herbs are activated by a spirit force. As we have already found, not all entities can be trusted and the Sacred Writings give clear guidance about this.[57]

Perhaps the most controversial issue relates to energy healing. Philip said that some believe there are positive scientific indicators for this energy.[58] Techniques such as reiki and therapeutic touch are premised on the notion that there is a unifying cosmic energy that can be tapped into and channeled. As we noted earlier, reiki healers claim that they are accessing the universal life force. Many New Age thinkers use this expression to refer to an impersonal cosmic force or power. The idea that all is one and all is divine is something we explore in our next chapter. However, just because your healer gives you testimony of how effective or helpful a treatment has been, this is no guarantee that it is truly right for you. As the master, Jesus, taught, even signs and wonders are not limited to the spiritually enlightened. Indeed, some practitioners may be deceived and in other ways mislead you.

Some critics of energy healing claim that the universal life force is unscientific and others link it to dark spirit powers.[59] This latter perspective does raise alarm bells about the need for caution and discernment. Such concerns seem to be even further warranted when the metaphysical teachings aligned with these techniques conflict with the Sacred Writings. Mikao Usui, the originator of reiki, tried to establish how Jesus healed people and found his answers in Tibetan Buddhism, not in the Sacred Writings.

Our colleague Harold Taylor, together with Philip, has been exploring a biblical approach to energy healing. The Sacred Writings indicate that God, in his general kindness to all humanity, makes provision for our basic needs (see Matt. 5:45, Acts 14:17). God's Spirit sustains all life, and if we are to speak of a universal life force, it is not an impersonal energy force but the person of the Spirit. The Sacred Writings disclose in a visionary way that there are rays that emanate from God's hands (see Hab. 3:3-4).[60] A Hebrew term that frequently appears in the Sacred Writings is *ruach*. This word can mean spirit, breath, or wind according to context. The *ruach* is the fountain of all life and is present everywhere in the creation.[61] There is the real possibility that what the energy healers are accessing may be a created energy, ultimately coming from God's Spirit. The difficulty we find is not if healings occur, but if the healer's teachings about energy are right.[62]

SOME GUIDELINES TO FOLLOW WHEN APPROACHING HOLISTIC HEALING

We offered Joanne and her friends some helpful tips:
- Be open to healing. A wise principle is that no thing is inherently evil and medical alternatives should be explored.
- Avoid excessive drug treatments. The body is to be the temple of the Holy Spirit.

- Seek healing by means of natural remedies where possible. Diet, herbs, and relaxation are examples of this.
- See diet in the framework of spiritual significance. Some Sacred Writings references to this are the feeding of the 5,000, Jesus' Last Supper, and the marriage supper of the lamb in Revelation 19:7-9.
- Stay in touch with reality and do not simplify the causes of illness. Diseases as an illusion or as the result of my thought patterns are two examples of such oversimplification.
- Beware of therapies that rely solely on personal endorsements in the absence of any careful testing.
- Read widely before experimenting. Test the spirits.
- If in doubt, leave it out! This is a useful—and ancient—common-sense principle.
- Go to the master physician, Jesus, in prayer. This can take place with you on your own.
- Remember that one can still overdose on an herb. It should be treated with the same care and caution as conventional medicines.

Laying on of Hands

Some may like to attend a healing service where there is laying on of hands and prayer in the name of Jesus. We conduct this sort of ministry at the festivals and, as hands are laid on the person, there is prayer for their particular complaint and petition that the Lord would deliver them in body, soul, and spirit.

Endnotes

Chapter 6

1   Edward A. Aviza, *Thinking Tarot*, New York: Simon & Schuster, 1997, p.19.
2   Marilyn Ferguson, *The Aquarian Conspiracy*, London: Paladin/Grafton Books, 1982, p. 282.
3   Paulo Coelho, *The Alchemist*, New York: HarperCollins, 1998; and Mircea Eliade, *The Forge and the Crucible*, 2nd edition, Chicago and London: University of Chicago Press, 1978.
4   Ted Andrews, *How to See and Read the Aura*, St Paul: Llewellyn, 1991.
5   John Warwick Montgomery, *Principalities and Powers*, Minneapolis: Bethany, 1973, pp. 141-142.
6   J. Gordon Melton, Jerome Clark and Aidan A. Kelly (eds), *New Age Almanac*, Detroit: Visible Ink, 1991, pp. 45-51.
7   Carl E. Armerding and W. Ward Gasque (eds), *A Guide to Biblical Prophecy*, Peabody: Hendrickson, 1989; R.J. Stewart, *The Elements of Prophecy*, Dorset: Element, 1990; and Jeane Dixon with Rene Noorbergen, *My Life and Prophecies*, New York: Bantam, 1969.
8   *A Course in Miracles*, London: Arkana, 1985.
9   Robert Skutch, *Journey Without Distance: The Story Behind A Course in Miracles*, Berkeley: Celestial Arts, 1984.
10 Gerald G. Jampolsky, *Love is Letting Go of Fear*, Berkeley: Celestial Arts, 1979; Kenneth Wapnick, *The Meaning of Forgiveness*, London: Arkana, 1983; and Marianne Williamson, *A Return to Love*, London: Aquarian, 1992.
11 Don Richard Riso, *The Practical Guide to Personality Types: Understanding the Enneagram*, London: Aquarian, 1991.
12 Sarah Rossbach, *Feng Shui*, London: Rider, 1984.
13 Stephen Skinner, *The Oracle of Geomancy*, Dorset and San Leandro: Prism, 1986.
14 Peter Proudfoot, *The Secret Plan of Canberra*, Kensington, New South Wales: University of New South Wales Press, 1994.
15 John Matthews, *The Elements of the Grail Tradition*, Dorset: Element, 1990.
16 Michael Baigent, Richard Leigh and Henry Lincoln, *The Holy Blood and the Holy Grail*, London: Jonathan Cape, 1982.
17 Rodford Barrat, *The Elements of Numerology*, Dorset: Element, 1994.
18 Will Parfitt, *The Elements of the Qabalah*, Dorset: Element, 1991.
19 David Carradine, *Spirit of Shaolin*, Sydney: Random House, 1991; Paul Crompton, *The Complete Martial Arts*, London: Partridge, 1989; and Da Liu, *T'ai Chi Ch'uan and Meditation*, New York: Schocken, 1986.
20 J. Gordon Melton, Jerome Clark, and Aidan A. Kelly (eds), *New Age Almanac*, pp. 351-352.
21 Interview with Annie Sprinkle, *Southern Crossings*, 12, 2, March-April 1992, p. 21.
22 Paul Twitchell, *Eckankar: The Key to Secret Worlds*, San Diego: Illuminated Way, 1969; and David Christopher Lane, *The Making of a Spiritual Movement: The Untold Story of Paul Twitchell and Eckankar*, Del Mar, California: Del Mar Press, 1983. On Lobsang Rampa, see Agehananda Bharati, "Fictitious Tibet: The

Origin and Persistence of Rampaism," *New Religious Movements Update*, 4, 4, 1980, pp. 21-35.

23 See Dan Korem, *Powers: Testing the Psychic and Supernatural*, Downers Grove: InterVarsity Press, 1988, pp. 25-56; and Andrè Kole and Jerry MacGregor, *Mind Games*, Eugene: Harvest, 1998.

24 Ronald Decker, Thierry Depaulis and Michael Dummett, *A Wicked Pack of Cards: The Origins of the Occult Tarot*, New York: St. Martin's Press, 1996.

25 Stuart R. Kaplan, *The Encyclopedia of Tarot*, volume 1, New York: US Games Systems, 1979, volume 2, Stamford: US Games Systems, 1986; Robert V. O'Neill, *Tarot Symbolism*, Lima, Ohio: Fairway, 1986; and Brian Williams, *A Renaissance Tarot*, Stamford: US Games Systems, 1994.

26 Joseph Campbell and Richard Roberts, *Tarot Revelations*, San Anselmo: Vernal Equinox Press, 1979, pp. 9-25.

27 Corinne Heline, *The Bible and The Tarot*, Marina del Rey, California: De Vorss, 1993.

28 Timothy Betts, *Tarot and the Millennium*, Rancho Palos Verdes: New Perspective Media, 1998.

29 Sallie Nichols, *Jung and Tarot: An Archetypal Journey*, York Beach: Samuel Weiser, 1980.

30 Mircea Eliade, *Yoga: Immortality and Freedom*, 2nd edition, Princeton: Princeton University Press, 1969.

31 John Warwick Montgomery, *Cross and Crucible*, 2 volumes, The Hague: Martinus Nijhoff, 1973.

32 J.B. Phillips, *Ring of Truth*, New York: Macmillan, 1967, pp. 118-119.

33 Arleen J. Watkins and William S. Bickel, "A Study of the Kirlian Effect," *The Skeptical Inquirer*, 10, 3, 1986, pp. 244-257.

34 Nevill Drury, *Dictionary of Mysticism and the Esoteric Traditions*, Dorset: Prism, 1992, p. 167.

35 John Warwick Montgomery, Principalities and Powers, Minneapolis: Bethany, 1974, pp. 121-129; and James Bjornstad, *Twentieth-Century Prophecy: Edgar Cayce and Jeane Dixon*, Minneapolis: Bethany, 1969.

36 J. Barton Payne, *Encyclopedia of Biblical Prophecy*, Grand Rapids: Baker, 1990.

37 *A Course in Miracles*, text, London: Arkana, 1985, p. 223.

38 Dean Halverson, "Coming out of the Course: A Personal Journey," *SCP Journal*, 7, 1, 1987, p. 32.

39 Barbara Metz and John Burchill, *Enneagram and Prayer: Discovering Our True Selves before God*, Denville, New Jersey: Dimension Books, 1987.

40 Mitchell Pacwa, *Catholics and the New Age*, Ann Arbor: Servant, 1992, pp. 95-109.

41 Richard Rohr, *Enneagram II: Advancing spiritual discernment*, New York: Crossroad, 1995.

42 Charles Williams, *War in Heaven*, reprinted edition, Grand Rapids: Wm.B. Eerdmans, 1980.

43 John Warwick Montgomery, *Principalities and Powers*, p. 89.

44 See John J. Davis, *Biblical Numerology*, Grand Rapids: Baker Book House, 1968.

45 Oswald Thompson Allis, *Bible Numerics*, Phillipsburg: Presbyterian & Reformed

Publishing, n.d., p. 24.

46 Da Liu, *T'ai Chi Ch'uan and Meditation*, New York: Schocken, 1986, p. 6.

47 Rachel Pollack, *The New Tarot*, London: Aquarian, 1989; and Terry Donaldson, *The Lord of the Rings Tarot*, Stamford: US Games System, 1997.

48 See A.E. Waite, *The Pictorial Key to the Tarot*, Stamford: US Games Systems, 1990, p. 157; and John Warwick Montgomery, *Principalities and Powers*, pp. 129-131.

49 T.S. Eliot, "The Waste Land" in *Selected Poems*, London: Faber & Faber, 1954, p. 52; and Charles Williams, *The Greater Trumps*, Grand Rapids: Wm.B. Eerdmans, 1980.

50 John Drane, Ross Clifford, and Philip Johnson, *Beyond Prediction: The Tarot and Your Spirituality*, Oxford: Lion, 2001.

51 Sympathetic introductions include Nevill Drury, *Healers, Quacks or Mystics?*, Sydney: Hale & Iremonger, 1983; Malcolm Hulke (ed.), *The Encyclopedia of Alternative Medicine and Self Help*, New York: Schocken, 1979; Edgar N. Jackson, *Understanding Health: An Introduction to the Holistic Approach*, London: SCM, and Philadelphia: Trinity, 1989; and the Australian Complementary Health Association's quarterly journal *Diversity: Natural & Complementary Health*—for subscription details www.vicnet.net.au/~acha.

52 See Stephen Parsons, *Searching for Healing*, Oxford: Lion, 1995; and Harold Taylor, *Sent to Heal*, Ringwood, Victoria: The Order of St. Luke the Physician, 1993.

53 S.I. McMillen, *None of These Diseases*, Old Tappan: Fleming Revell, 1963.

54 See the National Council Against Health Fraud at www.ncrhi.org/

55 Catherine L. Albanese, "The Magical Staff: Quantum Healing in the New Age" in James R. Lewis and J. Gordon Melton (eds), *Perspectives on the New Age*, Albany: State University of New York Press, 1992, pp. 68-84.

56 On Christian Science, see J. Stillson Judah, *The History and Philosophy of the Metaphysical Movements in America*, Philadelphia: Westminster, 1967.

57 John Weldon and Zola Levitt, *Psychic Healing*, Chicago: Moody, 1982; Stephen H. Allison and H. Newton Malony, "Filipino Psychic Surgery: Myth, Magic or Miracle," *Journal of Religion and Health*, 20, 1981, pp. 48-61; and Andrè Kole & Jerry MacGregor, *Mind Games*, Eugene: Harvest, 1998.

58 Ann Paterson, "Energy and Healing," *Diversity*, 2, 3, September-November 2000, pp. 2-9. Paterson is senior lecturer in nursing at RMIT University, Melbourne. For subscription details see note 51 above.

59 For a secular view, see Stephen Barrett, *The Health Robbers*, Buffalo: Prometheus, 1993. Christian critiques include Robina Coker, *Alternative Medicine: Helpful or Harmful?*, Crowborough: Monarch, 1995; Elliot Miller, "The Christian, Energetic Medicine, and New Age Paranoia," *Christian Research Journal*, 14, 3, 1992, pp. 24-27; and the Evangelical Alliance of the United Kingdom's website at: www.eauk.org/handlewithcare/index.htm

60 See Vladimir Lossky, *The Vision of God*, Crestwood: St Vladimirs Seminary Press, 1983.

61 R.C. Sproul, *The Mystery of the Holy Spirit*, Wheaton: Tyndale, 1990, pp. 77-90.

62 For a rudimentary discussion, see Philip Johnson, "Energy Healing: A Christian Theological Appraisal" at www.ozemail.com.au/~ptcsyd/JohnsonPage/

Chapter 7
Cosmic Oneness Paradigm

◆

There is one God. There is one intellect, which is God's intellect.
There is one body, which is God's body. You are a part of God.[1]

Does it make any difference that I call it Christ and she calls it the
Force? Force is energy. To my mind, it is of greater importance that
we recognize the light in each other—and this applies to anyone
with whom I come into contact.[2]

I and the Father are one (John 10:30, NIV).

◆

Jill and Linda are flatmates. As they were both twenty-nine
years of age, they were feeling a twinge of angst about turning
thirty. Although their jobs were interesting, neither Jill nor Linda
was content to be consumed by work. Relationships, travel, and
fitness are part of their agenda, but most importantly, they had
both been exploring personal development through spirituality.
They were involved in a weekly meditation and yoga class and had
undertaken some courses in aromatherapy. Most recently, they had
read James Redfield's *The Celestine Prophecy, The Tenth Insight*, and
The Secret of Shambhala. These novels crystallized for them a
desire to find the new spiritual common sense Redfield described.

Jill said that these novels meant a lot to her because they
pointed to a greater understanding about reality. She said that
most of us live with the basic awareness that people and objects
are separate entities. She indicated that, for functional purposes
of daily living, this awareness is necessary. However, there is a

higher or deeper level of awareness. At this deeper level we discover cosmic unity, where all of reality is one.

Jill illustrated that it is analogous to a lake. The lake (the universe) is made up of many different drops of water. At a simple or phenomenal level, you and I are small drops of water. We have our own identity, ego, and consciousness. At a cosmic or ultimate level, when all the drops of water merge, we form the lake. There is just one substance to reality. "I want to overcome the modern mental abstractions where all things are kept apart. I just sense my connection with this greater cosmic reality," she said. "I can send out a thought to the universe and an answer will eventually come. I try to tap into this higher awareness each day. For me, everything ultimately shares in the divine."

Jill then directed us to *The Celestine Prophecy* where Redfield's main character had this mystical intuition:

I sat down again on the rock, and, again, everything seemed close; the rugged outcrop on which I was sitting, the tall trees further down the slope and the other mountains on the horizon. And as I watched the limbs of the trees sway gently in the breeze, I experienced not just a visual perception of the event, but a physical sensation as well, as if the limbs moving in the wind were hairs on my body. I perceived everything to be somehow part of me. As I sat on the peak of the mountain looking out at the landscape falling away from me in all directions, it felt exactly as if what I had always known as my physical body was only the head of a much larger body consisting of everything else I could see. I experienced the entire universe looking out on itself through my eyes.[3]

Jill also referred to Marianne Williamson:

Just as a sunbeam can't separate itself from the sun and a wave can't separate itself from the ocean, we can't separate ourselves from one another. We are all part of a vast sea of love, one indivisible divine mind.[4]

Linda then interposed, "I see things a bit differently from Jill. I feel that the universe is really made up of different objects, but everything is linked to God. God is a real being and not just some force or consciousness. Everything is in God and God is everywhere, but not everything is identical with God."

Understanding Monism

We felt that it was important to further clarify their views. Jill's outlook that "all is one" is called monism. Although the term was coined by the 18th-century German philosopher Christian Wolff, it has a long pedigree. There have been several forms of monism in Eastern and Western philosophy. It is a metaphysical view, dealing with the philosophical question, "how many things are there?"

One version of monism is known as "substantival monism." Its advocates maintain that there is only one real substance or one real thing. The diversity of things we see in the universe is ultimately an illusion. The second version, known as "attributive monism," is where there is one type or category but many different things exist within this one category.

Monistic Roots

Some New Age seekers, but not all, embrace monist ideas.[5] There is substantival monism in classical Taoism, Mahayana Buddhism, and non-dualistic Vedanta in Hinduism.[6] Perhaps the best-known Eastern exponent of substantival monism was the Hindu teacher Shankara.[7] In Western philosophy, the pre-Socratic thinker Parmenides also taught substantival monism. A later variation on this was put forward by Benedict Spinoza (1632-77). He proposed that there is only one substance that underlies all things, so separate objects are just transitory forms of this one substance.

Some philosophers, such as Thomas Hobbes (1588-1679) and Bertrand Russell (1872-1970), held that all real things exist only in the category of matter or the material world. Other philosophers, such as the idealists Gottfried Leibniz (1646-1716) and George Berkeley (1685-1753), held that all real things exist only in the category of the mind or spirit.[8]

On reflection, Jill said that she identified with substantival monism, because she sees us all partaking of the same divine essence or substance. The lesson of life is to awaken our divine cosmic oneness. Linda, however, felt more inclined towards attributive monism, because she sees reality as being ultimately composed of many things that all fit into one category. For her the lesson of life is to see the seamless nature of the universe and that it is in this category where God encompasses all things.

All is God

Jill talked with Ross about her understanding of divine cosmic oneness. She told him that, as all is one essence or substance, all is God (pantheism). As all is God, everyone is a part of God. She said that God is ultimately not a personal being, but a force or energy. This force allows us to control our own lives, spiritually evolve, and create our own destinies. The ultimate goal is to return to the divine source. Jill identified with Shirley Maclaine on this point:

There is an urgent need for people to recognize the power within themselves, to know themselves as a spark of God . . . Begin with self; recognize the God within, and the result will be the recognition, with tolerance and love, that everyone else possesses God within as well. In other words, we are each part of God experiencing the adventure of life.[9]

The masters on oneness

Jill added that this cosmic oneness—where everything partakes of the same substance—appears to tally with what all of the world's great religious masters have taught: we are all divine. Ross spent some time with Jill exploring the teachings of major spiritual leaders and traditions. After some reflection, they then agreed that not all espoused oneness and inner divinity.

- Moses—He taught that God was personal and separate from creation. As the psalmist poetically portrayed, "What are human beings that you are mindful of them, mortals that you care for them? Yet you have made them a little lower than God . . . O Lord, our Sovereign, how majestic is your name in all the earth!" (Ps. 8:4-5, 9, NRSVB).
- Pharaoh Rameses—As Pharaoh of Egypt, Rameses was a human manifestation of one of the Egyptian gods, Amon-Re. Of all the people in Egypt, Pharaoh alone was considered to be a god. The religion of ancient Egypt was polytheistic (there were many gods).[10]
- Krishna—Krishna was the incarnation of Vishnu, a personal god of Hinduism.[11]
- Zoroaster—He believed that there is a good supreme being called Ahura Mazda and an equal entity of evil named Angra Mainyu: "From the beginning of existence there have been two inherently incompatible, antagonistic spirits in the world."[12]
- Jesus—He taught that God was a supreme and personal being, one with whom we can have a relationship. He saw that we are not gods in a divine sense, but rather his created children who are to worship him. The fact that there is evil in the world—that all is not one or of God—is seen in Jesus' rebuke of Satan: "It is written: 'Worship the Lord your God and serve him only'" (Luke 4:8, NIV). When Jesus stated, "I and the Father are one," he was not speaking of a cosmic oneness that we can all share in, but, rather, of his unique relationship with the Father.

- Paul the apostle—When a crowd desired to worship him and Barnabas as gods, he cried, "We too are only men, human like you" (Acts 14:15, NIV). Paul also believed in a supreme personal being.
- Muhammad—He taught that Allah alone was God and the only one worthy of worship. Allah is a personal Creator.[13]
- The Vikings—The Vikings of Scandinavia believed in the existence of various gods, such as Thor, the god of thunder. Viking warriors looked forward to a place in Valhalla, along with all other warriors, after death.
- 'Abdu'l-Baha—He was an early teacher of the Baha'i faith and taught that the other enlightened teachers were only messengers sent by the one God. The Baha'i hold to a separate Creator God.[14]

All is in God

Linda, however, sees God as the ultimate category in which all things exist. She told Philip that God is a personal being and the universe exists inside God's very being. She offered the analogy of a fetus (the world) inside the womb (God). The fetus is a real, distinct entity, but there is an umbilical cord that attaches it to, and it develops within the womb. The mother, however, is a larger, distinct being whose body includes the fetus but is, by definition, greater than the fetus. In the same way, the universe exists inside God and, as the universe develops, so God also changes and grows in an evolutionary process.

Linda's perspective is technically known as panentheism—all is in God. Panentheism should not be confused with pantheism. In pantheism, God and the universe are identical, whereas in panentheism the universe is part of God, but God has an identity that entails something more than the universe. Philosophers of the likes of Alfred Whitehead and theologians such as Charles Hartshorne have espoused this position with considerable finesse.[15]

Philip responded by exploring a few differences between Linda's panentheistic ideas and our own. He clarified that God is a personal, sentient being who created the cosmos. The cosmos, which contains many objects, is certainly the seamless handiwork of God. God is the ultimate reality, the eternal one who is present within the creation but is not identical with it. So, the creation is the category in which all finite things exist and would cease to exist without God's sustaining power.[16] The cosmos, however, is not part of God's being because God is eternal and the cosmos is not. Also, God's essential nature is constant and not subject to evolution. However, God is a passionate being who weeps over our suffering, laughs with us in the enjoyable things of the cosmos, and woos us in love.

Christ and cosmic consciousness

Jill and Linda then raised with us a common expression of New Age spirituality—the Christ consciousness. "Doesn't this support our argument? Isn't it another way of expressing cosmic oneness? Some see it as a divine spark in everyone that helps us to see we are all part of God. It shows us Jesus discovering the Christ consciousness, his own inner divinity and self-realizing being that can awaken this same consciousness in us. It is a spiritual rebirth," they suggested. This is what Jesus meant when he said, "the kingdom of God is within you" (Luke 17:21, NIV).

We responded along these lines. The author of these words, Luke, who also wrote Acts, was not directing us to a divine light within when he quoted these words of Jesus. As we have already seen, this same author records the denial that Paul and Barnabas had any divinity/Christ consciousness. The question remains, what do the words of Christ mean? It would be true to say that the words "within you" can also be translated from the Greek as "among you." When the context of the whole passage is considered, it is hard to escape the conclusion that Jesus is merely teaching that, if you know him, you are a part of his kingdom.

While Jesus' kingdom has an outward dimension that seeks to alleviate injustice, oppression, and spiritual poverty, it would be crippling to miss that it has an inner personal realm. This internalized aspect of the kingdom, though, is not about our own divine consciousness. Rather, what Luke records is the human being receiving the aid of the Holy Spirit for living the kingdom life (see Acts 2).

Another question concerns the very meaning of the word "Christ." In the Sacred Writings it means the "anointed one." It is the Greek translation for the Hebrew word "messiah." The Hebrews looked for just one future messiah, not a tribe of anointed/divine ones. To apply the concept of cosmic consciousness to the Sacred Writings is to give them a meaning that is not even available if you read them in a mystical way.

Even more compelling is the fact that Jesus, in his resurrection, is revealed as the one who is more than human. When Thomas the doubter received enlightenment about this, he affirmed Jesus as his God and was not driven to any sense of his own divine consciousness. The gospels conclude with a note of Jesus worship, not higher self: "When they saw him, they worshipped him; but some doubted" (Matt. 28:17, NIV-UK).

We are the "connected world"

We all agreed that the New Age value of oneness reminds us of our interconnectedness in a global village. As the poet John Donne so eloquently wrote, "No man is an island unto himself." As Paul today would admonish the church in Christ, "There is neither Jew nor Greek, slave nor free, male nor female, for you are all one in Christ Jesus" (Gal. 3:28, NIV). So concerns of oneness within a community are relevant to Christians.

Gaia

Jill and Linda find that a powerful motif for reconnecting us with each other and nature is Gaia (Greek goddess of the earth). Its classical myth-form is found in the ancient belief in an earth mother. Gaia now has a meaning beyond this and calls people to see the whole world as a living, interconnected entity.[17]

We acknowledged that real oneness is not just a human dimension, but involves the whole of nature. Genesis 1 brings us a sense of sacred solidarity with all of nature by reminding us that we ourselves are created from dust. As popular author and physicist Paul Davies tells us, the very dirt we are made of comprises stardust. Psalms 96, 98, and 148 declare that the trees, sun, seas, rivers, mountains, wind, stars and birds join in the dance of praise to God. Romans 8:22 announces that the whole of creation groans for the healing of the earth.

Another side of oneness

We proposed that, tragically, a journey along the path of cosmic oneness could be like a trip into a dark tunnel that gets deeper and deeper with no exit from the lostness. It can be a black hole that sucks everything into itself. Well-known writer on mysticism Karen Armstrong cautions, "Entering the depths of the mind can be extremely dangerous if the would-be mystic has not the mental or physical capacity for this interior quest."[18]

Tal Brooke, a former disciple of Indian guru Sai Baba, speaks of his own chilling exposures:

When a guru, a Rider, emerges from Explosion, you have his revelations, his claimed experiences and his non-human personality operating behind a poker face. Like a good screen actor, he can manipulate every button of human reaction, but behind it is a cold, unknowable, non-human intelligence. Who is the Rider? Who or what is occupying the body?[19]

Leap of Faith

In all of this excitement, we need to hear the word of caution from humanist commentator Bryan Appleyard. He reminds us that if the mechanistic theory has been "proven" wrong, no doubt this new "weird" science will one day be superseded too. While all of us have to rethink our cosmology in the light of the new physics, it would be unwise at this time for any group to base its path on the shifting sands of science.[20]

Quantum leap

Perhaps the most sophisticated expression of this concept today is found in the writings of the Austrian physicist Fritjof Capra.[21] He holds that current developments in science—relativity theory, chaos theory, quantum theory—have led to new insights in physics. He finds parallels between atomic matter and aspects of Taoist and Buddhist faith. Capra maintains that, as energy and matter are now seen to be one in process, the result is that there is no real distinction between them. The same can be said for the scientist (object) and his experiment (subject): all is one.

An American physicist who has quested beyond purely material explanations of matter is Fred Alan Wolf. In *The Eagle's Quest*, he joins together the ecstatic visions of the tribal shaman into other worlds with quantum physics. True consciousness is that there are no personal boundaries; we are all part of the energized "Big Dreamer." We script the universe.[22]

Understandably, some non-scientists are impressed by what Capra and Wolf have expounded. However, their views have not attained widespread acceptance among their peers.[23] Scientists agree that the new insights in physics are moving us out of the Newtonian-mechanical model of the world. Very few hold that it is leading us to monism. Even now, Capra admits that there is room for Christianity in his new paradigm.[24]

Charles Birch, an Australian biologist, suggests that the new science supports a theology of panentheism.[25] Biochemist Darryl Reanney speaks more of a cosmic consciousness that will transcend time with the elimination of our ego at death.[26]

Another influential concept offered in favor of cosmic oneness is the hologram, explicated by David Bohm and Karl Pribram. The hologram is a three-dimensional image of an object. Each fragment contains in it data about the complete object. When translated into a model of the universe, it is claimed that the whole universe is mirrored in each small part. This science, it is also believed, offers a model for monism.[27]

Parting friends

Our time of talking with Jill and Linda drew to a close. Jill indicated that, although she had held overly-generalized views about the world's religious traditions, she felt that Redfield's novels make sense of things. We reminded her how in Redfield's *The Secret of Shambhala*, the emphasis is on prayer energy as a key tool for cosmic harmony. We urged Jill and Linda to make prayer part of their daily regimen, and to be open to Jesus' response to them. As for Linda, she seemed content to affirm panentheism. They were due to attend a workshop, so we left them with some points to ponder.

- If all is purely one and we are part of an impersonal force, where does our capacity and desire to interact with each other come from?
- Why is it that we have our own personal tastes and dislikes?
- The whole idea of a seamless impersonal energy force raises the question where does our gift of love come from? The fabric of our very make-up knits us to a framework bigger than an impersonal cosmic oneness.

If we embrace the idea that the cosmos exists as part of God's very being, then we are left with some conundrums. If God and the cosmos develop in partnership, how is it that evil exists in the cosmos? For this to be true, we must assume that God commits evil as we commit evil, or neither does. Furthermore, as the earth is already in God, why would God enter our world as an avatar or incarnate being?

While affirming the road to global harmony, there is no need to lose a belief in a personal Creator God who is distinct from the cosmos. The Sacred Writings affirm this when Jesus taught that we can live in a personal relationship with a personal God. Through both the joys and strains of life, there is the abiding comfort of one greater than us whose "footprints" are alongside ours in the sands of time—"Never will I leave you; never will I forsake you" (Heb. 13:5, NIV).

Endnotes

Chapter 7

1 John Roger, *The Power Within You*, revised edition, Los Angeles: Baraka, 1984, p. 1.

2 Dawn Hill, *With A Little Help from My Friends*, Sydney: Pan, 1991, p. 42.

3 James Redfield, *The Celestine Prophecy*, Sydney and New York: Bantam, 1994, p. 98.

4 Marianne Williamson, *A Return to Love*, London: Aquarian, 1992, p. 29.

5 See Paul Greer, "The Aquarian Confusion: Conflicting Theologies of the New Age," *Journal of Contemporary Religion*, 10, 2, 1995, pp. 151-166; Irving Hexham and Karla Poewe, *New Religions as Global Cultures*, Boulder: Westview, 1997, pp. 5-6; Chrissie Steyn, *Worldviews in Transition: An Investigation of the New Age Movement in South Africa*, Pretoria: University of South Africa Press, 1994; and Michael York, *The Emerging Network: A sociology of the New Age and Neo-Pagan Movements*, Lanham and London: Rowman & Littlefield, 1995.

6 On monism in Buddhist, Hindu and Taoist philosophy, see Stuart C. Hackett, *Oriental Philosophy: A Westerner's guide to Eastern Thought*, Madison: University of Wisconsin Press, 1979, pp. 57, 112-113, 154; and Arvind Sharma (ed.), *Our Religions*, San Francisco: HarperCollins San Francisco, 1993.

7 On Shankara, see A.L. Basham, *The Wonder That Was India*, New Delhi: Rupa, 1981, pp. 330-331; and R.C. Zaehner, *Hindusim*, 2nd edition, Oxford: Oxford University Press, 1966, pp. 73-78.

8 On Berkeley, Hobbes, Leibniz, Parmenides, Russell and Spinoza see Frederick Copelston, A History of Philosophy,

9 Shirley Maclaine, *Going Within*, New York: Bantam, 1989, pp. 91, 108.

10 Sir Alan Gardiner, *Egypt of the Pharaohs*, London and Oxford: Oxford University Press, 1961, pp. 214ff.

11 R.C. Zaehner, *Hinduism*, pp. 92-99.

12 Yasha 45: 2. See Ninian Smart, *The World's Religions*, Cambridge: Cambridge University Press, 1989, pp. 217-218.

13 W. Montgomery Watt, *Muhammad: Prophet and Statesman*, London and Oxford: Oxford University Press, 1961.

14 Joel Bjorling, *The Baha'i Faith: An Historical Bibliography*, New York and London: Garland, 1985, pp. 15-24.

15 Alfred North Whitehead, Process and Reality, New York: Free Press, 1978; Charles Hartshorne, *Omnipotence and Other Theological Mistakes*, Albany: State University of New York Press, 1984; and Ronald H. Nash (ed.), *Process Theology*, Grand Rapids: Baker, 1987.

16 Gordon H. Clark, *Thales to Dewey*, reprinted edition, Grand Rapids: Baker, 1980, p. 231; and Edward John Carnell, *An Introduction to Christian Apologetics*, Grand Rapids: Wm.B. Eerdmans, 1948, pp. 40-41.

17 J.E. Lovelock, *Gaia: A New Look at Life on Earth*, Oxford: Oxford University Press, 1979; and James Lovelock, *The Ages of Gaia*, Oxford: Oxford University Press, 1988.

18 Karen Armstrong, *The English Mystics of the Fourteenth Century*, London: Kyle

Cathie, 1991, p. 4.

[19] Tal Brooke, *Riders of the Cosmic Circuit*, Tring: Lion; and Sutherland, New South Wales: Albatross, 1986, p. 170.

[20] Bryan Appleyard, *Understanding the Present: Science and the Soul of Modern Man*, London: Pan, 1992.

[21] Fritjof Capra, *The Tao of Physics*, 3rd edition, London: Flamingo, 1991.

[22] See Richard Leviton, "Through the Shaman's Doorway," *Yoga Journal*, July-August 1992, pp.48-55, 102.

[23] See Ernest Lucas, *Science and the New Age Challenge*, Leicester: Apollos, 1996; and Wouter J. Hanegraaff, *New Age Religion and Western Culture*, Albany: State University of New York Press, 1998, pp. 128-140.

[24] Fritjof Capra, David Steindl-Rast and Thomas Matus, *Belonging to the Universe: New Thinking about God and Nature*, Harmondsworth: Penguin, 1992.

[25] Charles Birch, *On Purpose*, Kensington, New South Wales: New South Wales University Press, 1990.

[26] Darryl Reanney, *The Death of Forever: A New Future for Human Consciousness*, Melbourne: Longman Cheshire, 1991.

[27] David Bohm, *Wholeness and the Implicate*, Order, London and New York: Ark, 1983.

Chapter 8
Near-Death Experiences

I was going towards a very bright light. And as I was travelling along I could see different-colored lights and then I got stopped, just stopped before I got to the light. And I felt this extreme presence of love, just absolute love. And I heard very clearly . . . I was being confronted by my Creator . . . I was told it wasn't my time to go on—that I had to come back. I had my life's work to do.[1]

The New Age has little to do with prophecy or the imaging of a new world, but everything to do with the imagination to see our world in new ways that can empower us toward compassionate, transformative actions and attitudes. If we remember this, then we can forget the New Age of channels, crystals, and charisma and get on with discovering and co-creating a harmonious world that will nourish and empower all of us on this planet and all our children who will be the inheritors of our future.[2]

In my Father's house are many rooms; if it were not so, I would have told you. I am going there to prepare a place for you (John 14:2, NIV).

Early one morning before the festival became crowded, Peter and Carol dropped by. They were exhibitors with a stand devoted to near-death experiences and members of the International Association for Near-Death Studies (IANDS).[3] As life partners in their late sixties, they had spent over a decade researching the phenomenon and the comfort such happenings have brought to many. We found that we could celebrate together that death is not itself the end of our existence. We were all aware of the prominence given to such encounters on TV shows such as *Oprah*.

Peter and Carol told us how Dr. Kubler-Ross, the recognized world authority on death and dying, was dramatically moved from doubt to faith with respect to near-death experiences.

Dr. Kubler-Ross was going to quit her position at the University of Chicago where she was dealing with terminal patients. As she was walking in the hospital, she encountered a former patient who had died eleven months previously. The patient spoke to her, walked with her, touched her hand and opened the door to her office. The patient asked, "Can you hear me?" and pleaded with Dr. Kubler-Ross, "Promise that you won't give up your work." Dr. Kubler-Ross says that this is the most important message she has ever received.

After these words, she stood in her study, still feeling doubt, and then this entity wrote a note for the pastor involved in this former patient's case. The note stated "at home, at peace." Dr. Kubler-Ross abandoned skepticism, and within a few weeks of this event, she began to write her best-selling book, *On Death and Dying*.[4] Peter and Carol directed us to Samantha Trenoweth's book *The Future of God* where Dr. Kubler-Ross recounts this story.[5]

Another benefit of near-death experiences for Peter and Carol is the move into the new paradigm of global consciousness. From the popular radio documentary "And When I Die, Will I Be Dead?" comes the story of Allan Lewis who, when he was fourteen, suffered a trio of successive heart attacks at school, departed his body, and entered the spirit world.[6]

On meeting his dead relatives and a being called the Light, he was taught about life after death. They indicated that there is no personal judgment at death and that all spiritual paths are valid approaches. In today's global civilization, Peter and Carol see the need for a spiritual faith that embraces all of the traditions.

Out of Body Experiences

Raymond Moody in his book *Life After Life* suggests fifteen common elements of near-death experiences, *The Aquarian Guide to the New Age* succinctly identifies these as follows: common denominators seem to be the sensation of passing through a tunnel, an out-of-body experience, a perception of light, and meetings with spiritual or biblical figures and/or dead friends and relatives. Individuals tend to interpret the experience in the light of their own cultural background.[7] When people experience the light, they often report being embraced by an immeasurable breadth of love that they find is indescribable. It can be a door to positive transformation.

Testimonies for near-death experiences

As we agreed with Peter and Carol, the case for near-death experiences is very strong and thrilling. The stage is being reached where a great many people know of someone who has had one. As well as this, there is the thorough documentation in the writings of Robert Monroe, Raymond Moody, Elisabeth Kubler-Ross and Cherie Sutherland.[8]

The subject has also attracted some serious scholarship, as evidenced in Carol Zaleski's doctoral work *Otherworld Journeys*. She states, "In nearly all cultures, people have told stories of travel to another world, in which a hero, shaman, prophet, king, or ordinary mortal passes through the gates of death and returns with a message for the living."[9]

Taylor's Testimony

Internationally renowned actress Elizabeth Taylor has spoken of her own near-death experience. She had kept quiet because it sounded so "weird":

> *Thirty years ago I was pronounced dead—I've read my own*
> *obituary. I had a terrible case of pneumonia and I stopped breath-*
> *ing for five minutes. And while I was dead, I went on and on*
> *through a long tunnel until finally I saw a light at the end of it.*
> *The light was wonderful and I wanted to go into it. But Mike*
> *Todd was standing at the end of the tunnel and he said: "You have*
> *to go back." So I did . . . I was painfully conscious of everything.*
> *Sounds, colors, objects, people . . . And when I heard that thou-*
> *sands of people had gathered outside the hospital and were praying*
> *for me, I felt an overwhelming sea of love being channeled into*
> *me. In a way that was almost mystical, I felt I was being accepted*
> *into humanity.*[10]

Margaret, who is an acquaintance of ours, has related how her
encounter had a fresh angle:

While in the tunnel I had a strange feeling, as though some-
thing—my soul, I imagine—was being vacuumed out of my body,
as if my body were a shell. Not painful, just strange. I remember
vividly hearing someone (I presume to be God) saying to me, "Are
you ready to die?" My response was "What about Deryck?" To
which I heard, "He'll manage." My next thought was, "It'll be a
large funeral" and so I said, "Yes, I am prepared to die."[11]

She found this to be an invigorating experience for her journey
with Jesus.

Even the prominent atheist philosopher Sir Alfred Ayer had a
near-death experience during a bout of pneumonia. It didn't
change his convictions about God, but, surprisingly, brought this
response: "My recent experiences have slightly weakened my

conviction that my genuine death, which is due fairly soon, will be the end of me, though I continue to hope that it will be."[12]

Philosophers Gary Habermas and J.P. Moreland have shown that near-death experiences are happening at all phases of medical demise. There are accounts of people having out-of-body experiences when they are close to being pronounced clinically dead. Then there are the ones when the heart stops and even after the brain stops. They conclude, "Since human consciousness does not depend on the central nervous system (or other bodily activity), NDEs are evidence of at least a short period of life after death."[13]

Theories Abound

Near-death traveler and researcher Professor John Wren-Lewis states, "A healthy discipline of skepticism is essential in evaluating NDE reports, and it's equally important when looking for patterns in the data that might provide clues to what these experiences are really all about."[19] He then gives a possible explanation for the phenomenon in terms of an "eternity consciousness." He interprets our modern busy lifestyle as acting as a block to confronting the existential reality of our own death. Instead, in the here and now we are solely concerned with survival. When people undergo a near-death experience, they may simply be coming in touch with a suppressed inner sense of eternity.[20]

Natural Explanations for NDE
Critics have pointed out a number of possible natural explanations for this phenomenon. These include the following:
- The possibility of time travel, where one moves out of linear time into another dimension of consciousness where past, present, and future are one. In this tunnel, we might be linking up with "past" comrades. A novel entitled *Many Dimensions* by Charles Williams has explored some of these possibilities concerning time, consciousness, and spirituality.[14]
- Carl Sagan, in *Broca's Brain*, suggests that near-death experiences are a

shadow recall of bliss in the womb. They are a reminder of our passage through the birth canal.[15]

- A cardiac surgeon has told us that when someone is under the effects of anesthetics, oxygen deprivation, or high fevers, strange things can happen. It is therefore not wise to give any real weight to post-operative recollections. Similar sensations can be experienced by using hallucinogenic drugs. It should be noted, though, that various tests have established that anesthetics, lack of oxygen, or drugs did not affect the substantial majority of those who had a near-death experience. As well, in many cases, there is no evidence of unusually high-body-temperature feverish delirium.[16]

- Some doctors note that when parts of the brain are shut down, patients do lose their bearings and a sense of drifting is common. The brain remains a frontier for research where mysteries and the seemingly inexplicable abound.

- Dr. Zaleski, after making a major cross-cultural study, states that other world journey stories are "through and through a work of the socially conditioned religious imagination." She further comments that we can no longer insist that such visionary experiences paint "a true picture of what occurs at the extreme border of life."[17]

- Dr. Zaleski does affirm the positive benefit of near-death experiences, but suggests they are symbols that reflect our religious heritage rather than actual events. This implies that, if you had lived in medieval Europe and had a near-death experience, you might see demons, hell fire, saints, and Madonnas. If you were living in India, you would most likely encounter Krishna, Ram, Ganesh, or Shiva. Consistent with Dr. Zaleski's insights are those of Zambian physician Dr. Nsama Mumbwe, who found that, among Africans, many interpreted such experiences as evil. Half thought the experience signified that they were somehow "bewitched." Another called it a "bad omen."[18]

Of all these natural explanations, near-death experiences expert Cherie Sutherland rightly says, "Overall they tend to be more evaluative than descriptive, and so far they can only be considered speculative at best."[21] We agree that science has not satisfactorily accounted for all these metaphysical travels. As Melvin Morse asserts, "The near-death experience remains a mystery."[22] While this is true, our awareness of the mystery of these experiences should be balanced by the excellent research work of those of the likes of Dr. Zaleski.

Messages from "the other side"

What we have noticed is that there are profound spiritual messages coming from those who have been beyond the grave and back. Many are stressing harmony and unity. Cherie Sutherland's three books—*Transformed by the Light, Within the Light,* and *Children of the Light*—are quite typical of this genre in recounting what near-death experience travelers affirm as the positive message and impact of these encounters.

Peter and Carol sought to enhance this outlook by pointing us to the teaching of leading near-death experience and out-of-body experiences researcher Robert Monroe. He believes that our common earthly experiences positively equip us all for the other side:

◆

This earth-life system is a predator world, so we can't help but be predators in order to exist in this world. We have come to this system for a very particular purpose, to learn certain things, and this system is exquisitely, beautifully adjusted to allow us to learn those things. We learn survival at a physical level, and we learn to manipulate energy. We also learn cause and effect, authority and responsibility—all those things we learn here as humans. But I can assure you that, once you graduate from this earth-life system and move into other realities, you are God. You are God in those other realities because of what you have gathered here.[23]

◆

While we understood Peter and Carol's ideas, we wondered about those who have had these experiences and found them not to be a good experience or a pointer to universal salvation. It is surprising that some current researchers of near-death experiences do not document some of these well-known cases. Perhaps this is because of their bias toward a global consciousness. In fact many, after having such experiences, have been driven back to the conviction that Christ is the path.

Dark and frightening near-death experiences

Dr. Maurice Rawlings is today one of the most talked about researchers of this area. He is a physician who has gathered together accounts of "negative" near-death experiences that actually drove him from skepticism to faith. He now even holds that some encounters during such experiences may be dark spirit directed. In his first book, *Beyond Death's Door*, Rawlings recounts:

I was resuscitating a terrified patient who told me he was actually in hell. He begged me to get him out of hell and not to let him die. When I fully realized how genuinely and extremely frightened he was, I too became frightened . . . Now I feel assured that there is life after death and not all of it is good.[24]

Rawlings's book created quite a stir at the time because virtually all the NDE literature emphasized positive experiences. Rawlings sustained the controversy with his sequel book in 1980, *Before Death Comes*, and again in 1993 with *To Hell and Back*.[25] Many researchers, as we shall see, have found Rawlings's work difficult to accept.

However, other researchers have confirmed the discovery of "negative" near-death experiences in modern times. Dr. Karlis Osis records the terrifying experience of a patient who cried out, "Hell, hell, all I see is hell." Then there was the patient who had the sensation of being burned alive.[26] Dr. Bruce Greyson is an American psychiatrist and editor of the Journal of Near-Death Studies.[27] Dr. Greyson, together with Nancy Evans Bush, President of IANDS, have studied fifty cases of hellish experiences gathered over a period of nine years.[28]

US psychiatrist George Ritchie had an extensive near-death experience where he saw people in a frightening place. It is interesting to note that a researcher of these experiences, Raymond Moody, has written the foreword to Ritchie's book *Return From Tomorrow* and describes it as "startling" and among one of the "three or four most fantastic and well-documented" cases known to him.[29] Moody is best known for recounting positive near-death experiences, although in his sequel *Reflections on Life After Life* he did refer to some new cases where people felt trapped in their experiences. Moody was goaded to explore the possibility of unpleasant experiences because of his friendship with Ritchie. Moody did later acknowledge that "nothing I have encountered precludes the possibility of hell."[30]

In interviewing patients, Dr. Rawlings has observed that there is a methodological problem with prominent near-death experience investigators such as Raymond Moody and Dr. Kubler-Ross. His remarks applied particularly to Moody's first book:

———————————— ◆ ————————————

It then occurred to me that Dr. Kubler-Ross, Dr. Moody, and other psychiatrists and psychologists were interviewing patients who had been resuscitated by other doctors several days to several weeks previously. Neither Kubler-Ross nor Moody, so far as I know, has ever resuscitated a patient or had the opportunity of recording immediate on-the-scene interviews.

After many interrogations of patients I have personally resuscitated, I was amazed by the discovery that many have had bad experiences. If patients could be immediately interviewed, I believe researchers would find bad experiences to be as frequent as good ones. However, most doctors, not wanting to be identified with spiritual beliefs, are afraid to question patients about their after-death experiences.[31]

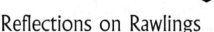

Reflections on Rawlings

As devotees of near-death experiences literature, Peter and Carol were acquainted with Rawlings's reputation and had dipped into his first book. As subscribers to the Journal of Near-Death Studies, they had also read the essay by Greyson and Bush. They felt that Rawlings's book was too anecdotal to be taken seriously. They also referred us to criticisms made by Cherie Sutherland. In her second book *Within the Light*, she wrote:

Of negative reports that have surfaced in contemporary times, Maurice Rawlings's work is perhaps the best known, taking as it does an extreme view. In 1978, Rawlings presented the thesis that hellish NDEs are simply repressed. Arguing as he does, however, from a "born-again" Christian perspective with the clear agenda of proving to readers the existence of hell and therefore the need to be "saved," his presentation is questionable.[32]

We responded by saying that there are a few points worthy of consideration about Sutherland's evaluation. She assumes at the outset that Rawlings's religious agenda makes his work suspect. This is not a good starting point for a scholar. One could easily propose that Sutherland's research must be suspect because she only reports positive experiences that are consistent with her own New Age beliefs. What she also fails to report is that Rawlings was converted to faith from skepticism about life after death after he had resuscitated a patient who had a negative near-death experience. Rawlings then went on to research for other possible cases of negative experiences.

We agreed with them that Rawlings's first book was highly anecdotal. However, the parapsychologist D. Scott Rogo made this astute observation: "No matter how Dr. Rawlings came to collect his data, the fact remains that negative or hellish NDEs have now been placed on record by obviously sincere witnesses . . . Facts are facts, no matter how one comes by them."[33]

Rawlings's findings have found some qualified support in research conducted by the famous US pollster George Gallup Jr. in his 1982 book *Adventures in Immortality*.[34] Tom Harpur is a Canadian researcher in this area who expresses some reservations about Rawlings's first book. However, Harpur is willing to make this concession: "Rawlings at least has raised the issue that possibly all is not light and bliss during the near-death experience."[35]

Sopranos, Simpsons, and Flatliners

Carol said to us, "I was watching a recent episode of *The Sopranos* and it was astonishing to see one of the younger Mafiosos have a bad NDE. This Young Turk, who had been shot, was very close to death. He had the usual tunnel experience, but when he encountered the light he was redirected to another place. I don't know if it was supposed to be purgatory or hell, but he met up with several deceased Mafia colleagues. They gave him a firm message about what will happen if he continues his life of crime."

"And did you ever see the episode of *The Simpsons* where young Bart had both a negative and a positive NDE?" Ross asked. Bart Simpson had quite a shock with his dark near-death experience. Philip then mentioned the chilling experiences of the characters portrayed by Kiefer Sutherland and Julia Roberts in the film *Flatliners*. We concluded that even TV shows and films are open to portraying the possibility of frightening or dark near-death experiences with no religious agenda in the scripts.

The illusion of negative near-death experiences

Peter and Carol moved the discussion on to the seminal and alternative insights of Kenneth Ring. His position is linked to the popular channeled work *A Course in Miracles*.[36]

"The Course" on Near Death Experiences

The Course, which was channeled by Helen Schucman between 1965 and 1973, attempts to explain the illusory nature of our ego. According to it we mistake the material world for true reality. The ego is transient, while our true identity is found in God. We are one with God in our very being for God is an impersonal mind. The Course also seeks to clear away our misconceptions about guilt. We have two choices in life: either love or fear.[37]

While affirming positive near-death experiences, Ring suggests that negative ones may be understood from psychological mechanisms that predispose a person to experience guilty feelings and believe there is a hell. However, he maintains that they are best understood via the revelation of the Course. As the Course explains the illusory nature of guilt and of our egos, negative near-death experiences are the products of illusory mental projections. In other words, the near-death traveler who encounters hell is only experiencing what the ego and subconscious mind have assented to. It is the detour of the mind away from love and into fear. The Course liberates us from these illusions. So, by studying the Course, a near-death experience survivor can be freed from these illusory bonds and experience transformation. The negative experience can then become a catalyst for growth through the medium of *A Course in Miracles*.

We told Peter and Carol that Ring's position, though interesting, is fraught with serious difficulties. Most significantly, his psychological theory about negative near-death experiences involves a form of reductionism. This is what the skeptics do to believers when they reduce all supernatural and paranormal phenomena to naturalistic categories. As the negative cases contradict his own spiritual pathway, Ring has fallen for the fallacy of dismissing them as mere psychological phenomena. Also, to agree with Ring's conclusions we would have to embrace the basic tenets of the Course. Can we take it for granted that the Course is trustworthy in what it says about God and ultimate reality? Despite the Course's widespread popularity, many postmodern pilgrims, like us, have not found it as being true for them. As J.G. Melton reports, "many metaphysically inclined students have been puzzled by the Course's language" and another difficulty "is the teaching that the body is but 'the instrument the mind made in its efforts to deceive itself.'"[38] We said to Peter and Carol that we have a bigger view of who we are.

Peter and Carol were not unaware of the concerns we raised. Carol knew of the apparent inconsistencies. For example, Ring only applies the principles of the Course to account for the negative near-death experiences, but how do we know that positive ones are not also the product of illusory experiences? For Ring, positive experiences are exempt because of the Course's principle of choosing love rather than fear. If the positive near-death experience yields an experience of love, then, according to Ring, it must be true. Carol understood the claim that Ring begs the question. Surely the very subjective nature of all these experiences opens up the possibility of self-deception or even wish fulfilment. The Course portrays God as an impersonal universal mind. However, for an authentic love relationship to exist, two personal beings must reciprocate. Unidirectional human love with an impersonal mind might simply be a detour into self-delusion. Clearly Ring's prior commitment to the Course's worldview shapes the way he understands all near-death experiences.

New Age acceptance

Our conversation then turned to the research of P.M.H. Atwater. She has had a near-death experience and is self-consciously committed to New Age spirituality. She began her research into near-death experiences in 1978 and, from the outset, has pursued negative cases. In her essay, "Is There a Hell?" Atwater points out that she has found 105 negative cases out of 700 reported experiences. She argues that they are probably more frequent than researchers have been willing to acknowledge.[39] Atwater has also drawn attention to negative cases in her two popular books *Coming Back* and *Beyond the Light*.[40] Even though Atwater is not convinced that there is a hell, she encourages people to come forward with their negative stories. She admits that these hellish encounters show us that there is much more to near-death experiences than any of us know.

Finally, we chatted about Margot Grey, the humanistic psychologist who has no religious ties whatsoever. In her book *Return from Death*, Grey documents several cases of negative near-death experiences where people had feelings of fear and panic. She reports that such negative experiences involve a black void, a sense of an evil force, and encounters with a hell-like environment. Her British study disclosed that 12 percent of near-death experiences she examined were negative. As Grey holds no religious beliefs and offers a Jungian reinterpretation of them, she can scarcely be criticized as being motivated by an agenda to convince her readers of the existence of hell.[41]

We concluded with Peter and Carol, then, that not all the messages from the other side uphold global consciousness.

The Last Laugh?

After our encounter with Peter and Carol at the festival, someone drew our attention to a book by Raymond Moody which was then just hot off the press: *The Last Laugh*. Moody expresses some crankiness with his publishers over his original book *Life after Life* because they had refused to let him take up the issues he is finally addressing in *The Last Laugh*. He takes to task three different interest groups with respect to near-death experiences: the true believers, the skeptics, and fundamentalist Christians. His argument is that each of these interpretive groups is flawed in their understanding of near-death experience phenomena.

Moody's primary complaint is that no existing interpretative model can adequately account for the paranormal experiences of near-death experience travelers. He argues that the paranormal is so peculiar that using any current methodology to account for the phenomena is utterly nonsensical. In effect, near-death experiences are beyond our reach because our present methods for interpreting them are flawed. Moody is implying that if we are ever going to understand near-death experiences we will all have to undergo a major paradigm shift over the criteria we use to evaluate the paranormal.

So Moody examines the psychology of the near-death experience skeptic. He excoriates Carl Sagan's dogmatic commitment to naturalistic explanations of the paranormal and the near-death experience as hopelessly flawed. He likewise chides the work of other parapsychologists, and near-death experience researchers affiliated with IANDS, for concluding that near-death experiences are objectively real evidence of life after death. He maintains that the data are too elusive to permit these conclusions and disputes the validity of the interpretive matrix near-death experience researchers use. Perhaps his most scathing criticisms are reserved for fundamentalist Christians who posit a demonic explanation for most of the near-death experience phenomena.

Moody offers no solution to the interpretative dilemma he underscores. He refers to near-death experiences as inexplicable but amusing phenomena. At times his own analysis seems to be a self-indulgent sideswipe at just about everyone else who has written about near-death experiences. Although Moody underscores some important points for all near-death experience interpreters to grapple with, it appears that in this book he is manifesting something of the same rigidity that he finds fault with in those he criticizes.

Lazarus unveils the other side

Indirectly, the Sacred Writings touch on these kinds of life-after-death experiences. There are the records of Paul's vision of the third heaven, Lazarus, the brother of Mary and Martha, being raised from the dead, and Jesus' teaching about the rich man and Lazarus. Although near-death experience exponents sometimes refer to these passages, it is interesting to note that none of them explicitly deals with the concept. Here, all the characters involved in the experience affirmed their need of Christ. There is no indication that they had a sense that all is well in the after life. In fact, Paul went on to explicitly teach otherwise.

We suggested to Peter and Carol that, rather than entering into dogma, we should let the narrative of the poor man Lazarus speak to our hearts. We paraphrased Luke 16:19-31 this way:

There was a baby boomer who enjoyed the best things in life, but showed no compassion for the poor beggar Lazarus (perhaps because the baby boomer saw this was Lazarus's "script" in life). Both the baby boomer and Lazarus died. The baby boomer found his destiny had brought him into a place of great alienation and torment, whereas Lazarus entered into a peaceful and wholesome rest. The baby boomer recognized the folly of his life and begged to be rescued. He pleaded that his soulmates might be warned as to what lies beyond the grave. He was told that the Sacred Writings are already there to enlighten them. Lazarus, on the other hand, in his peaceful rest, communed with the great sage Abraham.

Celebrating life ever after

Near-death experiences are helping people like Peter and Carol to cope with the trauma of death. They awaken us to the reality of eternity. People differ as to their meaning. When discussing this, we have found it helpful to suggest that this is because the near-death traveler is still only on the fringe of the city, glimpsing the city lights, and is yet to fully explore the center. The first impressions are therefore limiting and subjective. Is there anyone who can guide us through this labyrinth? Is there anyone who has been to the center of town and back? The master, Jesus, is the only one to guide us through the labyrinth.

Endnotes

Chapter 8

1 Cherie Sutherland, *Transformed by the Light*, Sydney: Bantam, 1992 p. 10.

2 David Spangler, "Defining the New Age," *The New Age Catalogue*, New York: Doubleday, 1988.

3 See the website at www.iands.org.

4 Elisabeth Kubler-Ross, *On Death and Dying*, London: Tavistock, 1970.

5 Samantha Trenoweth, *The Future of God*, Sydney: Millennium Books, 1995, pp. 37-59.

6 Bruce Elder, *And When I Die, Will I Be Dead?*, Sydney: Australian Broadcasting Corporation, 1987, pp. 9-33; and "Hal's Story" in Cherie Sutherland, *Children of the Light*, Sydney: Bantam, 1995, pp. 166-187.

7 Eileen Campbell and J.H. Brennan, *The Aquarian Guide to the New Age*, London: Aquarian, 1990, p. 224.

8 See Robert A. Monroe, *Journeys Out of the Body*, London: Souvenir, 1972. Raymond A. Moody, *Life after Life*, New York: Bantam, 1976; and Cherie Sutherland, *Within the Light*, Sydney: Bantam, 1993.

9 Carol Zaleski, *Otherworld Journeys*, New York and Oxford: Oxford University Press, 1987, p. 3.

10 Elizabeth Taylor, in *The Australian Women's Weekly*, June 1992, p. 8.

11 Margaret's story has not been published anywhere. Her remarks were summarized in a written note to Ross Clifford, who at the time was the minister at her church.

12 "What I Saw When I Was Dead," in Terry Miethe and Antony Flew, *Does God Exist?*, San Francisco: HarperCollins San Francisco, 1991, p. 228.

13 Gary R. Habermas and J.P. Moreland, *Immortality: The Other Side of Death*, Nashville: Thomas Nelson, 1992, p. 104.

14 Charles Williams, *Many Dimensions*, Grand Rapids: Wm.B. Eerdmans, 1979.

15 Carl Sagan, *Broca's Brain: Reflections on the Romance of Science*, New York: Random, 1979.

16 Ian Wilson, *The After Death Experience*, London: Corgi, 1989, pp. 164-200.

17 Carol Zaleski, *Otherworld Journeys*, p. 190.

18 James Mauro, "Bright Lights, Big Mystery," *Psychology Today*, July-August 1992, p. 57.

19 John Wren-Lewis, "Eternity Now," *Simply Living*, 6, 5, 1992, p. 60.

20 Wren-Lewis relates how his near-death experience has altered his personal worldview in "The Dazzling Dark: A Near-Death Experience Opens the Door to a Permanent Transformation," *What is Enlightenment?*, 4, 2, 1995, pp. 39-44.

21 Cherie Sutherland, *Transformed by the Light*, Sydney: Bantam, 1992, p. 18.

22 Melvin Morse and Paul Perry, *Closer to the Light: Learning from the Near-Death Experiences of Children*, New York: Bantam, 1992, p. 226.

23 Robert Monroe as interviewed by Nevill Drury, *The Visionary Human*, New York and Sydney: Bantam, 1991, p. 130.

24 Maurice Rawlings, *Beyond Death's Door*, New York: Bantam, 1979, pp. xii-xiii.

[25] Maurice Rawlings, *Before Death Comes*, Nashville: Thomas Nelson, 1980; and *To Hell and Back*, Nashville: Thomas Nelson, 1993.

[26] Karlis Osis and Erlendur Haraldsson, "Deathbed Observations by Physicians and Nurses," *Journal of the American Society for Psychical Research*, 71, 1977, pp. 237-259.

[27] This is the official journal for IANDS. See the organization's website at www.iands.org/jndsind.html.

[28] Bruce Greyson and Nancy Evans Bush, "Distressing Near-Death Experiences," *Psychiatry*, 55, 1992, pp. 95-110.

[29] Raymond Moody, Foreword in George Ritchie with Elizabeth Sherrill, *Return From Tomorrow*, Eastbourne: Kingsway, 1978, p. 9.

[30] Raymond Moody, *Reflections on Life after Life*, New York: Bantam, 1978, p. 36.

[31] Maurice Rawlings, *Beyond Death's Door*, p. 46.

[32] Cherie Sutherland, *Within the Light*, Sydney: Bantam, 1993, p. 141.

[33] D. Scott Rogo, *Return from Silence: A Study of Near-Death Experiences*, London: Aquarian, 1989, p. 136.

[34] George Gallup Jr. with William Proctor, *Adventures in Immortality*, New York: McGraw-Hill, 1982, and London: Souvenir, 1983, pp. 73-87.

[35] Tom Harpur, *Life after Death*, Toronto: McClelland & Stewart, 1991, p. 51.

[36] See Kenneth Ring, "Solving the Riddle of Frightening Near-Death Experiences: Some testable hypotheses and a perspective based on A Course in Miracles," *Journal of Near-Death Studies*, 13, 1994, pp. 5-23.

[37] *A Course in Miracles*, London: Arkana, 1985.

[38] J. Gordon Melton, Jerome Clark, and Aidan A. Kelly, *The New Age Almanac*, Detroit: Visible Ink, 1991, p. 54.

[39] P.M.H. Atwater, "Is There a Hell? Surprising Observations about the Near-Death Experiences," *Journal of Near-Death Studies*, 10, 1992, p. 150.

[40] P.M.H. Atwater, *Coming Back: The After-Effects of the Near-Death Experience*, New York: Dodd, Mead, 1988; and *Beyond the Light: What Isn't Being Said about Near-Death Experience*, New York: Birch Lane, 1994.

[41] Margot Grey, *Return from Death*, London: Arkana, 1985.

Chapter 9
Past Lives

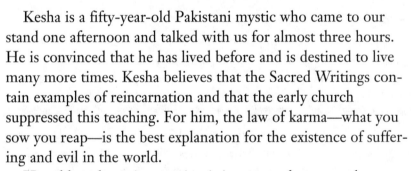

That Origen (the early church leader) taught the pre-existence of the soul in past world orders of this earth and its reincarnation in future worlds is beyond question.[1]

You must be born again (John 3:7, NIV).

Kesha is a fifty-year-old Pakistani mystic who came to our stand one afternoon and talked with us for almost three hours. He is convinced that he has lived before and is destined to live many more times. Kesha believes that the Sacred Writings contain examples of reincarnation and that the early church suppressed this teaching. For him, the law of karma—what you sow you reap—is the best explanation for the existence of suffering and evil in the world.

He told us that reincarnation is important because, when we go into our past lives, we discover the karma that is catching up to us. This is therapeutic as it allows us to understand ourselves and perhaps to re-script our fate by positive creative visualization. Kesha himself explored his past lives by rebirthing. He went on to explain that our path of spiritual evolution is to progress through many lifetimes. Eventually we will reach a state of balanced karma and God-consciousness.

Ross could relate to Kesha's ideas about the healing that comes from looking back. Ross mentioned that, in his early teens, while he lived on the streets of a city for a short time, he had suffered much abuse, hurt, and rejection.

The pain this produced had caused him to suppress the memory of this time. This had stopped him from dealing with questions of self-esteem and rejection that had come out of his teenage experience. It was only some twenty-odd years later when visiting the city that, in a divinely dramatic way, the events were revived. That resulted in an immediate understanding of why he lacked the empowerment he needed to assert himself in life. Regressing back revealed a hurtful past from which he could now be healed and released.

We thus acknowledged with Kesha the healing that flows from looking back. Kesha then asked us if our path, which certainly allows for regression, also embraces reincarnation?

Clarifying some key terms

We felt it was prudent at the outset to clarify what certain key words mean because they can be confusing: metempsychosis, transconception, transmigration, reincarnation, and rebirth.

- *Metempsychosis* is a term used by ancient Greek philosophers such as Pythagoras, Plato, and Plotinus. It refers to the passing of the soul at death from one body to another. Irving Hexham in his *Concise Dictionary of Religion* points out that metempsychosis "is found in Hinduism and Jainism but not Buddhism where the doctrine of reincarnation is similar but in important respects different."[2]
- *Rebirth* is a term defined quite differently in Christianity, Hinduism, and Buddhism. In Christianity, it refers to the moment of conversion when God's Spirit regenerates our spirit. However, rebirth means something very different to Hindus and Buddhists. Hexham and Poewe draw out these distinctions:

    Within the Yogic tradition, ideas of rebirth are logically related to belief in karma. Traditionally, rebirth is explained in two ways. Hindus believe that when human beings die, their souls pass (transmigrate) into another body. Buddhists, in contrast, deny the existence of the soul. They believe that the continuation of sense impressions at the point of death deludes those who suffer near-death experiences into thinking that they have an essence or soul. Buddhists postulate reincarnation rather than transmigration. Those who popularize new religions in the West, however, typically fail to convey these distinctions. They tend to define reincarnation as rebirth in human form and transmigration as rebirth in non-human form.[3]

- *Reincarnation* literally means to come again in the flesh. For modern Hindus, reincarnation is now used as a synonym for the transmigration of the soul. For the Buddhist there is no soul (anatta) or permanent self (anicca). So, at death, the illusory self that is shaped by karma reincarnates, in the same way that one candle may be lit by another candle. For Hindus and Buddhists, reincarnation takes place between all forms of animal life. In the West, reincarnation is popularly used to mean that your soul transmigrates from one human life to the next in an upward evolutionary spiral.

- *Transconception* is another Western philosophical synonym for metempsychosis.

- *Transmigration* is a term used in both Western and Eastern philosophical traditions, and is synonymous with metempsychosis. At death, the soul transmigrates from one body to another.

Kesha was aware of the subtle nuances in terminology, and he indicated that he believed in the soul's existence. He was happy to use the words metempsychosis, transmigration of the soul, and reincarnation as interchangeable synonyms, even though he acknowledged there really are technical differences in their meanings.

John the Baptist's past life

Kesha directed our attention to reincarnation in the Sacred Writings. He suggested that reincarnation is found in Matt. 17:10-13:

> *The disciples asked him [Jesus], "Why then do the teachers of the law say Elijah must come first?" Jesus replied, "To be sure, Elijah comes and will restore all things. But I tell you, Elijah has already come, and they did not recognize him, but have done to him everything they wished. In the same way the Son of Man is going to suffer at their hands." Then the disciples understood that he was talking to them about John the Baptist.*

In ancient Israel, there was an expectation that the prophet Elijah would return again as a herald of great deeds. He would bring healing to his people: "See, I will send you the prophet Elijah before that great and dreadful day of the LORD comes" (Mal. 4:5, NIV).

This is a developing theme in the New Testament, where the people were looking for his return. Elijah's return would prefigure the arrival of the messiah. When Jesus spoke about John the Baptist, he said, "And if you are willing to accept it, he is the Elijah who was to come" (Matt. 11:14, NIV).

The American trance medium Edgar Cayce posed the following question about these passages: "What logical thought process induced the disciples to draw such a conclusion so promptly, unless Jesus had made them thoroughly familiar with the laws of reincarnation?"4

We pointed out to Kesha that there are hurdles to be overcome with the above passages. The texts do not support the reincarnation of Elijah in the person of John the Baptist. As Elijah lived a truly enlightened life, he bypassed death and was taken directly to heaven (see 2 Kings 2:11-12). Such a sage has surely moved beyond the wheel of reincarnation.

In the Matthew 17 passage, the story is also told of how Jesus appears on a mountain with the "spirits" of Moses and Elijah. John the Baptist was already dead at this time. In reincarnation, the latest incarnation is the next stage. If John the Baptist was truly Elijah reincarnated, then that incarnation would have appeared.

John the Baptist himself specifically denied that he was literally Elijah: "They asked him, 'Then who are you? Are you Elijah?' He said, 'I am not'" (John 1:21, NIV).

Numerous passages in the gospels speak of John the Baptist being "like Elijah" and the Sacred Writings clarify what they are all about (see Mark 1:2-3, Matt. 11:10, Luke 7:27). They reveal that John came "in the spirit and power of Elijah" (Luke 1:17, NIV). In other words, when Jesus was talking about John and Elijah, he was not speaking about reincarnation, but the similarities in their ministries. So, when Jesus said that John "is the Elijah who was to come," he was simply confirming that John had fulfilled the role of God's promised forerunner to the messiah. Elijah was not literally coming, but one like him, namely John the Baptist.[5]

Another Sacred Writings passage may appear to lend support to reincarnation. Jesus told Nicodemus that "no one can see the kingdom of God unless he is born again." Nicodemus was puzzled by this and thought that he had to re-enter the womb. Jesus made it plain that this was not so. He said, "I tell you the truth, no one can enter the kingdom of God unless he is born of water and the Spirit. Flesh gives birth to flesh, but the Spirit gives birth to spirit" (John 3:5-6, NIV).

Here, Jesus does not refer to any cycle of reincarnation, but is indicating that, to belong to God's Kingdom, the Spirit of God must embrace you. In fact, the meaning of the Greek word is more correctly translated as "born from above" or "born anew" than "born again."

An integrating experience

As we talked, Kesha could see that, for us, the greatest stumbling block with reincarnation is its incompatibility with resurrection. A careful comparison of various New Testament passages shows that Jesus and his disciples believed in the resurrection of the body from the dead (John 11:21-25, Luke 24:36-47, Acts 2:24, 32; 1 Corinthians 15).

There is a real difference between reincarnation and resurrection. First, resurrection implies you die once (see Heb. 9:27). Second, resurrection assumes that our eternal destiny is not lived separate from some bodily experience. In Judaism and Christianity, because God creates the body, it is good. In Gnostic, Hindu, Buddhist, and New Age thought, it is more along the lines of the Greek philosophy that the body is rudimentary and needs to be escaped. The late Princess Diana's astrologer, Penny Thornton, expressed this simply: "The planets seem to be pointing to an era when we transcend the lower 'animal' passions."[6]

The resurrected body in the Sacred Writings is certainly a transformation from what we now know, but it can never be reduced to an "out-of-body" destiny. As the Sacred Writings promise:

But our citizenship is in heaven. And we eagerly await a Savior from there, the Lord Jesus Christ, who, by the power that enables him to bring everything under his control, will transform our lowly bodies so that they will be like his glorious body (Phil. 3:20-21, NIV).

Significantly, the concept of the resurrection alters our life in the here and now. For example, as the body is indispensable, it means that we must help the starving and the oppressed in practical ways. Surely this is seen in the devotion of "saints" such as the late Mother Teresa. The resurrection also endows our inner psyche with the hope that our whole personality will live forever.[7] Reincarnation, in contrast, only offers that our soul—after numerous journeys—will find a home in a depersonalized consciousness.

A tampering church

Kesha refocused our thoughts by returning to a commonly expressed concern about the Council of Constantinople (A.D. 553). The Council, he felt, censored the enlightened teaching of the early church father, Origen. They also scandalously heightened their sin by tampering with the reincarnation narratives in the Sacred Writings.[8]

We suggested our first port of call be what Origen really said. A number of facts can be set out. In his earliest writings, Origen expressed a belief in the pre-existence of the soul.[9] By "pre-existence," he meant that the soul was created in heaven before our earthly conception. He believed that souls fell away from God in heaven and then took on human flesh. He only believed that souls had one earthly sojourn.

Origen's belief in the pre-existence of the soul was only a personal speculation of his, not an official church dogma. Origen derived his idea about the soul's pre-existence from neo-Platonic philosophy and transplanted that into his own teachings. As a matter of principle, the pre-existence of the soul has nothing to do with whether or not we are reincarnated. Joseph Trigg, an authority on Origen's life, makes two key points:

Origen seems to have considered corporeality as a single, unrepeatable stage in the road of spirits back to God . . . At the same time Origen was careful to repudiate a doctrinal speculation of which some accused him but which he did not in fact hold, namely, the transmigration of souls into new bodies in this world.[10]

Origen specifically denied the concept of the transmigration (reincarnation) of the soul after it had taken flesh. In one of the last works he composed, Origen commented on the relationship between Elijah and John the Baptist:

———————————— ◆ ————————————

In this place, it does not appear to me that by Elijah the soul is spoken of, lest I should fall into the dogma of transmigration [reincarnation], which is foreign to the church of God and not handed down by the Apostles, nor anywhere set forth in the Scriptures.[11]

———————————— ◆ ————————————

At the Council of Constantinople, Origen's belief in the pre-existence of the soul was condemned. The Council did not tamper with the Sacred Writings.[12]

Kesha was persuaded that Origen's friend and student, Jerome, embraced reincarnation. He pointed to David Christie-Murray who states, "St. Jerome is supposed to have supported reincarnation in his letter to Avitus."[13] Yet Jerome's letter actually entails a scathing critical assessment of Origen's teaching on the soul's pre-existence. Again, in his letter to Demetrias, Jerome rejects the teaching about the soul's pre-existence. In neither letter does he endorse the transmigration of souls.[14]

We noted with Kesha that it is evident from the above that the early church did not support reincarnation. In fact, the first mention made of it is by Justin Martyr who was born in about A.D. 114. Before he adopted Christianity, Justin "studied in the schools of the philosophers, searching after some knowledge that should satisfy the cravings of his soul."[15]

Justin agreed in his dialogue with Trypho the Jew, that souls do not "transmigrate into other bodies."[16] Several other prominent church leaders who rejected reincarnation and lived before this "infamous" Council of Constantinople include Irenaeus (c. 175-195), Tertullian (c. 160-220), Lactantius (c. 260-330), Gregory of Nyssa (c. 335-395) and Augustine (354-430).

Out-of-space reincarnation

Kesha said some modern theologians have proposed new ideas about life after death.[17] Their efforts are based on a desire to integrate the Western idea of resurrection with the Eastern idea of the immortality of the soul as expressed in reincarnation. The end product is that our bodies after death are replicated in another dimension or galaxy where the soul is linked with the new body (resurrection). This process, seemingly, is repeated in various "beyond earth" pilgrimages until we attain nirvana, cosmic oneness, or face the last judgment.

On the one hand, we have here a noble attempt to bring together the East and West. On the other hand, people are trying to explain how the resurrection of the dead can take place in a real way. Even so, they are holding to the teaching of the Sacred Writings that we only die once on this earth plane.

Ross said that a major problem for this unifying position is that neither the Christian Sacred Writings nor the Eastern Sacred Writings acknowledge such a merger between reincarnation and resurrection. This view is not part of the received body of the traditional teachings of the Masters. Clearly, it has logical inconsistencies—we have already seen that there is a difference between reincarnation and resurrection.

Philip said that the Hindu and Buddhist views of the person after death differ significantly from each other. In classic Hindu thought, there is a soul that transmigrates, while in classic Buddhist thought, there is no soul, but instead a bundle of karmas that reincarnate. Similarly, their positions on human salvation—moksha in Hinduism and nirvana in Buddhism—offer different remedies to differently perceived problems. This means that there isn't just one model but several different Eastern models of reincarnation. These Eastern views of personhood and salvation not only differ considerably from that of Christianity, but also diverge from New Age views.

Finally, in response to what some modern thinkers say, there is the teaching and experience of the great master, Jesus. He taught and experienced one complete resurrection and did not refer to out-of-space reincarnation. He is the one who has a verifiable experience of life after death.

Reworking evil

Kesha raised an important issue about the reason for people suffering in this world. He believed that whatever we do in this life determines the conditions and quality of our next life. It is an automatic feedback system that eventually leads to balance and spiritual growth. This explains why young children in Africa are dying of starvation. They apparently had undeveloped souls in their previous lives so the law of karma is now catching up with them.

Our minds went on to the apostle John and his report on the blind man. Some suggest that here is an example of the law of karma: "As he [Jesus] went along, he saw a man blind from birth. His disciples asked him, 'Rabbi, who sinned, this man or his parents, that he was born blind?'"

Isn't suffering here equated with past lives and deeds? Jesus' answer says otherwise: "Neither this man nor his parents sinned," said Jesus, "but this happened so that the work of God might be displayed in his life" (John 9:1-3, NIV).

Elsewhere, the Sacred Writings acknowledge that karma in this life can affect our well-being. Paul's answer was, "you reap whatever you sow" (Gal. 6:7, NSRVB). The Sacred Writings does give some other answers for suffering, one being the world's and our chosen alienation from God. Whenever we are divorced from God's will, things go wrong. Another factor is that, because of our fallenness, we treat each other badly, and others hurt us. The history of the world bears testimony to this.

It must also be admitted that the Sacred Writings indicate that suffering in God's hands can sometimes be a cause for spiritual growth. As Paul declares, "And we know that in all things God works for the good of those who love him, who have been called according to his purpose" (Rom. 8:28, NIV).

We have found that these rational answers will not normally satisfy an aching heart. We are hearing that many who are feeling comforted in reincarnation are not finding it in past lives explanations, but in the hope it brings of a continuing existence.

Lord Hailsham, the former Lord Chancellor of England, and one who has known several personal tragedies in his own journey, reveals a certain hope:

---◆---

When, in the autumn of October 1969, I saw the ruined homes in Belfast, burned out by my own fellow-citizens and fellow-Protestants out of sheer hatred of the occupants, I was deeply moved with horror and rejection, and all the cruelty and suffering which has gone on there since has only intensified my feelings on the sub-ject. I will not, if I can avoid it, read stories of violence, or attend films or plays, or look at programs that portray evil. This is not because I believe such portrayals are damaging to the soul, although I think they are, but simply because they hurt me too much. How can a good God permit such dreadful things to happen, I ask myself helplessly.

The only thing which keeps me sane in such moods of black despair is the memory of Christ's passion, his shameful conviction, his cruel mishandling, his slow death, and the ultimate hopelessness of his cry of dereliction from the opening words of the 22nd Psalm, and the belief, which I have as a Christian, that this was not simply the despairing cry of a good man, shamefully abused, but a matter of cosmic significance, a statement that God the invisible, the Creator, the ground of all being, without body parts or passions, enters into human suffering with us, and somehow agonizes in all our private Gethsemanes.

I know, of course, that this must necessarily be folly to the Greeks, who can visualize a God in human form well enough, as did Euripides when he visualized Dionysius in the Bacchae, but cannot visualize a God in suffering.[18]

---◆---

The law of karma

In our conversation with Kesha, we raised some problems we saw with his view of suffering, the initial one being that many postmodern seekers hold that karma is not transmitted from a past life (see sidebar). Another point concerns the original spiritual context for the concept of karma. In the religious traditions of India, karma is conceived of as a moral law. Within these traditions, there are several theories of karma, each with subtle nuances. At its most basic level, karma is properly concerned with the "moral basis on which action past and present is predicated."[19]

What Goes Around

A number of "Mind Powers" devotees accept the concept of karma, but only believe we live on the earth once. These pilgrims claim that, by the power of our thoughts, we script for ourselves either good or bad karma in the present and this determines our non-earthbound future. (We will revisit this issue in our chapter on the power of the mind.)

Fundamental to karma is a chain of cause and effect that encompasses time, nature, consciousness, the will and soul, the living and the dead, the past and the present. Karma stops us from totally controlling our lives. It operates in a cyclical view of reality, not a linear view, because we are not evolving. The focal point is finding release and avoiding rebirth in this hellish world. For the Hindu and Buddhist, terminating rebirth is essential to achieving the ultimate goals found in the transcendent realm.

These ancient Indian traditions stand in contrast to the position Kesha takes with respect to karma and rebirth. Kesha told us that we create our own realities every time we are reborn. He quoted Louise Hay:

---◆---

Each one of us decides to incarnate upon this planet at particular points in time and space. We have chosen to come here to learn a particular lesson that will advance us upon our spiritual, evolutionary pathway.[20]

---◆---

We put it to Kesha, how does his view of the automatic feedback of karma fit in with this claim that we freely choose the circumstances of our next incarnation? If karma is a universal law, how can the individual exercise free will before being reborn in this world? Kesha's view clearly entails a redefinition of karma, basing it on the notion of progressive spiritual evolution, and fails to adequately explain this anomaly.

We then raised the question, if his view of karma is correct, why do we not have any conscious memory of our past deeds so as to avoid repeating them in this present state? It is quite crippling if, as is sometimes suggested, we "forget" our past life as soon as we are reborn. Neither a session of hypnotic regression (recalling past lives under hypnosis) nor a rebirthing course (technique for awakening primal experiences of pain) will reveal all or even most of our alleged past misdeeds. Without this vital knowledge, we are powerless to progress along the New Age path of spiritual evolution.

Another problem is the seeming absence of the need for compassion for the victims of this world. When asked about such infamies as the Nazi death camps, famine victims, refugees and the victims of Hiroshima, Kesha's reply was, "You don't have to worry about them at all! It is their karma!" So suffering is not to be explained but merely forms part of life and spiritual progress. This is in stark contrast to the compassion of Jesus, when he fed, healed, and delivered those who were oppressed and suffering.

Finally, we felt the major problem with karma is that it requires us to pull ourselves up by our own bootstraps. We can never really be certain about the life we've lived or of reaching the final goal of release from this cycle of birth, death, and rebirth. It all rests on our own performance and an impersonal cosmic law. In contrast, the Sacred Writings affirm an "alien" new birth, a deliverance from our misdeeds by the death and resurrection of the master, Jesus. There is no need for another incarnation.

The testimony of the many

Kesha continued to plead for reincarnation on the basis that it was in tune with the teachings of the "enlightened." It was indisputable that many teachers in Buddhist, Gnostic, Hindu, Jain, neo-pagan, and Taoist traditions, as well as the ancient Greeks, have believed in some version of reincarnation.

Nonetheless, many other teachers, such as those of Moses, Isaiah, Jesus, Muhammad, and Viking sages have not accepted it. In this case, we suggested, the spiritual path couldn't be resolved by counting numbers; the truth lies elsewhere. Sad to say, 60 million Britons, 260 million Americans—or a billion Chinese—can all be wrong!

Plausible evidence of past lives

Kesha offered various types of evidence to prove we have lived before. One of these is the common experience we have had of déjá vu—entering a place that appears familiar, even though you have never been there before. Some simply cite their own "memory" of a past life. Another proof is past-life recall under hypnotic regression.

Then there is the revealing of a past life through contact with the spirits of the dead. This same proof often comes with those who claim to have had contact with extraterrestrial beings. Finally, there is the explanation that there is not enough time to complete our "mission" in a single life.

There is a basic physiological explanation for déjá vu. It is the rapid assimilation of information by the senses before it is fully processed in the brain. In a split second, you have the sensation of seeing or hearing something, then it is repeated. Therefore, your reaction can precede your mind's processing of data. We are learning just how remarkable our minds are and how often the answer lies within us, not in some paranormal explanation.

On top of all this, it is possible to identify many of the sources that act as a catalyst for these experiences. Could it not be a picture previously observed but forgotten or a prior visit to a similar place?

There are several feasible explanations of a memory "flash" that appears to take us to another life. One is déjá vu, another is the gift of psychic powers, like that of the Dutch crime-solver Peter Hurkos (1911-88).[21] Then there is the idea that a foreign spirit has influenced us.

Ian Stevenson is a prominent reincarnation advocate and researcher. He admits that the foreign spirit theory must be taken seriously, even though he prefers the reincarnation hypothesis. In support of the foreign spirit view is the corroboration Stevenson has compiled. He has cases of people having memory flashes of living a life of someone who is not yet dead.[22] The memory flash raises more questions than it answers.

The most interesting argument for reincarnation is hypnotic recall. Some cases involve people speaking in ancient or foreign languages and recalling historical events. One must not be dismissive of such remarkable phenomena, unless the evidence demands otherwise.

Psychologists writing on these phenomena have instructed us about the reliability of recall. One typical report asserts:

During hypnosis, imagined events can seem as authentic as reality, images can be extremely vivid, and there is a heightened level of fantasy . . . although hypnosis increases recall, it also increases errors. In their study [Bowers and Dywan], hypnotized subjects correctly recalled twice as many items as did unhypnotized members of

a control group, but also made three times as many mistakes . . .
During hypnosis, you are creating memories.[23]

———————————◆———————————

A further point concerns the reliance on the recent phenomenon of "repressed memory syndrome" as evidence of reincarnation. A number of experts, such as Elizabeth Loftus and Richard Ofshe, have underscored several limitations of human memories. Within the courts, where repressed memories are being cited in child sex abuse cases, corroborating evidence is now regarded as indispensable. (This is not to deny that memories are suppressed, but it highlights the fact that some external evidence must support repressed memories.) Thus, to base one's belief in reincarnation solely on repressed memories is not at all satisfactory evidence.[24]

Ross said another difficulty with recall concerns the fact that there is at present more than one claimant to the past life of Cleopatra. Also, many claim to have been in a stable around 2,000 years ago! This evidence leaves us with the question, Are past lives a creative wish fulfilment?

What must also be taken into consideration are the documented claims of such celebrated cases as Bridey Murphy. In the 1950s, great excitement was associated with the case of American housewife "Ruth Simmons," alias Virginia Tighe, who recalled, under hypnosis, a previous life as Bridey Murphy in 19th-century Ireland. She went into great detail as to place names and even spoke in an Irish accent.[25]

Numerous critics have pointed out that, as a young child, Virginia Tighe spent much time with an Irish nanny who taught her the "other language," Gaelic, and told her stories about old Ireland. Another investigator, William Barker, went to Ireland. He found that the account given of the culture and times was accurate, but no records of Bridey Murphy or her family came to light. Nevill Drury has remarked, "The case remains controversial."[26]

What of the claim that reincarnation is confirmed by the advice received from extraterrestrials and spirit beings? There is one salient obstacle. These reports are unsubstantiated, even to the satisfaction of many New Age seekers.

The final argument for reincarnation is the need to have more time than life gives to fulfil our goals and so give meaning and purpose to our existence. We are all moved by the tragic loss of unfulfilled and seemingly incomplete lives. The trouble is that fulfillment could equally take place in another dimension—that of being face to face with God, for example. Why limit it to the earthly plane? Followers of the master, Jesus, find comfort in the fact that their unfulfilled loved ones are maturing in the resurrected life found in the loving energy of Christ.

We were at a gathering where an African leader touched the audience as he opened up about the death of his young son. He found strength in the vision that his son is like a bud who will now blossom before the very heart of God. He intimated that they would be reunited and he would have the joy of discovering his son as a perfected personality.

Group encounters and psychic unity

After our discussion about individual reincarnation, we drew Kesha's attention to group past-lives encounters. There are several cases coming to the fore. It appears that, under hypnotic regression, members of a community recall past times together and mention similar data. One of the most popular pioneers of this, in the context of group hypnosis for past-life regression, is Dick Sutphen. He and his ex-wife Trenna discovered that they had shared past lives in Mexico and France. He proposes that relationships between couples can occur in successive incarnations.[27]

We recapped our previous concerns about the reliability of hypnotic regression. We mentioned one major case where both the facilitator and those involved did not accept that the experience was of a past life. Rather, they thought it was an expression of untapped psychic unity that has them playing out similar dreams to one another's. This suggests that we want stories to live by—a theme that we explored in chapter 4.

Life through a rearview mirror

As our tête-à-tête with Kesha came to a close, we urged him not to be like those who are so overwhelmed by hurts that they limit themselves to the cleansing of past memories. Such can be a mediocre and contorted journey.

Popular writers Stan Katz and Aimèe Kiu put it delightfully:

It's a bit like trying to drive a car while looking only in the rearview mirror. You don't get very far that way and you run the risk of a crack-up. I prefer to check the rearview from time to time, making sure that the reflection is accurate, but concentrating most of my attention on the road ahead.[28]

We have found strength in Jesus' exhortation to live an empowered life by putting our hand to the plough and not looking back. Paul the apostle is of the same mind: "Forgetting what is behind and straining toward what is ahead" (Phil. 3:13, NIV).

Transcending karma

Kesha, in a most open way, shared with us his deep feelings about reincarnation. Reincarnation affirms the belief we hold in common with Kesha: that there is life after death and that existence is more than material. The illuminating call of today is for people to rediscover eternity. We shared our view that he was mistaken in his belief that reincarnation is mentioned in the Sacred Writings and that it was taught by Jesus and his early followers.

As we shook hands, there was the embracing warmth experienced by those who know what it is to yearn for healing. We offered Kesha an eternal healing of mind, body and spirit. This is found in the one who has transcended all our karma and the burden of the cycle of the wheel of life.

Endnotes

Chapter 9

1 J. Head and S. Cranston, *Reincarnation: The Phoenix Fire Mystery*, Pasadena: Theosophical University Press, 1994, p. 145.

2 Irving Hexham, *Concise Dictionary of Religion*, Downers Grove: InterVarsity Press, 1993, p. 147.

3 Irving Hexham and Karla Poewe, *New Religions as Global Cultures*, Boulder: Westview, 1997, pp. 101-102.

4 Noel Langley, *Edgar Cayce on Reincarnation*, New York: Warner, 1967, p. 173.

5 See Robert J. Miller, "Elijah, John, and Jesus in the Gospel of Luke," *New Testament Studies*, 34, 1988, pp. 611-622; and Walter Wink, *John the Baptist in Gospel Tradition*, Cambridge: Cambridge University Press, 1968.

6 Caroline Bing, "Di's Astrologer Looks Ahead," *The Australian Women's Weekly*, September 1992, p. 12.

7 On these resurrection themes, see Ross Clifford and Philip Johnson, *Riding the Rollercoaster*, Sydney: Strand, 1998.

8 Kesha's point has been raised by Elmar R. Gruber and Holger Kersten, *The Original Jesus: The Buddhist Sources of Christianity*, Dorset: Element, 1995, p. 93; J. Head and S. Cranston, *Reincarnation*, pp. 156-160; and Shirley Maclaine, *Out on A Limb*, New York: Bantam, 1984, pp. 181-182.

9 Origen, "On First Principles," Book 2, chapter 9, sections 6-8, in Alexander Roberts and James Donaldson (eds), *The Ante-Nicene Fathers*, volume 4, Grand Rapids: Wm.B. Eerdmans, 1979, pp. 291-293.

10 Joseph Wilson Trigg, *Origen: The Bible and Philosophy in the Third-Century Church*, London: SCM, 1983, pp. 107, 213; and Jean Danielou, W. Mitchell (translator) *Origen*, New York: Sheed & Ward, 1955, pp. 249-250.

11 *Origen's Commentary on Matthew*, Book 13, chapter 1, in A. Roberts and J. Donaldson (eds), *Ante-Nicene Fathers*, volume 10, p. 474.

12 On "The Anathemas Against Origen," see Philip Schaff and Henry Wace (eds), *Nicene and Post-Nicene Fathers*, Second Series, volume 14, Grand Rapids: Wm.B. Eerdmans, 1979, pp.318-319.

13 David Christie-Murray, *Reincarnation: Ancient Beliefs and Modern Evidence*, London: David & Charles, 1981, p. 59.

14 "Letter 124: To Avitus" and "Letter 130: To Demetrias" in Philip Schaff and Henry Wace (eds), "The Principal Works of St Jerome," *Nicene and Post-Nicene Fathers*, Second Series, volume 6, Grand Rapids: Wm.B. Eerdmans, 1979, pp. 238-244, 260-272.

15 A. Cleveland Coxe, "Introductory note to the First Apology of Justin Martyr," in A. Roberts and J. Donaldson (eds), *The Ante-Nicene Fathers*, volume 1, p. 160.

16 "Dialogue with Trypho," chapter 4, in A. Roberts and J. Donaldson (eds), *The Ante-Nicene Fathers*, volume 1, p. 197.

17 See Paul Badham, "Recent Thinking on Christian Beliefs," *The Expository Times*, 88, April 1977, pp. 197-201.

18 Lord Hailsham, *The Door Wherein I Went*, London: Collins, 1975, pp. 40-41.

[19] Wendy Doniger O'Flaherty (ed.) *Karma and Rebirth in Classical Indian Traditions*, Delhi: Motilal Banarsidass, 1983, p.xi.

[20] Louise Hay, *You Can Heal Your Life*, Sydney: Specialist Publications, 1988, p. 10; and Jane Roberts, *The Nature of Personal Reality*, Englewood Cliffs: Prentice-Hall, 1974, p. 28.

[21] Hurkos's career was a mixed bag of successes and colossal failures—see Colin Wilson, *Psychic Detective*, San Francisco: Mercury House, 1985.

[22] Ian Stevenson, *Twenty Cases Suggestive of Reincarnation*, Charlottesville: University of Virginia Press, 1966, pp. 48, 228-229, 340-347. Stevenson's work has been analyzed by Paul Edwards, "The Case Against Karma and Reincarnation" in Robert Basil (ed.), *Not Necessarily the New Age*, Buffalo: Prometheus, 1988, pp. 107-110.

[23] Elizabeth Stark, "Hypnosis on Trial," *Psychology Today*, February 1984, p. 34.

[24] Elizabeth Loftus and Katherine Ketcham, *The Myth of Repressed Memory*, New York: St. Martin's Press, 1994; and Richard Ofshe and Ethan Watters, *Making Monsters: False Memories, Psychotherapy and Sexual Hysteria*, New York: Charles Scribner's Sons, 1994. On recovered memories and satanic ritual abuse, see James T. Richardson, Joel Best and David G. Bromley (eds), *The Satanism Scare*, New York: Aldine De Gruyter, 1991; and "Satanic Ritual Abuse: The Current State of Knowledge," special issue, *Journal of Psychology and Theology*, 20, 3, 1992.

[25] Morey Bernstein, *The Search for Bridey Murphy*, New York: Doubleday, 1956.

[26] Nevill Drury, *Dictionary of Mysticism and the Esoteric Traditions*, revised edition, Dorset: Prism, 1992, p. 213.

[27] Dick Sutphen, *You Were Born Again to Be Together*, New York: Pocket, 1976.

[28] Stan Katz and Aimèe Kiu, *The Codependency Conspiracy*, New York: Warner, 1992, p. 106.

Chapter 10
The Power of the Mind and Human Potential

◆

Your mind creates your reality. You can choose to accept this or not. You can be conscious of it, and get your mind working for you, or you can ignore it, and allow it to work in ways that will hinder and hold you back. But your mind will always, and forever, be creating your reality.[1]

I am learning to alter my perceptions and therefore change my 'reality'. This was not easy when a mugger lunged at me on First Avenue with the clear intention of doing whatever he deemed necessary to get my handbag. I remember my flash reaction that I, by God, did not like playing the part of a victim. Instinctively I changed my 'part' and lunged back at him, shrieking like the Wicked Witch of the West until the mugger thought my insanity was something he didn't want to tangle with. I changed the script.[2]

Everything is possible for him who believes (Mark 9:23, NIV).

◆

We took time off from our stand and went to the exhibitor's lounge for a coffee break. Charlie, a young executive type, joined us as we sat down. Like us he was taking a rest from serving at his stand, which was promoting a self-development course based on the power of the mind. He sketched for us an overview of the state of mind in which people exist—"unconsciousness." He defined this as using only 10 percent of your mental powers. We agreed that most of us underuse our minds.

Charlie then spoke of how we can be empowered to operate on a higher level of consciousness. If we enter into this altered state of consciousness, we will be guaranteed profound enhancements in our work, relationships, life goals, and religion. Charlie's sales pitch was an enthusiastic endorsement of what this had done for him.

We asked Charlie how we could we enter into this higher state of consciousness. He explained that this could be done by participating in his program. It was ultimately about equipping us to realize that our mind creates our reality. We write our own life scripts. Charlie accepted karma from a past life as influencing each person's script. Later, we met others who only focused on the present. Some devotees added that we would only achieve what we desire when we find we are one with the unlimited, creating, "universal mind." The universal mind is whatever you perceive God to be.

Our conversation with Charlie returned to a fairly earthy, base level. We mutually felt the need to reach the bottom line of his philosophy.

Ross: Charlie, are you saying that through our minds we can be totally in control of our destiny and your program could allow us to achieve that?

Charlie: Yes.

Ross: If I desire a new relationship, can I mentally create it?

Charlie: Sure.

Ross: If it failed, would it be my own fault?

Charlie: In the sense that you have allowed yourself to have that experience. Probably you must have it for your own growth.

Ross: And would that be true for the failure of my own small business? The recession is not the problem, but my dream?

Charlie: Yes, I guess that has got to be the bottom line.

Philip: Charlie, I realize it's an extreme example, but I want to explore the depths of rescripting. I'm Hitler reincarnated.

Knowing what my karma is likely to produce, I come to you for guidance. How do I recreate this life's path through mind control? Could you help me?

Charlie: You wouldn't know you were Hitler.

Philip: No, I've just been to the clairvoyant's stand. She has disclosed to me that I was Hitler in my previous life.

Charlie: Oh. I don't think I can answer you. [Charlie found this a difficult scenario, so we returned to perhaps more current examples.]

Ross: Charlie, there is one place in the world where we would not expect to find a power of the mind program operating. That is in the refugee camps that darken our globe. [Charlie did not deny this. We had one last puzzle.]

Ross: Charlie, there is a four-year-old girl starving in Ethiopia. Is she a victim of world apathy, oppression, poverty, or her own visualization?

Charlie: It's basically her choice.

Powers of the mind players, principles, and stated benefits

There has been a remarkable spread of different organizations employing power of the mind and human potential theories. Some of these groups are not so doctrinaire as Charlie. (Still, their emphasis is that we have to "get it"—as we think, so we are, and we are responsible for our own lot.)

These organizations include Avatar, CALM, Delfin, the Forum, Insight Transformational Seminars, Pacific Institute, Silva Mind Control, Supercamp, and Winners' Camp. They offer their services to the business world, education, sports, armed services, and the general community.

Player Principles

The principles employed by these players are the following:

- *Creative visualization*—This is where you learn to create, by the power of thought, your own desired reality, such as envisaging winning an Olympic gold medal. You believe your thoughts have materialized in the physical world.
- *Self-hypnosis*—This involves training yourself to go deep within your mind to tap into your subconscious creative powers.
- *Neurolinguistic programming (NLP)*—This is a form of educational psychology that focuses on the three main forms of communication. These relate to three learning styles—some are good listeners and learn well by hearing (auditory learners); others see things better and learn by demonstration (visual learners); the remainder learn by doing things (kinesthetic learners). Further, by reading a person's body language (such as eye movements, gestures, postures, and other non-verbal cues), we can understand how to communicate better. We can assess someone's character by the style and choice of words they use. NLP's Richard Bandler says that it "teaches people to run their own brains instead of letting their brains run them."[3]
- *Centering*—This is a technique designed to harmonize the "left brain" (the rational, analytical side) with your "right brain" (the intuitive, creative side). Using relaxing music, meditation, and breathing exercises can achieve this.
- *Virtual reality and subliminal tapes*—One tool allied to power of the mind principles is the virtual reality relaxation machine. You wear a headset of specially designed dark glasses that block all outside vision and sound. Charlie said the glasses are plugged into a laser disk that plays a dazzling light and sound show across the lens. The flashing light show has the effect of lowering the activity of the brain and a state of quiescence is achieved. In that state of calm, the practitioner can then focus on visualizing or centering. These synchro-energizing machines are also meant to synchronize the right and left sides of the brain. Another tool is cassette tapes with subliminal messages that are played during sleep or while in an hypnotic trance. The tapes' contents convey messages or affirmations that register in the listener's subconscious. These messages

are designed to program the mind to operate at an optimum level of power so that success will be achieved.

- *Firewalking*—Charlie had tried firewalking as a tool for confronting and conquering fear and proving his innate powers. He strode across a cricket pitch of heated coals without the sensation of pain or injury. We have noted that coal is a poor conductor of heat, which explains in part why those with swift feet will not be singed.

Charlie passionately emphasized the blessings of the power of the mind. He underscored these benefits as being:

- greater productivity and creativity in the workplace
- control of stress
- removal of illness
- reduction of blood pressure
- increased efficiency
- enhanced ability to study
- better lovemaking
- peak performances
- the certainty of winning

The Eternal Flame Foundation espouses earthly immortality as being a fruit of the power of the mind. While this might appear to be a bizarre claim, it is a logical outworking of the concepts of the power of the mind. The Foundation claims that death brainwashing is fed into us from the time of our birth, "from ancestry that accepted death as inevitable. The truth is our bodies are beautifully and wonderfully designed and without limitation."[4]

Superlearning

At the festival, we met a number of parents and teachers who work to transform education by means of a process they call "Superlearning."[5] We gathered that it draws on a variety of theories, principles, and practices to enhance learning and memory retention.

During the late 1960s, George Lozanov of Bulgaria experimented with new ways of learning. He found that, by combining yogic breathing exercises with the "beat" of classical (baroque) music playing in the background, his students could learn foreign languages in a matter of weeks. The belief is that tone and language go hand-in-hand.

Lozanov's pioneering studies have developed a more New Age direction in the West. This is apparent in Supercamp and Winners' Camp. Some participants told us how they were encouraged to improve their self-image and no longer view themselves as failures. They were shown how to apply meditation, creative visualization, self-hypnosis, neurolinguistic programming, and New Age techniques to their studies. We listened to the praises of some thiry parents and pupils who claimed that these programs had powerfully transformed them.

The Creator of Winners' Camp and Supercamp is Eric Jensen. In his book *Superteaching*, he unfolds the recent emergence of the right brain/left brain concept. Jensen looks at the two hemispheres of our brain. Some suggest that there are two centers, which relate to our analytical (left-brain) and intuitive (right-brain) capabilities. Jensen aims to produce wholly integrated students who can master their minds. To do this, students must focus on the creative right brain as too much stress is generally placed on the left brain.

Our experience has confirmed that contemporary education tends to be analytical at the expense of the creative. Still, Jensen's approach reflects a love of the intuitive as against the logical and is sacrificing a balanced pattern by overemphasizing right-brain activities. Many educators believe that holistic education involves both reason and creativity, whether it is in the area of mathematics, language, or spiritual studies. It is a both/and, not an either/or area.

One process of power of the mind that surfaces in education is values clarification as a foundation for a healthy mind. This concept, which can be quite helpful, calls for teachers and educators to assist pupils in identifying their own values.

However, at times, a dogma emerges in this process. Some educators instruct their pupils that there are no absolute values, that life is purely about finding your own values and accepting other people's views. That in itself is a New Age value statement. We wonder how such educators would respond to a classroom comprising bigots, misogynists, and those whose values have been formed by hurtful childhood experiences. Is our motto to be "What I do is right" or "I do what is right"? The former idolizes self-discovery.

Metaphysical mastery

Charlie's pathway is focused on ultimately attaining metaphysical mastery. He said we have to reshape our self-awareness by reengineering our belief systems. This involves fundamental adjustments to self-esteem—such as being challenged to take positive responsibility for our lives and desisting from playing the role of a victim. Interpersonal skills of communication will also be imparted. Then our fears, boundaries, and belief systems will undergo major shifts. It may entail accepting that we are part of a seamless holistic universe—we are the universal mind—or a concept of inner enlightenment framed around Buddhist ideas about the lack of a soul and the goal of nirvana. Within this process of reengineering, Charlie said we would undoubtedly see some remarkable personal changes and experience profound creative effects with respect to states of mind and relaxation.

The steps to reaching this goal often remain secret until the aspirants have signed a contract containing a non-disclosure agreement. The motivation for this practice is generally not sinister, but is intended to protect the course's integrity from plagiarism. An example of this is Harry Palmer's Avatar program.[6]

One difficulty we raised with Charlie is that, for many seekers, the promise of transformation is never experienced. Rachael Kohn, a sociologist of religion we both know and respect, has pointed out a paradox within certain human potential, self-religion-type groups. Her point is that, within some groups, the creator or leader is the only one to have attained the state of enlightenment. The coursework holds forth the promise that we can be like the creator or leader, and yet the promised transformation remains elusive. She suggests that, in certain groups, this is because the teaching makes it impossible for a devotee to ever stand side-by-side with the creator or leader's spiritual accomplishments. So, one outcome is that some aspirants become "seminar junkies," shifting from one group to the next without ever really making much progress.[7]

Caring sharing companies

It is common for major corporations to utilize power of the mind workshops for the benefit of their staff. Not satisfied with corporate henchmen, companies are hunting for creative, confident visionaries. The huge success of Stephen Covey's *The 7 Habits of Highly Effective People* bears this out.

The impact of workshops in the corporate sector has been further borne out by a major newspaper consulting us in the course of its research into the power of the mind. Its article was concerned with employees being forced to participate in these workshops.[8] Some of the distinguishing marks of these business seminars are:

- visualization is the key to success
- positive affirmations where participants engage in self-congratulation
- the use of psychotechnologies, such as mantras, rebirthing, soul travel, as a means of reducing stress
- the promise of unlimited success
- large fees for attendees
- long, intensive sessions held over a weekend

- in some seminars there is a strong component of emotional confrontation designed to shatter preconceptions and self-images in order to reconstruct participants into truly enlightened ones—Werner Erhard's EST programme was noted for this, with statements such as "Your life doesn't work!"[9]

Some businesses are also relying on tools such as astrology for their motivation and planning. Newspapers even carry horoscopes for businesses. Other companies consult clairvoyants. In the midst of this pursuit for survival and profit, there is as well the industrial chaplain who works alongside employees in the company as a caregiver.

Reach for the sky

Charlie was intrigued to find that the Sacred Writings disclose that we are the pinnacle of creation and are made in the image of God. Job 28 reveals our wisdom, vision, and ability to explore even the depths of the earth for minerals. We travel into realms beyond the reach of the greatest bird or beast. We said how the Sacred Writings encourage us to have a healthy self-image, as we are loved by the most significant person in the universe. With God on our side, nothing is impossible!

We said to Charlie that the Sacred Writings have a threefold practical emphasis, which departs from his understanding of the power of the mind. First, we do not control everything, nor are we necessarily responsible for our predicaments. We interact with forces and circumstances and suffer from the actions of others. We are interconnected. We simply do not create our entire destiny by thought. The story of the Good Samaritan tells how thieves waylaid an innocent man (see Luke 10:29-37). What happened to him was not his fault.

He put to us a Sacred Writings text that Louise Hay often cites: "As he thinketh in his heart [mind], so he is" (Prov. 23:7, KJV). "Isn't this speaking of mind control?"

We replied, "The verse in the passage where it is found refers to a stingy person who acts as a dinner host. He is obsessed with the cost of the meal. What the proverb is saying is that such a person will only give you scraps. This is not advocating mind control, but giving us a warning: beware of Scrooges!"

Charlie was a step ahead of us and ready to pounce on our second point: "I suppose you are now going to tell me that there is a God up there who orders and sustains everything."

We responded, "That's how we understand the world. We've had some tremendous personal experiences where God has clearly guided us. For us, Jeremiah speaks the truth when he says, 'Before I [God] formed you in the womb, I knew you, before you were born, I set you apart'" (Jer. 1:5, NIV).

Finally, we turned to servanthood. It is not about mere words such as "change your script," but involves deeds and costly action. In the story of the Good Samaritan, two religious characters avoided the victim, but the Samaritan reached out. Jesus saw servanthood as the ultimate path to wholeness:

"Which of these three do you think was a neighbor to the man who fell into the hands of robbers?" The expert in the law replied, "The one who had mercy on him." Jesus told him, "Go and do likewise" (Luke 10:36-37, NIV).

We suggested to Charlie that it is servanthood that makes a person, family, business, team, and nation "great."

Pat your dog and dig in your garden

Charlie reminded us that we live in a stressful world. What techniques beyond the power of the mind can we discover to handle stress?

We joked about two of the best-known "bush" remedies. One is to pat your dog—our pets are kind of in-house therapists. The

second is to go dig in your garden. Professional healthcare work-
ers tell us these really do work. We can also personally testify to
this with respect to dogs! They relieve tension and aggression and
produce a state of relaxation.

Apart from these home remedies, the Sacred Writings give us
at least six basic insights:

- *Have balanced goals*—Don't get uptight about material things.
  Jesus said, "Therefore I tell you, do not worry about your
  life, what you will eat or drink; or about your body, what you
  will wear. Is not life more important than food, and the body
  more important than clothes?" (Matt. 6:25, NIV).

- *Give yourself space*—Jesus, in his own hectic times, would say,
  "Come with me by yourselves to a quiet place and get some
  rest" (Mark 6:31, NIV).

- *Confront the hurt*—Paul was a model for coming to grips with
  what emotions, people, or situations were causing him stress.
  He would identify the cause and positively confront it. In his
  various letters, he identifies undermining spirits and seeks to
  tackle the problems.

- *Don't keep anxieties to yourself*—Healing and strength are
  often found in opening ourselves to trusted friends and/or
  professional helpers and talking the issue through. As the life
  song of the Travelling Wilburys echoes, "Everybody got
  somebody to lean on," and as Galatians 6:2 says, "Carry each
  other's burdens" (NIV).

- *Be aware that God cares*—Jesus said, "Look at the birds of the
  air; they do not sow or reap or store away in barns, and yet
  your heavenly Father feeds them. Are you not much more
  valuable than they?" (Matt. 6:26, NIV)

- *Trust the power of prayer*—Paul, an apostle of Jesus, wrote,
  "Do not be anxious about anything, but in everything, by
  prayer and petition, with thanksgiving, present your requests
  to God. And the peace of God, which transcends all understanding, will guard your hearts and your minds in Christ
  Jesus" (Phil. 4:6-7, NIV).

Power of the mind guru finds grace

It now seemed opportune to discuss with Charlie the journey of a power of the mind guru. Michael Graham is probably one of the most ardent and disciplined spiritual seekers we have ever met. He has rubbed shoulders with the leading luminaries of both Eastern spiritual practice and the human potential movement (see sidebar).

All the Right Connections

In 1969, he was one of the three original Western disciples at Swami Muktananda's Siddha Yoga ashram in India. Over the next sixteen years, he worked in or managed the ashrams in Ganeshpuri, Melbourne, New York, Miami, and Los Angeles. Between 1982 and 1985, he was the international tour manager for Swami Nityananda, the ill-fated joint successor of Muktananda.

Although principally committed to Muktananda, Michael sought to supplement his spiritual quest with other gurus. He was a personal guest at the private apartment of Bhagwan Shree Rajneesh (later known as Osho) and studied under him ten years prior to his international notoriety. He joined, for a time, both Swami Rudrananda and Da Free John in their respective American ashrams. He met briefly with the anarchic teacher U.G. Krishnamurti and, during Muktananda's 1970 world tour, shared a room for three weeks with Baba Ram Dass. In the early 1990s, he spent time in satsangs (master/disciple dialogues) with H.W.L. Poonja.

Michael explored the human potential movement via Silva Mind Control, the Forum, Avatar, and the Hoffman Quadrinity Process. He spent some 900 hours experimenting with the mind-relaxing tapes of Zygon, Master Charles, and a course known as the End Program. He interacted with Barry Long's teachings about metaphysical enlightenment. He also encouraged former Siddha Yoga devotee Michael Rowlands when he began to emerge as a power of the mind teacher. He also spent a year leading a group through *A Course in Miracles*.

When he enrolled in Avatar, two fellow participants were New Age luminaries—Marilyn Ferguson (author of *The Aquarian Conspiracy*) and Ingo Swann (the US psychic employed in the CIA's "remote sensing" espionage programme). He spent some time getting acquainted with both of them. After completing the course, Michael then did the wizard's course so he could be a licensed presenter of Avatar. He was a successful Avatar teacher in America, Switzerland, Australia and New Zealand. Then he taught his own patented program, known as the Decision Principle, in Canada, France, Australia and New Zealand.

For thirty years, Michael combined the best insights and experiences from Indian spirituality with the most sophisticated components of the human potential movement. However, as Michael told us, in all his dedication to Eastern spiritual practices and teaching of the power of the mind principles, he had not found personal transformation. Yes, he had had numerous spiritual experiences, altered states of consciousness, and reengineered his beliefs many times, but without any appreciable result. It was not working in his life, nor could he see the lives of those he taught being effectively transformed.

Michael's life finally reached a point of desolation and futility. During an isolated meditation retreat, he had a surprising and unexpected mystical encounter with the resurrected Christ. That encounter led him to discover the transforming power of divine grace and forgiveness. It was in that moment of decision to embrace Christ that Michael first understood and experienced within what had eluded him in his thirty-year quest.[10]

Charlie was impressed and sobered by Michael's story. He then remarked that he now had a lot to think about.

There are no accidents

We feel that there is one unresolved issue to be settled. The notion that Charlie shared about writing your own script can lead to some unrealistic, unhelpful, and disconcerting ends. Consider the following:

When it is no longer necessary to have a disease such as AIDS on the earth plane, when no one needs that experience any more, then someone from the spirit side may very well pass the idea to someone on the earth plane and a so-called "cure" will come forward. However, there will always be some other illness waiting in the wings, some other way to exit for the human being who is choosing to leave the earth plane. Cures come when the disease is no longer necessary. There are no accidents. As long as there are those who need to have the experience of leaving the earth by AIDS or have the need for the communication of AIDS (and changing their lives because of it), it will stay on the earth plane. Always. Those within the spirit dimension will not interfere in any way with the earth plane. It is always the choice of those on the earth as to their needs and their path.

As more and more individuals go within and discover their own inner guidance, work on themselves, take responsibility for their own lives, then less and less is there need for what some would see as catastrophe or tragedy. There will be those who choose to leave through earth changes, volcanic eruptions, airplane crashes, all forms of departure. When there is no further need for that illness or experience to be manifest, it will go away.[11]

During our time at the festival, we also spoke with various New Age celebrities. Chris James is a marvellous musician and singer. His theme song, based on the poetry of Wordsworth, means much to us: "We are angels, we have forgotten these things; trailing clouds of glory, we are remembering."

After one part of his performances, we discussed spiritual journeys. We asked him, "How do you explain that there are victims in this world whose despair is not of their own making? What about the refugee?" His response was that these sorts of conundrums are for the philosopher or theologian to work out. His calling is to focus on the positives. We appreciated that, but we still posed the question, "If your worldview has a substantial Achilles heel in it, is it not time for a new paradigm? Can we hide in the positives while some who are savaged by injustice are chained to crushing circumstances?" He understood our concerns.

Reality check

As we have mentioned, there are positive aspects to the power of the mind. All of us have benefited from positive thinking. The concern with the modern power of the mind movement is its unrealistic view of thought alone creating reality.

We agreed with Charlie that there is a new consciousness percolating in our midst—one we want to own. It is an altered state of consciousness not bound by the shackles of falsely programmed patterns of thought. The new human is lateral, positive, balanced within, and harmonized with the environment. The new human steps confidently into the future.

Affirmations of the new human

We suggested to Charlie and others the following affirmations for the new human, which integrate the insights of the power of the mind ideas and those of the Sacred Writings. They reflect an empowered mind in tune with the realities of life.

- I affirm that transforming/refocusing my goals begins with the renewing of the mind.
- I affirm that I am special, created in God's image, and have been given tremendous capabilities. I will positively use my gifts, intuition, and creativity.
- I affirm that I am dependent on circumstances, others, and God for life's fulfillment. This is a beautiful concept and is in touch with reality.
- I affirm that I am a shamrock of body, mind, and spirit. I only operate as a wholly integrated person when energized

by the one who is beyond us, yet near enough to personally comfort, guide, and strengthen us.

- I affirm that life is more than thought and involves adventure even beyond my own creativity.
- I affirm that love is more powerful than dreams.
- I affirm that servanthood and dying for others is the authentic path. I conceive people, families, and nations growing together in mutual service.

Endnotes

Chapter 10

1 John Kehoe, *Mind Power*, Toronto: Zoetic, 1987, p. 23.
2 Shirley Maclaine, *Going Within*, New York: Bantam, 1989, pp. 46, 47.
3 *The New Age Catalogue*, New York: Doubleday, 1988, p. 85.
4 Charles Paul Brown, Berna Deane, and James Russell Strole, *Together Forever*, Sydney: Pythagorean Press, 1991, p. 72.
5 Sheila Ostrander, Lynn Schroeder, and Nancy Ostrander, *Superlearning*, London: Sphere, 1981.
6 Harry Palmer, *Living Deliberately: The Discovery and Development of Avatar*, Altamonte Springs: Star's Edge, 1994.
7 Rachael Kohn, "Radical Subjectivity in Self Religions and the Problem of Authority" in Alan W. Black (ed.), *Religion in Australia: Sociological Perspectives*, Sydney: Allen & Unwin, 1991, pp. 133-150.
8 Sally Macmillan, "Dark Side of the New Age," *The Australian Weekend*, 13-14 January, 1990, pp. 1-2.
9 On these points see Douglas Groothuis, *Confronting the New Age*, Downers Grove: InterVarsity Press, 1988, pp. 163-165.
10 For the full story, see Michael Graham, *The Experience of Ultimate Truth*, Melbourne: U-Turn Press, 2001. Available at www.u-turnpress.com.
11 *The New Age Catalogue*, p. 157.

Chapter 11
Jesus' Missing Years

———————◆———————

*Of course, the 'truth' about the missing years in Jesus' life cannot
be historically proven and, therefore, will always be subjective for
each individual who explores it—which is the way it should be. We
have no need to prove anything about this story.*[1]

*Christ traveled through many countries teaching and performing
all kinds of miracles before arriving in Judea to teach the doctrine
formulated in Japan. This provoked the Romans who sentenced
Jesus to death by crucifixion, but Jesus' brother, Isukiri, voluntarily
sacrificed himself on the cross.*

*At the age of 36, Christ went on a four-year journey to north-
ern Europe, Africa, Central Asia, China, Siberia, Alaska, down
through both Americas and back to Alaska. He then arrived at
Matsugasaki Port in Japan (now part of Hachinohe in Aomori
Prefecture) on 26 February in the 33rd year of Suinin, together
with many followers from all the countries he had visited on the
way. Christ's final years were spent in Herai, where he died at the
age of 118.*[2]

*When they had gone, an angel of the Lord appeared to Joseph in a
dream. "Get up," he said, "take the child and his mother and escape
to Egypt" (Matt. 2:13, NIV).*

———————◆———————

Colin, who was in his late forties, raised with us some interesting points about the life of Jesus. Like so many others, Colin had
seen the television documentary *The Lost Years of Jesus*. This film

217

suggested that Jesus spent his missing years—between the ages of 13 and 29—studying and preaching in India, Kashmir, Nepal, and Tibet. Colin said that there were actual scrolls in Tibet telling of Jesus' travels to these places in Asia. He challenged us to go beyond the limitations of the Sacred Writings and embrace these other scrolls. There we would find the full teachings of the great master.

At our stand we were to talk a lot with many "Colins" about the international travels of Jesus. This subject is one of the most interesting and mysterious to explore. It was stimulating to talk to those who were trying to get in touch with the true Christ.

Apart from the locations mentioned in our introductory quotes, Jesus is said to have traveled to many other places, including Greece, Persia, and Stonehenge.[3] The Sacred Writings indicate that Christ did go beyond Palestine—he at least found his way to Egypt as a child.

What is the documentary evidence for Jesus travelling to all of these other places? The fact is that the evidence is slight. This does not worry people such as Janet Bock, who stress that Jesus' travels are based on subjective insights. The weakness with this approach is that history is recast as romance that fits our own hidden fantasies. It is just as valid for us to see Cleopatra and Mark Antony embracing on a sandy beach at Ibiza. Such subjective imaginings might at times enliven our dreaming, but have no bearing on our understanding of what influenced Jesus.

Jesus in Tibet

Colin knew that the focus of the historical material for these international travels is Nicholas Notovitch's *The Unknown Life of Jesus Christ*. Notovitch was a Russian journalist who visited India, Kashmir, and Tibet in the 1880s. When he visited a Tibetan Buddhist monastery, the head abbot told him how the great master Jesus was honored in one of their scrolls.

According to the abbot, Jesus (known to them as St. Issa) came to India and Tibet during his early years and studied the Vedas and Buddhist sutras. Once he had mastered these Sacred Writings and their spiritual practices, he went back to Palestine to preach. Notovitch asked if he could be shown these scrolls, but the abbot was reluctant to do so on that occasion. He told Notovitch that, if he ever revisited the monastery, he would be allowed to look at the scrolls.

As fate would have it, Notovitch left the monastery but was thrown from his horse and broke his leg. As the only safe place was the monastery, he was brought back there and, while recuperating, was granted his wish. The abbot would sit with him reading the stories about St. Issa as Notovitch made notes. Later, Notovitch arranged them in the format of a biblical book. He was to report such incidents as this:

In his fourteenth year, young Issa, the Blessed One, came to this side of the Sindh and settled among the Aryas, in the country beloved by God. Fame spread the name of the marvelous youth along the northern Sindh, and when he came through the country of the five streams and Radjipoutan, the devotees of the god Djaine asked him to stay among them.[4]

Notovitch went on to publish the story of his travels, including the new "Gospel" document he had discovered. It first appeared in French in 1894 and in English shortly thereafter.

Two later major works that show a literary dependence on Notovitch are Levi Dowling's *The Aquarian Gospel of Jesus the Christ* and Elizabeth Clare Prophet's *The Lost Years of Jesus.* Even though Dowling's work was "downloaded" from the psychic realm, scholars have noted the links with Notovitch.[5] Prophet's work is a recent defense of the whole Notovitch saga. She also documents other teachers, such as Swami Abhedananda and Nicholas Roerich, who later went to the same monastery and claimed to have seen the scrolls. Their versions of the scrolls have some variations in them when compared with Notovitch's translation.[6]

Elizabeth Clare Prophet reproduces a photo of the alleged parchment, taken in 1939 by Elisabeth Caspari, with this caption: "These books say your Jesus was here."[7] Sadly, the photographed parchment is unreadable. In the absence of any scholarly translation, the photo hardly confirms the authenticity of Notovitch's work.

As was to be expected, the skeptics quickly followed in pursuit of Notovitch's work. One initial response came from the comparative religion scholar Friedrich Max Muller (1823-1900). In deference to Notovitch, he thought that he may have been the victim of a practical joke by the Buddhist lamas. Muller expressed his opinion in the popular British journal *The Nineteenth Century*.[8] Notovitch, in a fresh English edition, responded to Muller's article with this challenge: "Let it even be proved to me that I am wrong."[9]

We told Colin about Archibald Douglas, who was a professor at Government College in Agra, India. He had no axe to grind, but decided to spend his holiday retracing Notovitch's steps. Douglas wanted to view the scrolls for himself. In 1895, he arrived at the same monastery that Notovitch had referred to. Douglas was accompanied by a translator who interacted between himself and the head abbot. In dialogue form, the following was asked.

◆

Q: Have you or any of the Buddhist monks in this monastery ever seen here a European with an injured leg?

A: No, not during the last fifteen years. If any sahib suffering from serious injury had stayed in this monastery, it would have been my duty to report the matter to the Wazir of Leh. I have never had occasion to do so.

Q: Have you or any of your monks ever shown any Life of Issa to any sahib and allowed him to copy and translate the same?

A: There is no such book in the monastery and during my term of office no sahib has been allowed to copy or translate any of the manuscripts in the monastery.

Q: *Are you aware of the existence of any book in any of the Buddhist monasteries of Tibet bearing on the life of Issa?*

A: *I have been for forty-two years a lama and am well acquainted with all the well-known Buddhist books and manuscripts, and I have never heard of one that mentions the name of Issa. It is my firm and honest belief that none such exists. I have inquired of our principal lamas in other monasteries of Tibet and they are not acquainted with any books or manuscripts that mention the name of Issa.*

Q: *M. Nicholas Notovitch, a Russian gentleman who visited your monastery between seven and eight years ago, states that you discussed with him the religions of the ancient Egyptians, Assyrians, and the people of Israel.*

A: *I know nothing whatever about the Egyptians, Assyrians, and the people of Israel, and do not know anything of their religions whatsoever. I have never mentioned these peoples to any sahib. (I was reading M. Notovitch's book to the lama at the time and he burst out with, "Sun, sun, sun, manna mi dug!—which is Tibetan for "Lies, lies, lies, nothing but lies!")*

Q: *Is the name of Issa held in great respect by the Buddhists?*

A: *They know nothing even of his name; none of the lamas has ever heard it, save through missionaries and European sources.*

---◆---

Douglas concluded:

---◆---

I have visited Himis, and have endeavored by patient and impartial inquiry to find out the truth respecting M. Notovitch's remarkable story, with the result that, while I have not found one single fact to support his statements, all the weight of evidence goes to disprove them beyond all shadow of doubt. It is certain that no such passages as M. Notovitch pretends to have translated exist in the monastery of Himis and therefore it is impossible that he could have "faithfully reproduced" the same.[10]

It should be noted that Notovitch made no response to Douglas's report and, in fact, disappeared from the stage.

But Elizabeth Clare Prophet does not let the matter rest. She suggests that the lama may have been reluctant to be up-front with Douglas as he wished to protect his scrolls. She speaks of others who have journeyed to Himis and viewed the scrolls. Ross said the problem is that she paints the lama as a liar of convenience. Also, not one of the other travelers has publicly submitted any photographic slides of the parchments to scholars of Tibetan culture for verification. All they give us is their own translation of an unseen document.

Apart from Douglas's research, the greatest obstacle to Notovitch's story is the fact that Buddhism did not reach Tibet before the seventh century A.D. As Christmas Humphreys, the popular Buddhist writer notes:

Before the seventh century, the sole religion of Tibet was the Bon [Shamanism] . . . Some time in the fifth century A.D., a number of Buddhist books were brought into Tibet from India, but they seem to have been ignored, and it was not until the reign of King Srongtsen Gampo, in the middle of the seventh century, that Buddhism became a force in Tibet.[11]

There was simply no Buddhist monastery in Tibet for Jesus to visit.

Then there is Notovitch's linguistic problem. He claimed that the scrolls he saw were translated into Tibetan from the sacred Pali language. The fact of the matter is that no Buddhist literature of Tibet was ever translated directly from Pali; instead they came from Sanskrit or Chinese. The Pali language is the sacred tongue of the Theravadan Buddhists of Sri Lanka and southern India.[12]

Problems with Notovitch's translation

He refers to the Jains (Djaines) as believing in God. The Jains, however, do not believe in the existence of any God.[13]

The document's spelling does not reflect first-century Asian geography, but contains 19th-century Western anachronisms, such as Nepaul for Nepal.

Notovitch and others claim that the document is the most accurate first-century A.D. source concerning the teachings of Jesus. In reality, the scrolls speak of many Jewish temples in Palestine, but archaeology establishes that there was only one in Jerusalem.

In the first edition of his book, Notovitch claims to reproduce a single scroll. However, in the second edition, in answering Max Muller, he wrote, "The truth, indeed, is that the verses of which I give a translation . . . are to be found scattered through more than one book without any title." The Caspari photograph, if it is genuine, shows several parchments bound together and casts more doubts on Notovitch's truthfulness.[14]

Jesus is supposed to have mastered Buddhist teachings. A careful reading of Notovitch's work shows that there is no real resemblance between Buddhist dogmas and what is on the lips of his "Christ." Arild Romarheim points out, "This manuscript, according to its contents, renounces Buddhism. What it actually preaches is a moderately Cabalistic Judaism."[15] It is also remarkable that the current leader of Tibetan Buddhism, the Dalai Lama, has never quoted from the Life of St. Issa in his dialogues with Christian leaders. If Jesus had been to Tibet and mastered Buddhism, it would be in the Dalai Lama's best interests to quote these primary source scrolls that Notovitch asserted the chief lamas as studying.[16]

Jesus in India

A number of modern-day gurus, such as Yogananda, Sai Baba, and Bhagwan Shree Rajneesh have taught that Jesus traveled to India.[17] They appear to base their knowledge on Notovitch and/or subjective intuition. Someone who goes further is Edgar Cayce, who, in his trances, tapped into psychic records in the spirit world or universal mind known as the Akashic Records. These records apparently talk of Jesus' Indian sojourn.

A passage that is sometimes referred to by these teachers is Luke 4:22, which indicates that the hearers of Jesus were amazed at his wisdom, asking, "Where did a carpenter's son gain such insights?" Colin asked, could this not be proof that he must have gone to India? Ross replied this is not the answer disclosed in the gospels. They indicate that Jesus was wise because he was God incarnate, and if he had any assistance, it was from the Holy Spirit. Such a person would not be dependent on earthly guides.

There is a further problem. While Jesus acknowledged the wisdom of the ancient writings in the Old Testament, he never spoke of the Vedas, Sutras, or Tantric materials. Nor do we see Jesus using the postures of hatha yoga or Buddhist prayer chants in the Gospels. If he traveled East, surely he would have shared these insights with his disciples and encouraged them to seek such learning. Some gurus cite Notovitch's work in support of their claim that Jesus agreed with the Vedas. However, Issa denied the divine origin of the Vedas, claiming they perverted the truth (Life of St. Issa 5:12, 26).

Ross said we should not overlook the fact that Christ lived in a Greco-Roman world. Most scholars find his concepts and phraseology relying on his Jewish culture and his Greco-Roman world rather than on any supposed Japanese, Tibetan, or Indian influences.

Colin then raised with us the variant story the Ahmadiyya Muslim sect has about Jesus coming to Kashmir after the crucifixion. This story arose in 1899. In his 1978 book *Jesus Died in Kashmir*, A. Faber-Kaiser offers this reconstruction of what occurred. Jesus did not die on the cross, but survived and fled to Kashmir with his wife Mary Magdalene. It is believed that the lost tribes of Israel are the ancestors of the inhabitants of Kashmir. Jesus' tomb is claimed to be in Srinagar. They claim to have Christ's tomb and a living descendant.[18]

Per Beskow, the Swedish expert in patristic studies, maintains that the Ahmadiyya claim is partly based on the faulty Notovitch work.[19] He further indicates that it also depends on the late medieval forgery, the gospel of Barnabas.[20] Paul Pappas, professor of history at West Virginia Institute of Technology, takes the matter further:

Although the Ahmadis claim to have the tomb of Jesus in Srinagar, India, no historical evidence has been offered to confirm its authenticity except for questionable works based on oral legends. In addition, the Ahmadis have failed to produce any archaeological or anthropological evidence that the grave . . . might be that of Jesus. Therefore, the Ahmadi thesis is based only on the revelation of Hazrat Mirza Ghulam Ahmad, the founder of the Ahmadiyya movement.[21]

One result of the Indian pilgrimage stories is that some have now combined the Notovitch claim with the Ahmadiyya claim, so that Jesus makes two visits—one before his crucifixion, one after. The *National Geographic* reflects this and further responds to the Notovitch tale:

When we were in Srinigar, we were told of a book written by a European [Notovitch] who advanced a strange theory. The author claimed to have found documentary evidence in Himis that Jesus Christ had been to Ladakh in his lifetime.

After the crucifixion, so the tale goes, Christ was not buried in the Holy Land, but was brought secretly to Little Tibet, brought to life by Himalayan herbs and later ascended to heaven from the Himalayas. We were also told that this author mentioned going to Himis and seeing the document with Father Gergen. But the venerable old gentleman [Father Gergen] assured us he knew of no such evidence. Though he remembered the author, he had never been to Himis with him.

*After reading the book, several European church dignitaries wrote to Father Gergen asking for corroboration and details of this matter. When we visited Himis, we asked about the document [Notovitch's scrolls], but the lamas didn't know what we were talking about. It was Greek to them!*22

Remarkably, Edgar Cayce, who claimed the Akashic records revealed Jesus' Indian sojourn, maintained that works such as Notovitch's scrolls were forgeries. Cayce denied that there was any true written manuscript of Jesus' Indian travels in the world.23

Philip said, most psychic authorities affirm that tapping into the Akashic records takes one directly to the universal mind, the ultimate source of truth. This is what Levi Dowling and Edgar Cayce claimed they resourced. Rudolf Steiner, the founder of anthroposophy, averred, "It is only the reading in the Akashic record which can guarantee the right text of the gospels."24 Recently, two French psychics, Anne and Daniel Meurois-Givaudan, have tapped into the Akashic records and recalled their past lives as eyewitnesses to Christ's missing years.25

Despite Steiner's assurances, we have encountered a fundamental problem with the Akashic records. When we compared the eyewitness recall of Anne and Daniel Meurois-Givaudan with Dowling's *Aquarian Gospel* and Rudolf Steiner's and Edgar Cayce's readings, we discovered that they contradict each other on most of the major details. Dowling's *Aquarian Gospel* is riddled with historical anachronisms, such as Jesus' visiting Lahore, even though the city did not exist until the seventh century. Since the Akashic records are said to take us to the ultimate source of truth, which of the psychics do we trust?

Jesus in Japan and France

Colin asked what we thought about the Kirisuto Legend, which says that Jesus arrived in Japan at the age of twenty-one and spent ten years studying Shintoism. He returned to Judea to proclaim these teachings, but was opposed and his brother Isukiri was crucified in Jesus' place. Jesus then left Judea and returned to Japan at the age of thirty-seven and died at the age of 106 years. His tomb is said to be in Herai where an erected signpost outlines the legend. This claim, which has been repeated in several discrepant versions, has been extensively promoted within the Japanese new religion Mahikari.[26]

Philip pointed out that the twin visits to Japan mimic the 19th-century Ahmadiyya claims about twin visits to Kashmir. The legend is not found in any primary source historical documents, but comes from the Takenouchi family papers that began to be circulated in the 1930s. These papers revitalize religious ideas from the Tokugawa period (1603-1868). It was then that Christianity came to Japan. Winston Davis notes that, during the Tokugawa period, Christian beliefs were borrowed and reworked by popular Shinto movements.[27] Similarly the gospels do not show any traces of Shinto or Japanese folk teachings, such as ancestor veneration and shamanism.

Colin was also interested in the book *The Holy Blood and the Holy Grail*. The authors claim that Jesus survived on the cross and revived in the tomb. He then took his wife Mary Magdalene out of Judea and probably settled in France. The Merovingian royal dynasty, they claim, was the direct bloodline from Jesus. They claim that the suppressed truth about Jesus was preserved by a secret order known as the Priory of Sion. The authors also rely on the medieval Grail romances as primary evidence.[28]

Laurence Gardner has furthered these claims about Jesus in his book *Bloodline of the Holy Grail*.[29] Gardner believes that Jesus was married to Mary Magdalene and traces his lineage down to the English royal house of the Stuarts.

In his book *Leading Lawyers' Case for the Resurrection* Ross Clifford analyzes whether or not a man who has been subjected to torture, flogging, the cross, and a spear-thrust to the side could appear a couple of days later as large as life.[30] He would have to pretend to have conquered death for the fable of the resurrection to survive. We agree with the skeptic Strauss that such a scenario is more inconceivable as a miracle than the resurrection itself! As for someone taking Jesus' place on the cross, this would make him out to be a complete fraud. This is inconsistent with his character and status.

As to Jesus being married to Mary Magdalene, there is simply no evidence for this. Their inferences from the medieval Grail stories yield an utterly bizarre portrait of Jesus that has no historical support whatsoever. It seems that people who love conspiracy theories are easily impressed by these rather implausible claims. Gardner interprets the gospel records through the controversial writings of Barbara Thiering (see below), and fails to historically validate his conjectures about Jesus' life.

So, the Japanese and French accounts are based on legends. There is little, if any, historical base that you can check.

Jesus the Buddhist

At this juncture, Colin's son Richard joined in the conversation. He was interested in Holger Kersten's best-selling trilogy, *Jesus Lived in India, The Jesus Conspiracy*, and *The Original Jesus*.[31] In the first book, Kersten uses both Notovitch's story and the Ahmadiyya claims to affirm that Jesus made twin visits to India. He further argues that Jesus taught about reincarnation and that later church councils deleted this from the Sacred Writings.

In the second book, Kersten and his co-author Elmar Grubar argue that Jesus swooned, survived crucifixion, and the Turin

Shroud supports this. They maintain that the 1988 radiocarbon results, which indicate a medieval date for the Shroud, were deliberately faked. This implicates Vatican officials in a conspiracy to invalidate the Shroud because the evidence shows that Jesus survived death and so discredits belief in the resurrection.

In *The Original Jesus*, Kersten and Grubar argue that there are many parallels between the life and teachings of the Buddha and Jesus. They propose that the Essenes at Qumran taught Jesus. The Essenes, they claim, were clearly influenced by Buddhist missionaries. The conclusion reached is that Jesus was not a Christian but a Buddhist teacher.

We pointed out to Richard that there were many complex problems with Kersten and Grubar's views. Kersten's claims about Jesus' travels are undermined by his reliance on unreliable sources, such as Notovitch and Faber-Kaiser. As we saw in chapter 9, Jesus taught about resurrection. Resurrection negates the need for reincarnation. The historical evidence also shows that the church did not delete reincarnation from the Sacred Writings. It was not something Jesus or the apostles taught.

Similarly, their case for Jesus swooning on the cross has all the same drawbacks we just discovered with *The Holy Blood and the Holy Grail*. Their conspiracy case is, likewise, implausible. As critics had long maintained, the Shroud was probably a medieval relic. The 1988 carbon-dating tests simply disqualified the Shroud as being Jesus' burial cloth. Those test results could not confirm or disprove if the primary source accounts of Jesus' death and resurrection are historically reliable.

Another major problem is their itinerary, for Jesus' life crams in too many impossible episodes. There simply wasn't enough time for Jesus to have traveled and lived in India, studied and mastered Buddhism with the Essenes in Israel, been an itinerant preacher, survive crucifixion, and return to India.

We agreed that we could draw parallels between the Buddha and Jesus. However, the discovery of similarities does not mean that Jesus' teachings came from the Buddha. Parallels do not prove causation. Kersten and Grubar fail to account for the significant differences between Buddha and Jesus.

Where Buddha and Jesus Don't Connect

Steven Rockefeller indicates how Buddha and Jesus differ:

- The Buddha saw no relevance for, nor gave any, revelation from God, whereas Jesus revealed a personal Creator.
- The Buddha taught that the root problem for humanity is ignorance; Jesus taught that the root problem is sin.
- The Buddha is not a savior figure, but rather points the way to attaining enlightenment; Jesus presents himself as the unique savior of the world.[32]

Kersten and Grubar basically select from the gospels what suits their theory and dismiss or ignore major sections that would undermine it. Their reconstruction of Buddhist missions in Palestine through the Essenes lacks primary source evidence. They claim to have uncovered the original Jesus, but in reality they do not allow him to speak for himself.

Jesus the Essene/Gnostic

Colin then wondered, "Well, what about the possible links between Jesus and the Essenes and Gnostics? Barbara Thiering makes a strong case for Jesus having been an Essene and she also looks at Gnostic sources. Could these paths, rather than the Buddhist-Hindu spirituality, have been Jesus' guiding light?"

The Essenes were a Jewish group, probably known to most through the famous Dead Sea Scrolls. The Dead Sea Scrolls bring fresh insights into the Jewish religious scene before and around the time of Christ, and for this we must be most grateful, as they help us better understand the world in which Jesus lived.

The Scrolls were found near Qumran on the Dead Sea in 1947. They deal mainly with the life of a particular Jewish sect in the last two centuries B.C. These scrolls, though, make no mention of Jesus, John the Baptist, or any other New Testament figure.

We told Colin that both of us had studied under and greatly respect Dr. Thiering. She is almost alone in her endeavor to link Jesus to the Dead Sea Scrolls and the Qumran community. Her books *Jesus the Man, Jesus of the Apocalypse*, and *The Book that Jesus Wrote* have caused some sensation.[33]

A couple of points need to be borne in mind. The first is that Dr. Thiering is not New Age and would be horrified to find any such connection. Second, there is no documentary evidence to directly link Jesus with the Scrolls. She relies on her own "pesher" method—that is, finding the hidden meaning in the text—to reconstruct the history of the early Christians. Third, she follows the path of theologian Paul Tillich, who held that religious statements were purely symbols pointing to something beyond themselves.

From this position, it is hardly surprising to find that she has reinterpreted the gospels and the Dead Sea Scrolls to fit a meaning not found on the surface. Most scholars of a variety of academic backgrounds, those with and without faith, have dismissed her theory about Jesus and the Scrolls.[34]

Finally, the Dead Sea Scrolls themselves do not speak of any cosmic consciousness, karma, and reincarnation. Neither do they correlate to any of the Hindu or Buddhist scriptures. There are also significant differences between the gospels and Essene teachings.

The Gnostic gospels are fascinating to study. Some of these books pick up various sayings associated with Jesus, and some speculate on the hidden aspects of his life. A large collection of the Gnostic writings were found at Nag Hammadi in Egypt in 1945 in a jar in a Greco-Roman cemetery. The problem with relying on these documents is that we are most uncertain as to their date, authorship, and reliability as records. They fail the basic historical tests set out below and just cannot stand up to Matthew, Mark, Luke, and John. To rely on the Gnostic books is like riding a bike when we are able to travel in a Ferrari.

Some venerate the Gnostic gospels in the sense that they place great stress on sayings that are not found in the traditional gospels. Yet, a striking contrast between the Jesus of the gospels who constantly affirms women is found in the final saying of the gospel of Thomas. "Peter" argues:

"Let Mary [probably Mary Magdalene] leave us, for women are not worthy of life." Jesus said, "I myself shall lead her in order to make her male, so that she too may become a living spirit, resembling you males. For every woman who will make herself male will enter the kingdom of heaven."[35]

Such an aversion to womanhood is hardly admirable. Some try to redeem the gospel of Thomas by suggesting that this saying is a later addition. The problem still remains in that it represents the thought of a Gnostic devotee.[36]

As Colin listened to our views on Gnosticism and the Essenes, he asked for our opinion on New Age writer Edmund Bordeaux Szekely. We were aware that Szekely claimed he had discovered a previously unknown text, called The Essene Gospel of Peace. Szekely was of French-Hungarian descent and was concerned with promoting a vegetarian lifestyle.

Szekely insisted that he had discovered fragments of an Aramaic manuscript at Monte Cassino, Italy, in the mid-1920s. Two more substantial versions were said to be found, one in Old Slavonic, held at the National Library of Vienna, and the other in Aramaic, held in the Vatican's archives. According to Szekely, Jesus was an Essene who believed in a heavenly father and an earthly mother.

◆

*It is by love that the heavenly father and the earthly mother and
the Son of Man become one. For the spirit of the Son of Man was
created from the spirit of the heavenly father and his body from the
body of the earthly mother. Become, therefore, perfect as the spirit
of your heavenly father and the body of your earthly mother are
perfect. And so love your earthly mother as she loves your body. And
so love your true brothers as your heavenly father and your earthly
mother love them.*[37]

◆

We put it to Colin that to be a devotee of Szekely is a trouble-
some journey. No one has been able to find the manuscripts that
Szekely said he had found and translated in Vienna and Rome.
Per Beskow notes that they should be easy to locate if they exist.
Further, Szekely was reluctant to assist anyone in their search for
this truth and supplied no catalogue or other library numbers.
Szekely alone has read them.[38]

Jesus—the pagan myth?

At the festival, other seekers asked us about the controversial
book *The Jesus Mysteries*. The authors Timothy Freke and Peter
Gandy argue that Jesus never existed but was invented by the
apostle Paul who borrowed from and freely adapted myths about
a dying and rising god. They argue that the Greco-Roman mystery religions were resplendent with rich stories and rituals about
figures such as Dionysius, Mithras, and Osiris. They claim that
Christianity was originally Gnostic, but, by the time of
Constantine, a literalist faction won the day, suppressed the
pagan/Gnostic connections, and turned Christianity into a literalist religion by making Jesus into a real person.[39]

We said that Freke and Gandy have simply dredged up an
old theory that has long since been discredited. Ronald Nash
has shown that there are parallels between Jesus' death and

resurrection and pagan myths. However, there are some important distinctions. He notes five concerning Jesus' resurrection:

- None of the pagan gods died for someone else.
- Only Jesus died for sin.
- Jesus died once and for all—in contrast the mystery gods died repeatedly.
- Jesus' death was an actual event in history—the New Testament documents carefully give the places and times of the events, as well as listing witnesses, whereas the deaths of the mystery gods appear in mythical dramas with no historical ties.
- Unlike the mystery gods, Jesus died voluntarily.[40]

Furthermore, Leon McKenzie has painstakingly shown how the archetypes of the mystery religions and pagan myths point towards a common yearning in humanity. That yearning is fulfilled in the historic reality of Jesus' death and resurrection.[41]

Freke and Gandy also claim that the church borrowed its ideas about Christ's sacrificial death from the taurobolium, or bull-sacrifice rites, of the mystery religion called Mithraism.[42] Edwin Yamauchi, Professor of ancient history at Miami University, Ohio, points out that the taurobolium is only attested around A.D. 160 and became a full blown bull-sacrifice in the fourth century A.D. He indicates that Mithraism did not influence Christianity but rather the reverse is more likely.[43]

The Secret Gospel

Colin and Richard then came to the writings of Morton Smith—*Clement of Alexandria and a Secret Gospel of Mark, The Secret Gospel,* and *Jesus the Magician.*[44] Morton Smith teaches ancient history at Columbia University. Several popular authors we have just considered, such as Freke and Gandy, Baigent, Leigh and Lincoln, Gardner and Prophet, rely on his books as part of their cumulative case for reinterpreting Jesus.

In 1958, Smith discovered an 18th-century manuscript at the Mar Saba Monastery near Jerusalem. The manuscript was a two-

and-a-half page letter in Greek copied on to some blank pages of a book. The letter is attributed to the early Christian leader Clement of Alexandria (A.D. 150-211).

This letter alleges that there is a secret version of Mark's gospel and quotes a short section from it. Jesus raises a young man from the dead and then teaches him about the mystery of the kingdom. Smith extrapolates from these fragmentary quotations that a secret gospel of Mark pre-dated the canonical gospels. He argues that Jesus initiated the young man via a secret baptism into a licentious mystery religion based in magical rites. Smith regards miracles as simply a form of ancient magic and uses third- and fourth-century Greek magical papyri for parallel illustrations of his hypothesis. He claims that this licentious secret tradition was so widespread that it explains the rise and proliferation of the Gnostic sects, especially in Egypt.

We said to Colin and Richard that Smith's case rests on a very fragile foundation. The first major problem is that we do not actually have an original manuscript of either this secret gospel of Mark or Clement's letter. The copy of Clement's letter could be a forgery, as Smith's own teacher A.D. Nock maintained. Other scholars do believe it is genuine, but we still lack any independent corroboration for the contents of the complete document—we merely have a short quotation of an otherwise lost text. Even if it is genuine, it does not prove Smith's elaborate hypothesis, but merely shows that another document purporting to be a gospel existed, but we cannot even be certain as to its full contents.

Secret's Fundamental Flaws

Edwin Yamauchi finds several historical and methodological flaws in Morton Smith's work:

Smith accepts at face value the contents of Clement's letter, yet Clement was notorious for his uncritical and credulous views about apocryphal literature.

His hypothesis of the Christians as a licentious sect ignores the pagan testimony of the Roman governor Pliny the Younger (A.D. 115), which shows the exact opposite was true of Christians.

Most Gnostic sects were ascetic and the development of licentious Gnosticism in Egypt can be accounted for without recourse to Smith's conjectures.

As there is no direct primary source of evidence to support his complex hypothesis, Smith postulates a conspiracy of suppression to conveniently explain the absence of evidence.

His use of third- and fourth-century magical papyri is anachronistic, particularly when using them to posit first-century historical conditions. These later texts are used to reinterpret the first-century canonical gospels, which is akin to using Hitler's *Mein Kampf* to interpret Napoleon Bonaparte's writings. Smith arbitrarily rejects the canonical gospels, even though as primary sources their evidence contradicts his hypothesis.[45]

We suggested to Colin and Richard that these scholarly considerations cast serious doubts on the plausibility of Smith's theory. Popular authors who quote Smith's work do so on a selective and sometimes arbitrary basis. The main implication with this is that, as Smith's case is very weak, it means that those who rely on him also have a weak case.

Jesus' various travels

Colin asked us—after our discussions about the various travels of Jesus—why not accept this multiplicity of journeys? We pointed out a major stumbling block: it would have been impossible for Jesus to have traveled, studied, and died in all these various places. A lot of the stories contradict each other, so we have to ask which story is true.

It is enriching at this point to apply basic historical criteria to the various stories of Christ. This is something we have found many seekers enjoy, as they like to get to the core of the Jesus path. Ross has documented the way to do this in *Leading Lawyers' Case for the Resurrection*. Briefly, there are three criteria.

THE TRANSMISSION TEST

Has the written document been carefully and reliably copied and recopied from one generation to the next? As we don't possess any of the original documents with respect to Jesus' life and journey, we must check the process of copying in the available manuscripts. In the case of the New Testament books, there are more than 5,000 Greek manuscripts that we can peruse to check on the copying process. When the copies are compared, they complement each other so that an original can be faithfully reconstructed. None of the other "lives of Christ" in any way pass this test. As British scholar Richard France comments:

All such reconstructions of Jesus necessarily have in common an extreme skepticism with regard to the primary evidence for Jesus, the canonical gospels, which are regarded as a deliberate distortion of the truth in order to offer a Jesus who is fit to be the object of Christian worship. Instead, they search out hints of "suppressed evidence," and give central place to incidental historical details and to later "apocryphal" traditions not unknown to mainstream biblical scholarship, but which have generally been regarded as at best peripheral and, in most cases, grossly unreliable. The credulity with which this "suppressed evidence" is accepted and given a central place in reconstructing the "real" Jesus is the more remarkable when it is contrasted with the excessive skepticism shown towards the canonical gospels.[46]

THE INTERNAL TEST

Do the documents claim to be written by eyewitnesses or those closely associated with the witnesses to the events recorded in them? In the case of the biblical books, both Matthew and John were eyewitnesses to the events, while Mark's gospel is believed to comprise the preaching of St. Peter. Luke's gospel begins by acknowledging that he has carefully checked things out with the original eyewitnesses:

Many have undertaken to draw up an account of the things that have been fulfilled among us, just as they were handed down to us by those who from the first were eyewitnesses and servants of the word. Therefore, since I myself have carefully investigated everything from the beginning, it seemed good also to me to write an orderly account for you, most excellent Theophilus, so that you may know the certainty of the things you have been taught (Luke 1:1–4, NIV).

The other stories on Jesus' life, if they have inspectable documents, do not have the eyewitness testimony. They tend to be legendary in form, speculative in nature, or bear the marks of a forgery.

THE EXTERNAL TEST

Is there any data outside the documents to confirm their claims or contents? With the biblical books, there are numerous archaeological remains, inscriptions, and sociological material to confirm their general details. There are also Greco-Roman and Jewish historical writings (such as Tacitus, Josephus, Pliny the Younger) that correlate with the gospel records.[47]

In contrast, we have noted above how Notovitch's work is inconsistent with external data with respect to names, places, and language.

So, we said to Colin that, when we look at the stories of the various journeys of Jesus, there is only one about which there can be any certainty. This tells us that Jesus was a refugee child in Egypt, that he lived, died, and rose again in Palestine. We accepted that we all have an inclination to embrace the mysterious tale rather than settle for the trustworthy, but sometimes incomplete, historical narratives. We also explained that gospel investigation was not simply a matter of dredging through crusty old books, but was also something of an existential reality. We illustrated this with the case study of John (see sidebar).

A Case Study

We encountered John at a seminar we were conducting. At the end of the seminar, there was a time for storytelling. John said that he had engaged in astral travelling for a long while, but the exhilaration wore off. He grew desperate, as he had found no strength or meaning in his journey into his inner self. In fact, he was at the point of no return. He decided to take a final astral travel before committing suicide.

In this journey, he encountered a bright light that he could not look at. He then heard a voice that he recognized as someone who had comforted him when he was sick in his youth. The voice said, "You have encountered the Godhead. You cannot look upon it. Go back into your body and read the gospels."

He re-entered his body, read the gospel of John, and found that it transformed his life. It self-authenticated itself to him. He stood up in the power of the Spirit as a new disciple of the master, Jesus. "Read them [the gospels] for yourself," he pleaded, "and by so doing encounter the real Jesus."

Embrace the traveler

We said to Colin, "Suppose that Jesus really did journey to India and other places and mastered all these religious pathways. Would that not only add credence to his followers' assertion that he is the enlightened one? He must truly be the master of all wisdom. Before him, of all the ancient sages, we must truly bow."

Of himself, Jesus says this is who he is and why he had come:

- "I tell you the truth, I am the gate for the sheep. All who ever came before me were thieves and robbers, but the sheep did not listen to them" (John 10:7-8, NIV).
- "I am the way and the truth and the life. No one comes to the Father except through me" (John 14:6, NIV).
- "I am the resurrection and the life. He who believes in me will live, even though he dies" (John 11:25, NIV).
- "I am the bread of life. He who comes to me will never go hungry, and he who believes in me will never be thirsty" (John 6:35, NIV).
- "For even the Son of Man did not come to be served, but to serve, and to give his life as a ransom for many" (Mark 10:45, NIV).

It was Thomas the doubter who fully expressed the magnitude of Christ when he said to the resurrected Jesus, "My Lord and my God!" (John 20:28). Rhineland medieval mystic Meister Eckhart has put it nicely:

The greatest good God ever did for man was that he became man himself. Here I shall tell you a story that is relevant to this.

There was once a rich man and a rich lady. The lady had an accident and lost one eye, at which she grieved exceedingly. Then the lord came to her and said: "Wife, why are you so distressed at losing your eye?" She said: "Sir, I do not mourn because I have lost my eye. I mourn for fear you might love me the less." Then he said, "Lady, I love you." Not long afterwards, he put out one of his own eyes and, going to his wife, he said: "Lady, so you may know I love you I have made myself like you. Now I, too, have only one eye."

This is like man, who could scarcely believe that God loved him so much, until God put out one of his own eyes and assumed human nature.[48]

It is apparent that we know little about Jesus' life between the ages of thirteen and twenty-nine years. The gospels are silent. The temptation has been to have him journeying to other countries to find wisdom and to validate all other religions.

As we said to Colin, the straightforward explanation for these years is that Jesus was sanctifying the ordinary. When Luke speaks of Jesus growing in wisdom, no doubt he simply means that, in his life as a child, student, carpenter, and adult, he learned how to appreciate the ordinary things of life—just as we must do.

As his Jewish ancestor wrote in Ecclesiastes, "A man can do nothing better than to eat and drink and find satisfaction in his work. This too, I see, is from the hand of God" (Eccl. 2:24, NIV). From this mastery of the ordinary, Jesus has been able to relate to all. That is why he lives on.

Potholes to transformation

Colin, by his words and movements, was signifying his openness to Jesus. There were, however, potholes in the road to recovery in Christ—not academic potholes, but ones that touched his very being, stumbling blocks that we ourselves had agonized over, genuine concerns that penetrate the very nature of faith.

He took his first step: "What about those who haven't heard about Jesus? Is it fair that they miss out on eternal life simply out of ignorance?" We said to Colin that there are various differing views on this matter. The scriptural view, in our opinion, is that we are judged on the basis of the light we have received and not on the revelation we have not received (Rom. 2). In other words, as Romans 1 makes clear, all know of God and his attributes. Those who have not heard of Christ will be judged on what they know of God. Still, we encouraged him to place his faith in Christ. After all, who would want to stand before God with their own karma?

His second pothole related to sin. He found the concept obnoxious. Was he really that unacceptable to God? We responded by asking if sin wasn't really the best explanation of the human predicament. Don't we feel that at times we fail ourselves, others, and the One beyond us? How else do we make sense of the anger, hurt, and hatred in the world? Has not sin been with us since time immemorial? Simply to see wrongdoing as an illusion or a step for correction is not to do justice to the human cry for forgiveness and cleansing from guilt.

M. Scott Peck has reflected on these realities in his own journey:

◆

One of the reasons I very gradually gravitated towards Christianity is that I came to believe that Christian doctrine has the most correct understanding of the nature of sin. It is a paradoxical, multidimensional understanding, and the first side of the paradox is that Christianity holds that we are all sinners. We cannot but sin. There are a number of possible definitions of sin, but the most common is simply missing the mark, failing to hit the bull's-eye every time. And there's no way we can hit the bull's-eye every time.[49]

◆

We said to Colin that, in our interactions with New Age seekers, many have divulged that they just cannot "positively affirm" away the dark side or shadow of their inner being and community life. We concluded by emphasizing that Jesus takes the sin problem seriously. When he hung on that cross, he did what we could not do—he paid the price for our sin. In him alone is the positive affirmation that I am liberated from sin.

On the matter of sin and evil, Colin focused the discussion on *A Course in Miracles.* This work, which, as we saw earlier purports to be channeled teachings from Jesus, has no negative concept of sin. For example, "No one is punished for their sins and the Sons of God are not sinners."[50] "All our sins are washed away by realizing they were but mistakes."[51]

Our concern with *A Course in Miracles* is that it is just not in touch with reality. The denial of sin and evil is one of its greatest flaws. Scott Peck observes:

---◆---

The reality is that there really are people out there who like to maim, to torture, and to crush other people. There are people who want war because they profit from war. And you can get into serious trouble if you believe that there aren't. Because sooner or later you will be accosted with real evil, and dealing with it will not be as easy as some New Age books imply . . . While A Course in Miracles *purports to be Christian, it distorts Christian doctrine. It is not all the truth; rather, it is a half-truth, and in failing to deal with the problem of evil, it leaves out a major part of the picture.*[52]

---◆---

We reflected with Colin that the message of Jesus as found in the gospels when compared with *A Course in Miracles*, leaves us with two irreconcilable core teachings. The Jesus found in the gospels touched, healed, and transformed people by tackling the reality of their brokenness, guilt, and sin. The "Jesus" found in *A Course in Miracles*, on the other hand, undermines and contradicts the very heart of this. We also reiterated other drawbacks about the *Course* that we discussed with seekers elsewhere in this book.[53]

Former power of the mind guru Michael Graham spent a whole year leading a group of friends through *A Course in Miracles*. He provides this sobering insight:

---◆---

I was fascinated by the fact that such a brilliant work could bear no good fruit whatsoever. That I could understand it, believe it, see the compelling value of it, the coherence of it, the brilliance of it, agree with it, understand it, and yet not be changed one jot . . . and not

one of the people that I spent a year with in the Course in
Miracles *were changed or bettered . . . it didn't change anyone.*[54]

———————————— ◆ ————————————

Michael later encountered the transforming grace of the real
Jesus, so utterly different from the prescriptions and denials of
the *Course.* We prayed that Colin would discover the filling in of
his potholes—that he would freely walk the path of Jesus.

Recovery in grace

Our intense dialogue continued, addressing some fundamental
questions: "What is the first step of recovery? Who can bring us
transformation? Who can we trust? Do we trust tarot cards, our
past lives, other earthly gurus, spirit guides, power of the mind,
and the unsubstantiated Jesus of the New Age?" Colin could see
where we were going. We said that the first step to recovery is
trusting Jesus: the one who said he was God and proved it by his
resurrection from the dead; the one who offered more than words
for salvation in that he gave his own life for us; the one who
invites us to embrace the free gift of divine grace—the pure bliss
of forgiveness from sin and guilt; the one who has given us the
greatest ideal for living—servanthood; the one who is unique in
comparison to all other religious leaders and gurus, still reaching
into the here and now and touching our lives through the Spirit.

We referred to Scott Peck, who says that, in his pilgrimage, he
has been thunderstruck by the one he found in the gospels. To his
amazement, he discovered a real person, not an embellished,
"mellow yellow" figure of spiritual fancies. Peck was so surprised
that he fell in love with Jesus.

We said to Colin that it takes courage to face who we really
are and grapple with the darkness inside. When we truly accept
our need for divine forgiveness, God welcomes us. In that
moment of self-abandonment, we begin to experience the power
of God's love. That love fills us up because the risen Jesus has the

power to forgive, renew, and transform so we can love God and love others—to truly forgive and be forgiven.

Our dialogue together moved us all. Colin acknowledged that the reconstructed stories about Jesus' many travels left him with many questions. We shook hands as new friends, learning together on the journey of life. He said that he was going home to read the gospel stories—to let Jesus speak for himself. He was on the threshold of genuine Christ-consciousness.

Endnotes

Chapter 11

1 Janet Bock, *The Jesus Mystery*, Los Angeles: Aura, 1980, p. 5.

2 A.K. Tebecis, *Mahikari: Thank God for the Answers at Last*, Tokyo: Yoko Shuppansha, 1982, p. 358.

3 See Levi Dowling, *The Aquarian Gospel of Jesus the Christ*, London: Fowler, 1964; and C.C. Dobson, *Did Our Lord Visit Britain as They Say in Cornwall and Somerset?* London: Covenant Publishing, 1974.

4 "Life of St Issa, 5:1-2" in Nicolas Notovitch, *The Unknown Life of Jesus Christ*, reprinted edition, Joshua Tree, California: Tree of Life, 1980, p. 34.

5 Edgar J. Goodspeed, *Modern Apocrypha*, Boston: Beacon, 1956, pp. 18-19; and Arild Romarheim, *The Aquarian Christ: Jesus Christ as Portrayed by New Religious Movements*, Hong Kong: Glad Tiding, 1992, p. 28.

6 Elizabeth Clare Prophet, *The Lost Years of Jesus*, Malibu: Summit University Press, 1984, pp. 46-47; and Per Beskow, *Strange Tales About Jesus*, Philadelphia: Fortress, 1983, pp. 62-63.

7 Elizabeth Clare Prophet, *The Lost Years of Jesus*, photo facing p. 313.

8 "The Alleged Sojourn of Christ in India," *The Nineteenth Century*, October 1894, pp. 512-521.

9 Elizabeth Clare Prophet, *The Lost Years of Jesus*, p. 101. Prophet has reprinted Violet Crispe's 1895 translation of Notovitch's book, pp. 82-221.

10 J. Archibald Douglas, "The Chief Lama of Himis on the Alleged 'Unknown Life of Christ,'" *The Nineteenth Century*, April 1896, pp. 671-672, 677.

11 Christmas Humphreys, *Buddhism*, Harmondsworth: Penguin, 1962, pp. 190-191.

12 See the chief lama of Himis remarks in *The Nineteenth Century*, April 1896, p. 672; and John Powers, *Introduction to Tibetan Buddhism*, Ithaca: Snow Lion, 1995, pp. 128-129, 134.

13 A.L. Basham, *The Wonder That Was India*, New Delhi: Rupa, 1981, p. 292.

14 Elizabeth Clare Prophet, *The Lost Years of Jesus*, pp. 16, 94.

15 Arild Romarheim, *The Aquarian Christ*, p. 29.

16 See The Dalai Lama, *The Good Heart*, London: Rider, 1996; and Elizabeth Clare Prophet, *The Lost Years of Jesus*, pp. 183, 185-186.

17 Paramahansa Yogananda, *Man's Eternal Quest*, Los Angeles: Self Realization Fellowship, 1975, p. 306; Sathya Sai Baba, *An Eastern View of Jesus Christ*, London: Sai Publications, 1982; and Levi Geir Eidhamar, "Rajneesh's Understanding of Jesus," *Update*, 9, 2, 1985, pp. 21-28.

18 A. Faber-Kaiser, *Jesus Died in Kashmir*, London: Abacus, 1978.

19 Per Beskow, *Strange Tales About Jesus*, pp. 63-64.

20 On the Gospel of Barnabas, see Per Beskow, *Strange Tales About Jesus*, pp.11-15; James Cannon, "The Gospel of Barnabas," *The Moslem World*, 32, 1942, pp.167-178; and Lonsdale Ragg, "The Mohammedan 'Gospel of Barnabas,'" *Journal of Theological Studies*, 6 23, 1905, pp. 424-433.

21 Paul Pappas, *Jesus' Tomb in India*, Berkeley: Asian Humanities Press, 1991, p. 154.

22 Enakshi Bhavnani, "A Journey to 'Little Tibet,'" *National Geographic*, 99, 1951, p. 624.

23 Jeffrey Furst (ed.), *Edgar Cayce's Story of Jesus*, London: Neville Spearman, 1968, p. 172.

24 Rudolf Steiner, *From Jesus to Christ*, London: Rudolf Steiner Press, 1973, p. 74.

25 Anne Meurois-Givaudan and Daniel Meurois-Givaudan, *The Way of the Essenes: Christ's hidden life remembered*, Rochester: Destiny, 1993, pp. vii-ix.

26 A.K. Tebecis, *Mahikari: Thank God for the Answers at Last*, Tokyo: Yoko Shuppansha, 1982, pp. 355-361. Curiously this section has been deleted from later editions of Tebecis's book.

27 Winston Davis, Dojo: *Magic and Exorcism in Modern Japan*, Stanford: Stanford University Press, 1980 pp. 83-84; and Gary R. Habermas, *Ancient Evidence for the Life of Jesus*, Nashville: Thomas Nelson, 1984, pp. 75-76.

28 Michael Baigent, Richard Leigh and Henry Lincoln, *The Holy Blood and the Holy Grail*, London: Jonathan Cape, 1982; and *The Messianic Legacy*, London: Jonathan Cape, 1986.

29 Laurence Gardner, *Bloodline of the Holy Grail: The Hidden Lineage of Jesus Revealed*, Dorset: Element, 1996.

30 Ross Clifford, *Leading Lawyers' Case for the Resurrection*, Edmonton: Canadian Institute for Law, Theology & Public Policy, 1996, pp. 101ff.

31 Holger Kersten, *Jesus Lived in India: His Unknown Life Before and After the Crucifixion*, Dorset: Element, 1986; Holger Kersten and Elmar R. Gruber, *The Jesus Conspiracy: The Turin Shroud and the Truth about the Resurrection*, Dorset: Element, 1994; and Elmar R. Gruber and Holger Kersten, *The Original Jesus: The Buddhist Sources of Christianity*, Dorset: Element, 1995.

32 Donald S. Lopez and Steven C. Rockefeller (eds), *The Christ and the Bodhisattva*, Albany: State University of New York Press, 1987, p. 258; and Irving Alan Sparks, "Buddha and Christ: a Functional Analysis," *Numen*, 13, 1966, pp. 190-204.

33 Barbara Thiering, *Jesus the Man*, Sydney: Doubleday, 1992; *Jesus of the Apocalypse*, Sydney: Doubleday, 1995; and *The Book That Jesus Wrote*, Sydney: Doubleday, 1998.

34 Edward M. Cook, *Solving the Mysteries of the Dead Sea Scrolls*, Grand Rapids: Zondervan, 1994, pp. 143-145; and N.T. Wright, *Who Was Jesus?*, London: SPCK, 1992, pp. 19-36.

35 *The Gospel of Thomas*, saying 114, from James M. Robinson (ed.), *The Nag Hammadi Library*, revised edition, San Francisco: HarperCollins San Francisco, 1988, p. 138.

36 On the Gnostic writings, see F.F. Bruce, *Jesus and Christian Origins Outside the New Testament*, Grand Rapids: Wm.B. Eerdmans, 1974, pp. 110-156; Craig A. Evans, *Non-canonical Writings and New Testament Interpretation*, Peabody: Hendrickson, 1992, pp. 162-168; and Edwin Yamauchi, *Pre-Christian Gnosticism*, 2nd edition, Grand Rapids: Baker, 1983.

37 Edmund Bordeaux Szekely, *The Essene Gospel of Peace*, volume 1, Cartago, Costa Rica: International Biogenic Society, 1978, pp. 22-23.

38 Per Beskow, *Strange Tales About Jesus*, Philadelphia: Fortress, 1983, pp. 82-91.

39 Timothy Freke and Peter Gandy, *The Jesus Mysteries*, London: Thorsons, 1999.

[40] Ronald Nash, *Christianity and the Hellenistic World*, Grand Rapids: Zondervan, 1984, pp. 170-173.

[41] Leon McKenzie, *Pagan Resurrection Myths and the Resurrection of Jesus*, Charlottesville: Bookwrights, 1997.

[42] Timothy Freke and Peter Gandy, *The Jesus Mysteries*, pp. 65-66.

[43] Edwin Yamauchi, *Persia and the Bible*, Grand Rapids: Baker, 1990, p. 513.

[44] Morton Smith, *Clement of Alexandria and a Secret Gospel of Mark*, Cambridge, Massachusetts: Harvard University Press, 1973; *The Secret Gospel*, New York: Harper & Row, 1973; and *Jesus the Magician*, San Francisco: Harper & Row, 1978.

[45] Edwin M. Yamauchi, "A Secret Gospel of Jesus as 'Magnus'? A review of the recent works of Morton Smith," *Christian Scholars Review*, 4, 3, 1975, pp. 238-251; and "Magic or Miracle? Diseases, Demons, and Exorcisms" in David Wenham and Craig Blomberg (eds), *Gospel Perspectives*, volume 6, Sheffield: JSOT Press, 1986, pp. 89-183. See also F.F. Bruce, *The "Secret" Gospel of Mark*, London: Athlone Press, 1974.

[46] Richard T. France, *The Evidence for Jesus*, London: Hodder, 1985, p. 14.

[47] See Gary Habermas, *Ancient Evidence for the Life of Jesus*, Nashville: Thomas Nelson, 1984, pp. 87-118.

[48] Sermon 53 in Meister Eckhart, *Treatises and Sermons*, with notes by J.M. Clark and J.V. Skinner, London: Faber, 1958.

[49] M. Scott Peck, *Further Along the Road Less Traveled*, New York: Simon & Schuster, 1993, p. 157.

[50] *A Course in Miracles*, text, London: Arkana, 1985, p. 88.

[51] *A Course in Miracles*, workbook, London: Arkana, 1985, p. 172.

[52] M. Scott Peck, *Further Along the Road Less Traveled*, p. 202.

[53] See our remarks in chapters 6 and 8 respectively.

[54] Michael Graham, as interviewed by Tal Brooke, "A High-level Insider Converts," *SCP Journal*, 23, 2-3, 1999, pp. 11, 12.

Chapter 12
Living Meditation

◆

All I really need to know about how to live and what to do and how to be, I learned in kindergarten. Wisdom was not at the top of the graduate-school mountain, but there in the sandpile at Sunday school. These are the things I learned: Share everything. Play fair. Don't hit people. Put things back where you found them. Clean up your own mess. Don't take things that aren't yours. Say you're sorry when you hurt somebody. Wash your hands before you eat. Flush.[1]

I am convinced that, by their nature, children live in Dreamtime. Most parents are given children as their spiritual directors.[2]

Anyone who will not receive the kingdom of God like a little child will never enter it (Luke 18:17, NIV).

◆

Over the years, we have participated in a variety of New Age exhibitions and shared with many pilgrims. It is, without a doubt, one of the most challenging and spiritually invigorating experiences a Christian could have. Time after time we have been in dialogue with earnest seekers who have honored us by sharing out of the depths of their souls what has been most precious to them. We have been challenged to honestly consider their questions and examine their tools for attaining transformation. We have assessed those tools in our previous chapters.

Postmodern seekers are people of the heart rather than the head. They are not immediately concerned with dogma and theory, but rather want a living encounter with God. They love to participate in practical exercises that will release them from their burdens, uplift their spirits, and connect their souls with God. When we encounter seekers, we invite them to explore our tools for transformation and try some of the spiritual exercises we have found most beneficial. Each exercise can be a catalyst for an earnest seeker who desires the everlasting healing Jesus Christ brings. What follows are the tools and exercises we use to enable seekers to make that marvelous discovery.

Tools and exercises to attain transformation

GRACE

We affirm that the discipline of divine grace to forgive and renew is vital. The Sacred Writings are threaded together with a powerful, unifying theme: grace. Divine grace is an undeserved merit or favor bestowed by God on those who are grateful to receive it. The scriptures center on the person of Jesus. They declare that Jesus' death on the cross has rescued us from evil, brought us forgiveness, and relieved us of guilt. The resurrection of Jesus is the assurance that this is so. Jesus died on the cross for our sin, in our place. By so doing, Jesus liberates us from the penalty of sin—death and separation from God. As a result, we are released from sin, and that brings an inner peace, which flows into our relationships. This is genuine reconciliation, a positive change in the relationship between God, human beings, and each other. Every day we find freedom. It is not transient but everlasting. The old hymn captures the wonder of it: "O happy day, O happy day, when Jesus washed my sins away!"

Acceptance of this gift has challenging lifestyle consequences, but the fact that it is grace means that it is God who changes your life's script.

A helpful starting point is to read this passage of scripture: "For it is by grace you have been saved, through faith—and this not from yourselves, it is the gift of God" (Eph. 2:8, NIV).

Now ask yourself, "Am I willing to acknowledge I cannot renew my spirit?" Are you open to having your spirit renewed? If you have answered "yes" to both questions, then you can receive the gift of grace by praying:

Creator God, I accept that you alone can make my spirit live forever. I acknowledge that in my brokenness and guilt I am helpless. I want to trust you and your ways. I am open to your love and mercy. I thank you for the love you have shown me through Jesus. Renew me now and flood me with your grace. Amen

PRAYER

We affirm that the discipline of prayer is greatly beneficial. Prayer is our way of talking to God. We live in an era characterized by technology and the diminution of God's power. The real need of our day is to encounter the living God, and this is achieved supremely in prayer. Sometimes it's a struggle. Spanish mystic Teresa of Avila understood this. She spoke of the four degrees of prayer. She likened them to various ways in which a garden is irrigated. The first way, drawing water out of a well, is a hard slog, where we appear to be relying on our own capacity. The last is rain, where one is overwhelmed by the showers of divine energies.

Prayer that touches us like rain is often enhanced by our postures. The Sacred Writings mention these:

- *kneeling*—a sign of homage, emptiness, and earnestness
- *hand movements*—raised hands, spread-eagled hands, palms turned upwards were signs of worship and that one was not closed to the divine blessing
- *eyes raised and open*—a sign that one was focused on the celestial realm and the strength and power therein

- *body work*—a sign of one's emotional status through drama, such as the beating of breast

Passages that can help us learn more about our own prayer postures are Ephesians 3:14, Philippians 2:10, Luke 5:8, Luke 22:41-42, Acts 7:60, Acts 9:40, 1 Timothy 2:8, Psalm 28:2, John 17:1, Daniel 6:10 and Luke 18:11-13.

Prayer is open to everyone and can be enacted in families, groups, or alone. The legendary Robinson Crusoe, shipwrecked on a desert island and physically alone, cried out for the first time in prayer. He found joy, inner peace, forgiveness, and comfort in his trials and burdens. Crusoe learned no one need be an island—even when on one!

Here is a brief practical exercise in prayer. To set the appropriate atmosphere, put on some instrumental classical music—it could be a Bach sonata or one of Liszt's Hungarian rhapsodies. As the music plays, be seated and close your eyes. Let the music filter out all background noises and distractions. As your body and mind relax, be aware that God's Spirit is in the room. Be willing to open your heart to the presence of God's Spirit. As the music concludes, open your eyes and begin to talk to God in prayer.

An Example for Meditative Prayer

In this prayer, pause briefly between each stage as the text indicates. Feel free to recite these words silently or audibly, whatever you feel most comfortable doing. Remember, what matters most is your attitude towards God.

Stage 1: Emptiness before God
Fill me with the deep wisdom.
Fill me with the great compassion.
Fill me with the serene peace. (Pause).

Stage 2: Peace with God
Let forgiveness flow.
Let love come forth.
Let energy return. (Pause).

Stage 3: Harmony with creation
  Deep peace of the quiet earth.
  Deep peace of the flowing air.
  Deep peace of the Son of peace. (Pause)
Stage 4: Belonging to God
  Eternal Creator keep me.
  Beloved companion, Jesus, hold me.
  Gentle Spirit smile on me. Amen[3]

FASTING

We affirm that the discipline of fasting can be helpful. Jesus at times fasted in order to attune himself spiritually. Fasting is good for our health—our digestive system has a break—and it enhances our opportunity for spiritual growth. It gets us in touch with our own bodies. Lynda Rose offers this practical advice:

Positively, a fast can purify the system and so make us more spiritually receptive. Not all fasts, however, need necessarily involve renunciation of food. Some fasts, for example, might involve restriction on the amount of time spent in talking to people. I once decided that for 24 hours I would restrict what I said to only what was absolutely necessary. A word of warning here, however! Do tell people if you are going to do this, because otherwise they might assume that you are being rude.[4]

READING THE SACRED WRITINGS

We affirm that the discipline of reflecting on the Sacred Writings is crucial to spirituality. Mysticism has rightly perceived that a full knowledge of God is beyond our intuition. We have discovered that this cloud of unknowing is pierced by spending time in contemplation of the scriptures. This discipline also leads us to an understanding of our own condition, knowledge of Jesus, detoxification of our inner spiritual impurities, and the presence of the Spirit residing in our hearts.

An Example for Reading the Sacred Writings

Relying on the perceptions of Ignatius of Loyola, for example, we recommend the following exercise when reading the Sacred Writings. It will bring wholeness, harmony, balance and dignity:

- Find a quiet place where you can relax. Do not fold your legs; unfold your arms. Play some therapeutic music, such as Antonio Vivaldi's "The Four Seasons."
- Choose a passage of scripture that speaks to you. For example, the story of the women who encounter healing:

  A ruler came and knelt before him [Jesus] and said, "My daughter has just died. But come and put your hand on her, and she will live." Jesus got up and went with him, and so did his disciples.

  Just then a woman who had been subject to bleeding for twelve years came up behind him and touched the edge of his cloak. She said to herself, "If I only touch his cloak, I will be healed."

  Jesus turned and saw her. "Take heart, daughter," he said, "your faith has healed you." And the woman was healed from that moment.

  When Jesus entered the ruler's house and saw the flute players and the noisy crowd, he said, "Go away. The girl is not dead, but asleep." But they laughed at him. After the crowd had been put outside, he went in and took the girl by the hand, and she got up (Matt. 9:18-25, NIV).

  Other suitable passages could include any gospel miracle stories, the book of Ruth, or a Psalm.
- Imagine becoming part of the scene by hearing the crowd, smelling the surroundings, and seeing the characters.
- Imagine becoming one of the characters (apart from Jesus) and live out their journey. As you do so, be in touch with how this touches your own emotions, hurts, and joys.
- Imagine letting Jesus touch the character—touch you.

The power of scripture to bring us to an awareness of the divine and uphold us is seen in the film *The Elephant Man*. The film portrays a hideously grotesque and deformed being wearing a bag over his head. One day as he is walking, some hoodlums pull the bag off. He begins to run and people chase him, laughing and spitting. More join the frenzied crowd. He runs into a toilet stall and finds himself lying in the urinal. He cries out: "I am not an animal; I am a human being!" The crowd falls silent and slinks away as they hear the Elephant Man's heartfelt cry of dignity.

Where did he find such understanding? Every night before he went to bed he used to say the Psalm 23, "The Lord is my shepherd . . . I will fear no evil, for you are with me." This man knew from his reflections on the Sacred Writings that the Lord of the cosmos accepted him. There our self-esteem is renewed, too.

MEDITATION

We affirm that the discipline of meditation is very beneficial. Meditation is an ancient way of entering into a deep spiritual awareness of God. It is a pathway to rest, peace, and the handling of stress, as well as to the energies of God—those times when we intimately experience God's presence. Modern society is out of harmony with the environment. Our urban jungle lifestyles disconnect us from the beauty of the natural world. As the Psalmist observed, there is great pleasure to be found in our enjoyment of nature (Ps. 104:1-30). Meditation is an excellent tool that, if done outdoors, brings us an appreciation of our natural surroundings.

An Example for Meditation

Lynda Rose has developed the following approach to achieving rewarding meditation:

• Prepare yourself by finding a quiet spot and identifying your purpose for meditation.

- Choose one or more of the following God-given aids as your focus. This can be a passage of scripture, a word, such as "peace" or "Jesus" (Some of have recommended all-embracing one-syllable words such as "God," "love," "sin"), the Eastern Jesus Prayer ("Lord Jesus Christ, Son of God, have mercy on me"), silence (that is, being still to allow God to talk to you—he leads the soul to pray), creation (seeing the handiwork of the supreme artist).
- Conclude your exercise. "The ending of meditation should be the same. It should be relaxed and end with a brief prayer of thanks and dedication, and the eyes should only then be opened, slowly."[5]
- Be prepared to face distractions, such as pain, headaches, and even falling asleep. Acknowledge them, don't be deterred, gently refocus your attention on your exercise, and the more experienced you become, the less these things will occur.

Here is a "creation meditation" designed to connect you with the Creator and creation. For this exercise you will need a portable player and a copy of instrumental music.

- Go to your favorite place outdoors—this may be a beach, park, or your own garden. Sit or lie down, turn on the music, and sit quietly, with your eyes closed. Let the music relax your mind.
- Once the track has finished, stop the player, sit quietly and listen to the sounds of nature—the breeze in the trees, the waves by the beach, bird and animal sounds.
- Recite these words of creation affirmation:

  For earth, sea, and sky in the harmony of color—I give thanks.
  For nature resplendent, companion pets, singing birds, and whales, verdant fields, and the energies of the world—I give thanks.
  For the person of Christ you sent to restore us when we fell away from you—I give thanks.
  For harmony restored through his Spirit moving on the turbulence of my life—I give thanks.
  For the honor you give me of life flowing in the rhythm of your tides—I give thanks.
  For setting me, like the stars upon their courses, within the orbit of your love—I give thanks.[6]

CENTERING

We affirm that the discipline of centering can help a great
deal. Throughout the ages, those with spiritual insight have
affirmed the importance of centering life on a true master. It is
the technique of detaching yourself from insignificant pursuits.
Jesus stands before us as we see his humanity, divinity, purity,
kindness, servanthood, love, grace, death, resurrection, and coming. As we concentrate on him, we are motivated to lead the
authentic path of the fully conscious and wholly integrated person. It is also as we center our focus on Jesus that we receive the
revelation that the coming "New Age" is dependent upon his
breaking into the lives of us all. Calvin Miller draws us into the
realm of a focus on Christ:

Fellowship with Christ is a table only for two—set in the wilder-
ness. Inwardness is not a gaudy party, but the meeting of lovers in
the lonely desert of the human heart. There, where all life and fel-
lowship can hold no more than two, we sit together and he speaks
as much as we, and even when both of us say nothing there is our
welded oneness. And suddenly we see we cannot be complete until
his perfect presence joins with ours.[7]

SPIRITUAL BREATHING

We affirm that the discipline of spiritual breathing is very
energizing. When our lives are fixed on Jesus, the Spirit joins
with us and fully immerses us in God. To reach the state of inner
calm, it can be helpful to breathe out our worries and ask the
Holy Spirit to fill us completely. This is when our leaden ways
are turned to gold (see Gal. 5:16-23).

IMAGINATION

We affirm that the discipline of imagination has a very important role to play. Dreaming is a tool that helps us contemplate

our future and envisage growth and improvement. It is best done by quietly assessing our gifts, talents, and desires, and recording in a journal where these could feasibly take us. As the writer of Proverbs said, "Where there is no vision, the people get out of hand" (Prov. 29:18, JERUSALEM). Imagination helps us set goals for life. Cliff Jones writes:

◆

In the area of personal achievement, imagination frees us from breaking one of the Ten Commandments, "Thou shalt not covet." The temptation is to desire our neighbor's achievement rather than achieving ourselves. We can be fatally eaten up in the selfish pursuit of obtaining what belongs to another. The doorway to growth is to be found by releasing ourselves from this desire and by applying our own gifts and abilities to accomplish something uniquely ours.[8]

◆

WORSHIP

We affirm that the discipline of worship is very important. Worship involves the aspects of rest, music, interconnecting, praise, and everyday life. All are involved with worship, be it self-worship or divine worship. Rest is an intrinsic part of divine worship. It is captured in the symbol of the sabbath.

We suggest that rest is best exercised by taking time each week to be inactive, sharing your time with Jesus, family, and friends. It brings physical release and calm to the body, mind, and spirit. Jesus, in the story of Mary and Martha, saw it as a therapeutic priority from which all else could flow.

Martha, as a socially conscious Jew, was busy preparing the meal, while Mary sat at the Master's feet. To Martha's critique of Mary's conduct, Jesus responded, "Mary has chosen what is better, and it will not be taken away from her" (Luke 10:38-42, NIV).

Brother Jeremiah is earthy in his appreciation of rest:

*If I had my life over, I would start barefooted earlier in the spring
and stay that way later in the fall. I would play more. I would ride
on more merry-go-rounds. I'd pick more daisies.*[9]

Worship is not purely an isolated thing, and it finds its best
expression in a community. It is also about what we offer to the
world, God, and each other in our everyday lives.

TOGETHERNESS

We affirm that the discipline of human togetherness is very
therapeutic. A major tool for recovery is community. In our era of
mobilization, the tendency is to live alone, even though surrounded by a maze of other housing. Jesus called us to form a
new community where there is support, encouragement, and a
sense of belonging. Regrettably, within our communities there is
today a superficial spirit. They have caught the modern malaise of
distancing in relationships and a lack of deep, honest communication. This shallowness is not confined to churches and finds a
place in families, community groups, and clubs.

We believe that, increasingly, more males in particular have
had enough of this:

*Men have discovered a new kind of pain—loneliness and longing.
For the first time, they are starting to hear from the boys inside
themselves who were imprisoned in suits of armor centuries ago
and told to be men. They can no longer block out the need for intimacy, friendship, tenderness, and creativity—those things dealing
with "being" rather than "doing." Having allowed the inner need
to reach the surface, it is demanding to be heard.*[10]

Psychodrama

One effective way of allowing our communities to be strengthened is a form of psychodrama. We suggest that the members gather and take time to relax. Oneness is then created by dividing into pairs and taking ten minutes to look into each other's eyes without comment. This closeness will draw us to ask meaningful questions of ourselves, such as "Why, as a male, do I find it difficult to share in this closeness?" and "How long is it since I have just been in the presence of my children?"

After this period of emotional intimacy, those involved can take time to form a human sculpture of how they felt—to choose someone to play their part and indicate what stance they should take to represent themselves. For example, they can have palms open, indicating they want to be accepted, or back turned, showing a fear of closeness. Then, other members in the group can be placed around the central "player," representing how the "director" believes his family and friends relate to him. Into this drama, Jesus can be asked to come to take our fears, heal and create what we truly desire.

SERVANTHOOD

We affirm that the discipline of servanthood is a key tool. As we have discussed, transformation is like a river that flows from our personal self to flood our global village with healing and recovery. The catalyst for this is the tool of servanthood. Its dimension is the breaking down of the racial, social, and sexual barriers that bind people to poverty in body, mind, and spirit. It loathes starvation, deprivation, political oppression, and ecological abuse.

The discipline of servanthood begins in a surrender of the self to Jesus, who was the ultimate servant. Then, we can move on to concentrate again on him, not in the sense of personal growth but for cosmic transformation. Jesus embraced the call of servanthood in the words, "Greater love has no one than this, that he lay down his life for his friends" (John 15:13, NIV).

Prayer of a Servant

The essence of the personalized servanthood path is in the prayer of Francis of Assisi:

> Lord, make me an instrument of your peace.
>   Where there is hatred, let me sow love,
> Where there is injury, pardon,
>   Where there is doubt, faith,
> Where there is despair, hope,
>   Where there is darkness, light,
> Where there is sadness, joy.
>   O divine master, grant that I may not so much seek
>   To be consoled as to console,
> Not so much seek to be understood as to understand,
>   Not so much seek to be loved, as to love;
> For it is in giving that we receive,
>   It is in pardoning that we are pardoned,
> It is in dying that we awake to eternal life.

As the festival concludes

One of the most memorable and poignant experiences we have ever had was in an instructive little drama that unfolded on the edge of our exhibitor's stand. Diagonally across from our stand was the public stage. Every half-hour, there was a performance by either a presenter or an exhibitor. A crowd of several hundred had gathered for the day's final performance. Suzy, the coordinator of a stand devoted to Kahuna—a form of Polynesian massage—was at the microphone. She and three female assistants were attired in Polynesian costumes. Suzy narrated the physical, emotional, and spiritual benefits of this technique while her assistants massaged a male volunteer.

As the demonstration ended, Suzy's assistants came to the microphone. The audience was rapt as each one told her own story. They had all been in deep emotional and spiritual distress, but when they met Suzy and followed her teachings on Polynesian massage they were radically changed. Now they were happy and contented. They had found healing and purpose in life through massage. Polynesian massage was a life-changing thing. This was just like testimony time in a revival meeting!

After the last woman spoke, there was a spontaneous standing ovation from the crowd. Their applause and acclaim affirmed these women. Although Polynesian massage might not "work" for all those applauding, the crowd was enthusiastic that at least it was working out for these women.

Once the applause ended and the crowd began to disperse, Ross felt a sudden tug on his trousers. He looked down to see a very small boy who said, "Mister, I'm lost." We escorted the young lad to the information desk where he was soon reunited with his mother. As we made our way back to the stand we were struck by the curious synergy of events.

Here we were amidst 60,000 people who had paid their entry fees for this spiritual supermarket, looking for healing and spiritual succor. We had just witnessed the testimonies of three young women giving thanks for the transforming power of Polynesian massage. There were so many seekers reaching out for spiritual renewal, with some settling on massage as the answer. The child's plight, "I'm lost," and his need of a guide is surely the heart-cry of everyone who attends such a festival.

We felt burdened to weep for these lost ones. It is why we come to these festivals. We have something far better to offer. This is our God-given opportunity to be among postmodern seekers and speak, sow, and reap for the kingdom of heaven. Come and join us in declaring the good news and making disciples.

Endnotes

Chapter 12

1 Robert Fulghum, *All I Really Need to Know I Learned in Kindergarten*, London: Grafton/Collins, 1989, p. 6.
2 Matthew Fox, "Creation Spirituality and the Dreamtime" in Catherine Hammond (ed.), *Creation Spirituality and the Dreamtime*, Sydney: Millennium, 1991, p. 4.
3 Adapted from Ray Simpson, *Celtic Worship Through the Year*, London: Hodder & Stoughton, 1997, p. 34.
4 Lynda Rose, *No Other Gods*, London: Hodder, 1990, pp. 138-139.
5 Lynda Rose, *No Other Gods*, p. 155.
6 Adapted from Ray Simpson, *Celtic Worship Through the Year*, p. 30.
7 Calvin Miller, *The Table of Inwardness*, Downers Grove: InterVarsity Press, 1984, p. 22.
8 Cliff Jones, *Winning Through Integrity*, Nashville: Abingdon, 1991.
9 Brother Jeremiah in Ted Engstrom, *The Pursuit of Excellence*, Grand Rapids: Zondervan, 1982, p. 90.
10 Terry Colling, *Beyond Mateship*, Sydney: Simon & Schuster, 1992, p. x

Chapter 13
Conclusion: Sharing in the Marketplace

In this book, we have traversed a wide range of ideas and practices embraced by today's postmodern spiritual seekers. We have recreated conversations we actually had with seekers to demonstrate their mindsets, and what issues and questions crop up. In this presentation of our dialogue with these people we have offered a practical model of how to present Jesus' gospel to today's seekers. Each discussion illustrates how you can direct conversations apologetically to the gospel.

Now it is one thing to contemplate all this and it is entirely another thing for us actually to go out and do it. In keeping with the intent of our book, we now want to present some of the practical steps that we have taken to reach seekers. By a process of trial and error, we have experimented with a variety of displays and techniques. We do not claim that the examples cited are a recipe or panacea for contemporary evangelism. What we outline are the things both our colleagues and we have found work the best. However, we stress that these are only examples and those who would like to do the same will need to consider their own cultural context before imitating us.

We also offer a sermon outline that we have found most effective in evangelistic programs. What we have set out need not be confined to an exhibition, but can also be adapted to other venues and settings. We further suggest that, in tandem with what we present here, you wrestle with John Drane's two challenging and provocative books *Faith in a Changing Culture* and *The McDonaldization of the Church*.[1]

One final point. In recent times, we have invited visitors to our stand to complete a brief survey form that preserves anonymity but allows them to indicate their age group, past religious affiliations, and current spiritual pursuits. We have found the results to be quite startling and yet indicative of the postmodern quest:

- 81 percent of visitors to our stand are women,
- 61 percent of visitors are aged between 20 and 40 years
- 22 percent of visitors are aged between 40 and 60 years
- 11 percent of visitors are aged between 16 and 19 years
- 58 percent of visitors have come to the exhibition for the first time
- 50 percent were formerly (or still are) Roman Catholics
- 19 percent were formerly Protestants
- 48 percent have explored New Age ideas
- 32 percent have explored Buddhism
- 95 percent have had a tarot reading

Two obvious issues arise from these figures. One is the high percentage of women looking for spiritual nurture beyond the church, as well as the substantial number of those who used to participate in the church. If ever there was an incentive for both women and youth to be mobilized for mission, New Age festivals offer a wonderful opportunity. It is certainly one area of mission where the laity can be encouraged to help out. We have found that one of the greatest results of our ministry at the festivals lies in the personal growth of the Christian who shares.

The other issue concerns theological education. We affirm the need for rigorous standards of academic excellence in theological education. However, we are persuaded that Bible colleges and seminaries must also take students beyond the classroom and into the postmodern world. We feel that a holistic education in theology must prepare students to minister in the outside world. If a candidate for the ministry does not have some practical experience in meeting non-Christian devotees of other worldviews, then how can that student lead a congregation into mission?

Irving Hexham is troubled by the Christian community's inability to discern cultural trends and to educate clergy vis-à-vis other faiths: "This failure to understand modern culture reflects the narrowness of contemporary theological education which, in general, leaves ordinands totally unprepared for meeting people of other faiths."[2]

One of the small steps we have taken to redress this problem in our respective colleges, which are Baptist and Presbyterian, is to invite our theological students to work on "The Community of Hope" stand. Those who are enrolled in courses on alternative spiritual movements or apologetics can participate in the festival as part of their course assessment. After the festival, they must submit a report on how they would design an incarnational stand for their local congregation to run in a similar exhibition. The student feedback has been uniformly positive.

Models for ministry at festivals

Now a ministry of this kind requires the same sort of meticulous planning and preparation that goes into a NASA rocket launch. We stress this at the outset to encourage you. Your enthusiasm for evangelism should be positively matched with sober reflection on what you are going to do. What follows are several illustrations of what we have done or what others we know have done when setting up stands at markets and festivals. We want to emphasize that these illustrations can be adapted to other settings, including church functions where both laity and clergy are flexible about doing things a bit differently.

Prayer chair

For several years, we have coordinated a healing prayer chair ministry. Our stand's signage indicates that we offer "free positive prayer," and it is remarkable the number of people who are open to being prayed for. With a two-seater sofa suitably positioned away from the loud, bustling crowds, visitors can sit down to talk privately about their physical, emotional, and spiritual needs. We indicate that we pray to God through Jesus, then anoint them with oil, making the sign of the cross on their forehead. With hands lightly placed on the person's head or shoulder (men must take note of the need for sensitivity here about what sort of touch is appropriate when interacting with female visitors), we offer jargon-free prayer that affirms the person, gives God thanks for his or her life, then petitions for whatever the need happens to be. This exercise can be very moving, as tears flow and the burdens lift.

FACE IN THE SNOW

As we noted in chapter 6, we set up a blown-up photo of the famous face in the snow picture. The picture is based on a photograph taken of some burnt coals in the snow that, when developed, appeared to contain the shape of a face that resembles church art portraits of Jesus' face. Above this was another sign: "Life is a puzzle. He can make sense of it." The sign was interactive, requiring visitors to see if they could "spot" the face. This was a highly successful way of attracting people, making them stop and look, with the opportunity of starting conversations.

PURE RAIN WATER

Busselton is a small town located in the southwestern corner of Western Australia. The Margaret River irrigates this idyllic area and rainstorms over the region sweep up from Antarctica. The chemical composition of the rainwater is such that it contains few traces of pollutants. Skywater Pty. Ltd. is a Christian-run business that bottles and sells the Margaret River Rain Water. Long before the product became widely available, we offered water-tasting samples at our stand. We decorated the stand with a sign: "Try the Margaret River Rain Water. Pure, natural, and free. Just like the water Jesus gives." We dispensed samples in small Communion cups. Seekers of course responded warmly to the appeal of trying pure water, which also allowed us, like Jesus with the Samaritan woman (John 4), to elevate the dialogue from physical to spiritual water.

GOSPEL THROUGH THE TAROT

In chapter 6, we detailed how tarot cards were not originally created or used for fortune telling, but, rather, were playing cards that sprang out of medieval and Renaissance Europe. The cards were only used for fortune telling when French occultists hijacked the cards for such purposes in the 19th century. We pointed out how the best-known deck of all—the Rider-Waite deck—has very explicit biblical and Christian pictures.

We set up tables where we use a fourteen-card layout in the shape of the cross and, using the cards' pictures, start with Adam and Eve, and conclude with the resurrection of Jesus. Our book *Beyond Prediction* sets out the background and theory, as well as explaining the Christian meaning of the entire deck. We also run post-festival workshops where we explore the tarot's symbolism and its connection with the gospels in more detail.

To anticipate criticisms about the tarot, let us make the following clear:

- We do not use the cards for fortune-telling purposes and make that clear with visitors to the stand.
- The cards are not evil, nor is the deck inhabited by demons, though, like anything in creation, they can be used for good or perverted purposes. If it is claimed the cards cannot be used because occultists also use them, then perhaps we should shred our Bibles because the Mormons and Jehovah's Witnesses use the Bible to teach false doctrine. Using the cards is an application of Paul's strategy in Athens.
- We do tell the whole story, from creation, the fall, death, the last judgment, grace, incarnation, crucifixion, resurrection, and the giving of the Holy Spirit, illustrating each point from the very symbols on the cards. We are restoring the forgotten meaning of the cards.

God's Use of Pagan Symbols

In scripture, the Lord God and his servants often used pagan symbols to communicate truth:

- God used dreams to reach both Pharaoh (Gen. 41) and Nebuchadnezzar (Dan. 2).
- In Egypt and Babylon, dreams were a normal part of pagan religious revelation, and God authorized his servants Joseph and Daniel to act as interpreters.
- God spoke to the pagan Abimelech in a dream (Gen. 20:3).
- God revealed things to Laban through divination (Gen. 30:27).
- God gave the pagan prophet Balaam a messianic prophecy (Num. 24:2, 15-19).
- The prophet Hosea used the imagery of the pagan fertility cults to speak to the children of Israel—indeed, God likens himself to a green pine tree (Hos. 14:8)
- God used a cosmic sign to draw the Magi astrologers to Jesus.
- Paul quoted the Greek philosophers (Acts 17:28).

CRYSTAL DISPLAY AND COLOR THERAPY

Harold Taylor and Wim Kruithof are our colleagues who coordinate The Community of Hope in the city of Melbourne. Under their direction, the core group of volunteers has been developing a variety of interactive displays. Peter Jolly, for example, has developed a crystal display. The sacred crystals and gemstones of the Sacred Writings are displayed, with explanatory cards setting out the spiritual and symbolic meaning of each stone.[3]

Sharon O'Neill of New Directions church in Launceston, Tasmania, inspired another display, known as color therapy. From her original concept, Harold and Wim's team has devised an attractive display. Several heart-shaped bottles filled with richly dyed water are arranged in rows. Visitors select whichever color appeals to them and the biblical meaning of the color is then unfolded. An explanatory tract setting out the spiritual significance of the colors is also distributed.

Harold is also involved in the healing ministry, the Order of St. Luke the Physician, and has written *Sent to Heal*.[4] Harold has taken his healing ministry to New Age exhibitions and also conducts workshops in this area for both seekers and Christians. He is on the cutting edge of developing an incarnational theology of healing that puts Christ in the midst of the complementary healers. His recent insights for a Christian approach to energy healing open up very fruitful possibilities for proclaiming the supremacy of Christ even here.

FOOT WASHING

A small group of mostly Salvation Army volunteers led by Lieutenant Cathy Hindle received training from us. They then designed their own stand called "Cleansing streams." At their stand, they washed the feet of visitors using essential oils. As they washed and massaged the visitors' feet, a time for talking and prayer unfolded. The symbolism of Jesus' servanthood, dramatized in the foot washing, combined with the oils is a very demonstrative way of inviting seekers to follow Christ. It is possible to develop such a stand focusing on aromatherapy, particularly as anointing with oil runs throughout scripture.

"THE PLAY OF LIFE" COUNSELING

Some Assemblies of God folk opened up a stand sponsored by one of their member's own professional counseling service. They created a good interactive stand involving visitors in a three-stage process of dealing with their mind, body, and spirit. This group used a patented method of counseling called "The Play of Life," devised by Argentinean Christian Carlos Raimundo.[5]

"The Play of Life" begins with a brief one-to-one chat about problems the visitor may be experiencing. The visitor is then invited to create on a small board a sculpture of how he or she feels using small plastic figures. After further dialogue, the visitor is encouraged to then create on another board a positive sculpture of how the visitor would prefer the situation to be. The boards constitute a "before" and "after" portrait, and a photograph of this is taken to mail to them subsequently. The person then moves over to a professional massage chair. During the massage, he or she is encouraged to quietly reflect on how God's Spirit could make a difference. After the massage, the person then moves to a third chair where a time of prayer occurs.

POINT OF REFERENCE BOOTH

A different model for booth ministry has been pioneered in Canadian New Age festivals. Gene Wilson, a graduate of Trinity Evangelical Divinity School in Illinois, has been active in church-planting strategies for the Evangelical Free Church in Montreal, Canada. In the 1990s Wilson helped to establish a booth ministry known as The Point of Reference: A Center for Christian Alternatives in Montreal. This venture has had volunteers from para-church groups such as Christian Direction, Operation Mobilization, and YWAM participate in booth outreach in Canadian New Age festivals. The approach taken by Wilson and his team has involved setting up a booth using a display centered on the theme "Christ—the Mystery of the Nations." Through the booth volunteers conduct client surveys about spiritual beliefs, and distribute leaflets and copies of John's gospel. The apologetic stance of this particular ministry appears to combine aspects of the heresy-rationalist model with spiritual warfare.[6]

CREATIVE ARTS IN MISSION

The creative arts go hand-in-glove with worship and mission. John and Olive Drane share a productive and successful ministry both inside the church and also with postmodern spiritual seekers in the United Kingdom and California. John is a lecturer in practical theology at Aberdeen University and is a visiting professor at

Fuller Theological Seminary. Olive holds a master's degree in theology and is one of Britain's leading clowns.

They co-present seminars on "the creative arts and the Bible" in which they set forth the relationship between theology and art and the role of the arts in worship. It is their thesis that worship and evangelism dovetail and so should not be considered mutually exclusive activities.[7] They explore the "craziness" of the Old Testament prophets, look at storytelling in Jesus' ministry, consider the place of humor in the Sacred Writings, and the place of clown ministries in early church history.

The Dranes have developed some powerful approaches using mime and clowning, liturgical dance, drama, and painting. For example, they have employed face painting to paint the cross on seekers into Druid spirituality with tremendous effect. John has used facemasks to graphically illustrate biblical stories, such as the way Abraham maltreats the women and children in his life. The masks have proved effective, particularly with an audience of women who have been abused. Even parachuting can be used as an experiential means of enabling people to take a leap of faith and begin the discipleship journey![8]

Olive has developed the clown persona Valentine as a response to her own painful experiences as a Christian. The clown opens people up and removes barriers and so can carry the message of the gospels in ways that a traditional preacher could not. She says, "Creative worship can speak powerfully to today's unchurched people; and at a time when few people care to listen to sermons, there are few who can resist the message of a Christian clown." Olive's clown ministry has been well received in the Presbyterian Church in Egypt, the Church of Scotland, and in theological institutions such as Fuller Seminary, Morling College, and Ridley College.

Another example comes with the band Rivertribe. Rivertribe composes and performs contemplative instrumental music in outdoor contexts. The aim is, via the music, to glorify God and build bridges with today's New Age seekers. The band includes both

Aboriginal and Anglo-Celtic members, who play a variety of unusual woodwind instruments, violins, metal, and wooden didgeridoos, drums and synthesizers. Rivertribe has performed in Southeast Asia and Australia. It was officially authorized to perform at various Olympic site venues during the Sydney 2000 games. The music picks up a lot of themes about God's creation, and the band has recorded two best-selling albums. The Irish group Iona, which plays music that is of the same genre as Enya, sings lyrics that speak powerfully to today's seekers.

WORKSHOPS

We have found that post-festival workshops that address the seekers' interests and are interactive bear much fruit. We have run workshops on angels and the spiritual meaning of the tarot. This has allowed us to continue contact with seekers we have met in festivals.

Genieve Blackwell is an evangelical Anglican priest who has shared her faith at our stand. She has presented a seminar entitled "A Woman's Spirituality: Hildegard of Bingen." Using color slides, Genieve's seminar is an illustrated commentary on Hildegard's visionary art, called the illuminations. It serves as a catalyst for exploring the gospels. Hildegard (1098-1179) was a very popular mystic, and her illuminations resonate with the rites of passage of many.

The Northside Community Church is in Sydney's northern suburbs. As a "Churches of Christ" congregation it is committed to evangelism, discipleship, and the personal growth of its parishioners. This congregation facilitates a lot of workshops designed to build bridges between Christians and seekers. It has run traditional courses, such as Alpha, but also experimented with programs on relationships, personality development (such as Myers-Briggs and enneagram), and divorce recovery.

Tom Glynn, an elder of the congregation, has for several years successfully coordinated an "Exploring the Road Less Traveled" course. The course uses a Christian study guide based on Scott

Peck's book and, over a twelve-week period, participants explore the concept of grace.[9] Tom has found that many seekers develop an interest in the gospels after completing this course.

TENTMAKERS AMONG THE NEO-PAGANS

Market ministries are event-specific activities, but what about maintaining a permanent presence among New Age seekers? Such ministries are being pioneered in various alternative lifestyle cultures. Warwick and Dianne Saxby, who are in the Assemblies of God, have a tentmaker ministry called Musterion (the Greek word for mystery). Their passion is to share the gospel with neo-pagans.

They started in the alternative culture at Nimbin, New South Wales, Australia. For just over two years, they built up solid and credible rapport with neo-pagans and mother goddess practitioners, but, due to their daughter's health, were compelled to relocate to another neo-pagan community situated in Katoomba, also in New South Wales.

Warwick and Dianne look and dress the part so as to fit in with the culture. Warwick derives income by carving jewelry from red wood and beef bone. He carves various sorts of Christian spiritual symbols and sells his handiwork from his studio as well as at local markets. As spiritual symbols are treasured in neo-pagan circles, Warwick has chosen an excellent way of incarnating his faith with them. Each carved item has a spiritual meaning, which Warwick explains to prospective customers. One of Warwick's prized items is a necklace of a man praying inside a large fish: this is the sign of Jonah, being a symbol of the death and resurrection of Christ.

Justin and Rebecca Whitecross are ministers in the Churches of Christ. They have established New Sight Community in the neo-pagan town of Byron Bay, New South Wales. The Whitecrosses' ministry, like that of the Saxby's, operates outside the typical denominational structures. They have established a small shop where they sell various products, such as aromatherapy oils, and they participate in local markets. Their shop is also a venue for small discussion groups and spiritual workshops.

Effective preaching in postmodernity

Preaching to a postmodern world represents a challenge, particularly when people are more accustomed to aural and visual stimuli than monologues and the printed word. Effective preaching has always been a communicative art, as preachers such as Billy Graham, Moody, Spurgeon, and Wesley attest. Whether today's preachers should opt for overhead slides, computer-aided presentations, or other visual aids is one issue we will not be tackling here. Should storytelling replace the sermon or not is, likewise, an issue we cannot discuss here.

Rather, we want to offer a sample sermon outline that we have found quite effective in outreach. If you go back to our chapters on angels and near-death experiences, you will find structured material that can be easily adapted into sermons.

SAMPLE SERMON: VALUES FOR LIVING ON LIFE'S ROLLERCOASTER

Here is a sermon outline that brings together the search for values and the power of the risen Christ.
• Text: 1 Corinthians 15:17-24.
• Introduction: Living life today is just like being on a roller coaster.
   We all relate to the stresses and pains of living.
   The past century was overloaded with tragedies and suffering.
• The paradigm shift
   We are living in the midst of a momentous shift in ideas as dramatic as the discoveries of Copernicus and Einstein.
   No longer satisfied with the "stories" of science, the shift is to the spiritual. The evidence of this is all around us—illustrate with TV (*Charmed*), movies (George Lucas's *Star Wars: The Phantom Menace*. In a *Time* magazine interview, Lucas said that the film is meant to stimulate us to reflect on the existence and search for God), books (*The Celestine Prophecy*), magazines (on astrology, tarot).

Why this search? People find life so difficult. It is a world where people feel very acutely a meaninglessness of life, as seen in drug abuse, suicide rates and so on.

• Jesus' values

The resurrection of Jesus shows that there is a personal God who is interested in the whole person. In 1 Corinthians 15, we discover that there is a connection between Jesus' pre-crucifixion body and his resurrection body. As Jesus is the first fruits, we too will be raised. Jesus gives us a holistic mind, body, spirit resurrection.

The resurrection of Jesus shows that, through the cross, there is genuine forgiveness. Why we need forgiveness—Scott Peck's conversion showed him that sin and guilt must be faced. (Refer to chapter 11 for Peck's remarks on sin.)

The resurrection of Jesus gives us hope for life, both now and forever. The promise is that we will be raised and spend eternity with him; he lives with us now. This impacts me as an individual, my family relationships and my career. People are into near-death experiences—the resurrection gives us certain hope about life beyond the tomb.

• The resurrection is God's seal on what Jesus taught.

Jesus calls us to the model of servanthood. It is servanthood not self-love that makes the difference in family life and community activity. It is this radical posture of love for those who hurt you the most that is powerful and transforming.

Jesus calls us to care for the powerless—illustration: every day 40,000 children die from starvation. In Luke 6, Jesus calls us to be on the side of the defenseless and poor.

• Conclusion

Invitation from Jesus is to follow. No matter what happens to me, God never abandons me. He is always there. The challenge is to face up to who I am and make the journey with Jesus. The resurrection shows that I can live in his strength and have real power to take the ride on life's roller coaster.

Endnotes

Chapter 13

1 John Drane, *Faith in a Changing Culture*, London: Marshall Pickering, 1997; and *The McDonaldization of the Church*, London: Darton, Longman & Todd, 2000.

2 Irving Hexham, "The Evangelical Response to the New Age" in James R. Lewis and J. Gordon Melton (eds), *Perspectives on the New Age*, Albany: State University of New York Press, 1992, p. 162.

3 Ruth V. Wright and Robert L. Chadbourne, *Crystals, Gems, and Minerals of the Bible*, New Canaan, Connecticut: Keats Publishing, 1988.

4 Harold Taylor, *Sent to Heal*, Ringwood, Victoria: The Order of St. Luke the Physician, 1993.

5 For more details, see the website at www.playoflife.com

6 For more details see Gene Wilson, "Reaching New Agers on their own turf" *Evangelical Missions Quarterly*, 31, 1995, pp. 174-180.

7 See John Drane, *Faith in a Changing Culture*, pp. 108-144.

8 Ronald Gagne, Thomas Kane, and Robert VerEecke, *Introducing Dance in Christian Worship*, Washington DC: Pastoral Press, 1984; Conrad Hyers, *And God Created Laughter*, Atlanta: John Knox Press, 1987; and Janet Litherland, *The Clown Ministry Handbook*, 4th edition, Colorado Springs: Meriwether Press, 1990.

9 Alice and Walden Howard, *Exploring the Road Less Travelled*, London: Arrow, 1996.

Appendix I
Dialoguing with Each Other

One of the enlightened people from the past we admire the most is Hugo Grotius (1583-1645). He was the 17th-century maverick, ambassador, philosopher, and founder of our modern international law. He awakened the world to this principle:

For my part, both here and elsewhere, I avail myself of the liberty of the early Christians, who had sworn allegiance to the sect of not one of the philosophers, not because they were in agreement with those who said that nothing can be known—nothing is more foolish—but because they thought that there was no philosophic sect whose vision had encompassed all truth, and none which had not perceived some aspect of truth.[1]

In this spirit, we desire to probe what forgotten truths the New Age and Christian devotees can learn from each other in dialogue.

Forgotten truths for New Age seekers

DIVERSITY
Diversity is a fact of life, and many New Age seekers celebrate the unity of human culture in its diversity. Some even portray their spirituality as a harmonious whole without the real conflict of ideas. While there is genuine warmth felt at New Age exhibitions that creates a sense of oneness, it is by no means the whole story. As you interact with other seekers, you quickly discover groups with contradictory approaches to life and differing

emphases, often competing with each other for disciples. One illustration of this "conflict" is found in reiki. There are several rival reiki grand masters, each claiming that they have received the true mantle of initiation from the founder Mikao Usui. This is an illustration of the need for New Age seekers to accept that, like the world, all is not one in spirit.

TOLERANCE

New Age and postmodern seekers often speak of Christians being intolerant of other paths due to their exclusive emphasis on Jesus Christ as the only way to God. The forgotten truth, though, is that, philosophically, tolerance doesn't demand acceptance of others' views; rather, its focus is on the right of people to hold them. It is summed up in this aphorism: "I may disagree with your view, but I'll defend your right to hold it." That's tolerance! It is intolerant to impose universalism on others.

TRUTH

On the whole, the New Age as a movement avoids the truth question. It simply claims that truth is found in all paths. Marianne Williamson decrees, "Religion is like a map. The route isn't important. It's the destination that matters."[2] The difficulty is that this in itself is an assertion that has not been proven. As well, we have identified that Jesus' teaching on life after death substantially differs from that of New Age practitioners. The New Age "plane" is not going to the same destination.

Another concern with this approach to religious endeavor is that it's disrespectful to the integrity of the basic claims of each major tradition. For example, for Muslims, Islam is the only true path to God and Muhammad was the final prophet. Orthodox Hindus regard Buddhists, Jains, and Sikhs as heterodox. Mortimer Adler, considered to be America's philosopher for the layperson, stated that the truth question in religion couldn't be avoided or trivialized. Adler has issued this clarion call:

◆

I would like to hear leading 20th-century theologians speaking as apologists for Judaism, Christianity and Islam [dare we add the New Age?] engage in a disputation. The question at issue would be which of these three religions has a greater claim to truth. It being conceded that each has a claim to some measure of truth, which of the three can rightly claim more truth than the other two?[3]

◆

Philosopher Francis Beckwith has this poetic, gentle rebuke:

◆

'All roads lead to God,'
  I've heard so many people say,
But when they get to Jonestown,
  They beg to look the other way.[4]

◆

The New Age still has to face Pilate's appeal to Jesus, "What is truth?"

Forgotten truths for Christians

ENJOYING GOD

One of the Christian catechisms states that our chief end is to glorify God and enjoy him forever. The New Age has perceived that the second part of the creed has been lost in parts of modern-day Christianity. Dry orthodoxy, dogma, and moribund rituals must never replace the joyful experience of the Spirit.

NINE-TO-FIVE SPIRITUALITY

Contemporary Christianity in some domains has lost the understanding of vocation. Ministry is seen as what is done for the church. The New Age, in contrast, has re-emphasized in many of its seminars the importance of people being encouraged and equipped for living in the workforce and at home. It seeks to make better salespersons, clerks, real estate agents, and so on.

The "Sunday" spirituality of contemporary Christendom is not part of its inheritance. The apostle Paul had a theology of everyday life where he talked about foods to eat, relationships, and the workforce, sexuality, and the world of nine-to-five. However, the path back to authentic spirituality is being addressed by contemporary theologians such as Robert Banks and must become part of the church's teaching ministry if New Age seekers are to find the Christian faith relevant.[5]

Another area of concern is that of guidance. Christians struggle in today's age to know the will of God. In contrast, clairvoyants and so on offer quick solutions. There is a real need for a practical theology of guidance. In chapter 11 we stressed how guidance can be found when we take up the tools of transformation.

CREATION-CENTERED SPIRITUALITY

Western Christianity has drifted into a humanized spirituality that is divorced from the rest of creation. It has compartmentalized faith by separating it from everything else. This is not good enough. Biblical justice is concerned about the liberation of all the creation—the trees, dolphins, and the refugee. The challenge is to hear again the words of Teilhard de Chardin, "Nothing here below is profane for those who know how to see. On the contrary, everything is sacred."[6]

THE "HUME" ATTACK

Christians tend to reduce the miraculous phenomena of other paths to natural explanations or fraudulent behavior. Have Christians forgotten that the 18th-century philosopher David Hume did the same to them? He suggested that, at all times, we should seek a natural explanation rather than accept the miracle stories of the Sacred Writings. The truth or otherwise of miraculous occurrences does not rest on our hostility towards a group. All miraculous phenomena need to be tested, not simply dismissed.

GROWING TOGETHER

We have encountered many seekers who, when they visit a church and identify themselves as New Age, have been immediately dismissed and rejected as evil or stupid. John Drane rightly suggests that the New Age is saying something to the church about its togetherness:

The church should be a place where we can be accepted as we are— children, women, and men together—a safe environment in which to discover more about ourselves, to experience personal growth, and to make a contribution to the growth of others. When so very few of our congregations even begin to approximate that ideal, need we be surprised that honest people look elsewhere?[7]

The church should continue to develop healing communities and strive against becoming cold, bureaucratic, and ecclesiastical ghettos. Let the Spirit of Christ reign.

DO NOT BEAR FALSE WITNESS

One sad fact is that, often when New Age seekers and Christians meet, misunderstandings arise and one another's views get misrepresented. We have already indicated in chapter 1 how Christian writers have sadly fallen into this trap. However, this problem is not unique to Christians. Some New Age writers have also fallen for this. Dick Sutphen, for example, tries to debunk Christian preachers using the discredited—yet popular—theory about religious conversions being a form of brainwashing.[8] In another way, Louise Hay makes careless remarks about Christian beliefs based on crude stereotypes:

I find it hard to believe that the vast, incredible Intelligence that created this entire Universe is only an old man sitting on a cloud above the Planet Earth . . . watching my genitals! Yet so many of us were taught this concept as a child . . . There are so many different religions to choose from. If you have one now that tells you you are a sinner and a lowly worm, get another one.[9]

Religious studies scholar Eric Sharpe draws our attention back to an important, foundational truth:

The best dialogue is one in which those old-fashioned virtues of courtesy and mutual respect are allowed to have the upper hand of what our culture seems to be best at: points-scoring and vilifying the opposition. I can think of no better way to conclude here than with a biblical word; the most frequently broken of the ten commandments is not the one about not committing adultery or stealing, but the one that follows it: "You shall not bear false witness against your neighbor." For the ultimate limitation on dialogue is that one must not bear false witness, either in your neighbor's hearing or more especially behind his or her back.[10]

How can New Age seekers hear about Jesus if Christians persist in bearing false witness about what they stand for? How can Christians feel welcome to enter into a dialogue if New Age writers also bear false witness by setting up and knocking down straw man views about the church?

It would be a narrow position that held that the church has nothing to learn from the New Age or the New Age from the teachings of Christ. Throughout these pages, we have suggested that Christians need to hear the plea for a workable spirituality and New Age seekers the cry of the uniqueness of Jesus Christ.

We leave you with these words from well-known writer James Sire. They are addressed to Christians, but human nature being what it is, they apply to all:

A siege mentality is at work. Those who hold cultic ideas are seen as the enemy, the great threat to humanity, to Christians—even, some seem to suggest, to God himself . . . So in response, anything goes: innuendo, name-calling, back-handed remarks, assumption of the worst motives on the part of cult believers. And thus the Christian dehumanizes the enemy and shoots him like a dog. But the Christian in this process is himself dehumanized.[11]

Endnotes

Appendix I

1 Hugo Grotius, *The Law of War and Peace*, Indianapolis: Bobbs-Merrill, 1925, Prolegomena, paragraph 42, p. 24.

2 Simon Sebag Montefiore, "Marianne Williamson: Who Is She and Why Do We Need Her Now?" *Psychology Today*, July–August 1992, p. 29.

3 Mortimer Adler, *Truth in Religion*, New York: Collier, 1990, pp. 109–110.

4 Francis Beckwith, *Baha'i*, Minneapolis: Bethany, 1985, p. 55.

5 Robert Banks and R. Paul Stevens (eds), *The Complete Book of Everyday Christianity: An A–Z Guide to Following Christ in Every Aspect of Life*, Downers Grove: InterVarsity Press, 1997.

6 Teilhard de Chardin, as cited in Leo F. Buscaglia, *Personhood: The Art of Being Fully Human*, Thorofare: C.B. Slack, 1978, p. 118.

7 John Drane, *What is the New Age Saying to the Church?*, London: Marshall Pickering, 1991, p. 237.

8 Dick Sutphen, *Radical Spirituality*, Malibu: Valley of the Sun, 1995, pp. 191–206. On brainwashing claims, see chapter 4, note 14.

9 Louise Hay, *You Can Heal Your Life*, Sydney: Specialist Publications, 1988, p. 136.

10 Eric Sharpe, "Faith at the Round Table," *Areopagus*, 7, 4, 1994, p. 34; and David Clark, *Dialogical Apologetics*, Grand Rapids: Baker, 1993.

11 James Sire, *Scripture Twisting*, Downers Grove: InterVarsity Press, p. 18.

Appendix II
Vicky's Story

One of the tremendous challenges Christians face in the 21st century is addressing those who have become disenchanted with the church. In our experiences we have encountered at least three kinds of disenchanted individuals. First, there are those genuine believers in Christ who struggle to maintain their involvement with the local congregation. These Christians are finding little connection between what happens in church services and their daily lives. Many of them would no doubt find themselves agreeing with a lot of the issues that John Drane has raised in his *The McDonaldization of the Church*.

The second lot of individuals are those who have become disenchanted with faith altogether and do not bother to explore any other spiritual options. The third type comprises those whose disenchantment leads them to move away from Christianity and to enter into other faiths, especially the do-it-yourself spirituality.

The reasons why these people become disenchanted are undoubtedly many and varied. Both secular and Christian sociologists have been interested in studying shifts in religious affiliation and defection. We do not intend to explore these broad and fascinating matters here, but we would suggest that any interested readers might like to delve into some pertinent literature.[1]

In this case study we are concerned with the story of one young woman who used to belong to a church but has found more meaning in Wicca. Vicky shares how throughout her life she has been very conscious of God's presence. She eventually found faith in Christ and began to eagerly participate in a local congregation. However, as Vicky tells her story, several events led her to move away from the church. Her story is both sobering and intriguing. Although she now sees life quite differently, Vicky nonetheless still believes that Jesus died to forgive her sins.

Vicky sent us an email after she read Philip's online article, "Wiccans and Christians: Some mutual challenges," at www.jesus.com.au. We were moved by what she recounted. Vicky has graciously given her consent to having her story told. We realize that people tell their own stories in their own way, selecting those events and issues that stand out to them. Those who hear another's story may respond in various ways, sometimes agreeing and sometimes objecting. We might feel that there were other issues or factors influencing her, and that may be so.

Often people who abandon one faith for another reinterpret their previous allegiances in very negative ways. However, that does not mean their negative experiences are all imaginary. It may well be that Vicky has reinterpreted some experiences, and certainly we only have a brief snapshot of her life. With these limitations in mind there is still a lot of value in reading what she has to say.

We recommend that you read her story first. You may then want to refresh your memory about Wicca by rereading our third chapter. Afterwards, we suggest that you look at the questions we raise at the end of this appendix. You might like to wrestle with these questions as part of a group exercise or on your own. We hope that by hearing Vicky's honest heart-cry and questions you may be goaded and motivated to reach out with love, compassion, and understanding to today's spiritual seekers. Now we will let Vicky tell her story in her own words.

Vicky the church exile

I've known God for a very long time, for as long as I can remember actually. Now this wasn't the God of the Sacred Writings or the God of Israel or the God of Islam. The God I knew was just God. I wasn't raised in any particular faith, although being of "Anglo-Celtic stock" it was just sort of assumed I was sort of vaguely Christian. But as a young kid, I didn't know anything of the Sacred Writings, of Church, or dogma, or even the basic commandments. I just knew God, intimately and simply, just like a kid.

Then I was "found" by some Christians. I got deeply involved, and along the way I became a Pentecostal. I spoke in tongues. (Later I realized that I had been able to speak gobbledygook long before my "spirit baptism.") I lost quite a few friends by bashing them (metaphorically) over the head with my Bible. I still knew God, the God I had always known, but now people were putting lots of restrictions on God. These restrictions were like "God is this. God is not that. God likes this. God hates that. If you are Christian you will believe this."

I admit I was full of somewhere between hate and self-righteous pity for all those "heathens" out there. I managed to grossly offend my boss—a lovely Muslim woman—by trying to convert her. I also offended many others with my holier-than-thou attitude.

My zeal and excitement for doing that died down. When the pastor of my church gave a huge hate-filled rant about the Buddhist temple that was about to be built in my area, something inside my brain screamed "no!" It was a downhill slide after that, with me questioning everything. I was unceremoniously kicked out for "not repenting of the spirit of doubt" or some such thing. But I still knew the God I knew from way back. That God hadn't changed at all.

Then in 1996 my best friend admitted she was gay. This shook my world up. I loved her for her, as well as her lover too (she was also a good friend). How could this good and wonderful person be evil and nasty? This set up another long line of questioning and doubting. I couldn't stand the church anymore. It was full of nasty, narrow-minded, bigoted, hypocritical, uncaring, unloving, un-Christlike, spiritually dead people. So I quit. I stopped calling myself a Christian. I still knew God, but no way was I going to classify myself with them.

I stumbled across Wicca. Honestly, it felt like I had come home. God, to me, was never just a "father," or "mother," or anything gendered. God was God, male and female, and both and neither. When Wiccans refer to the Goddess and God, I have no drama, because to me, the God and Goddess are just personifications of aspects of the same thing. This is the Deity I had always known.

Wiccans are quite happy to have women in charge of spiritual things if they want to be. It was good for me after having gone through a very abusive relationship where I was treated like "I am your husband so you have to obey me because the Bible says so. Now cook my dinner and do my laundry."

Wiccans often celebrate their spirituality out in nature, rather than in a stuffy old building. I have always felt closer to God out in nature. Wiccans celebrate their faith, just like the Psalms tell us to do: "Make a joyful noise unto the Lord." That is in contrast to trotting out the old and meaningless hymns that go for meekness and humility. I have sat in church, on a wonderful spring morning, wanting to scream and clap and laugh and be very thankful at the whole wonderfulness of life. But instead I was forced to sit and be quiet and listen to the same boring sermon I heard on the same Sunday as last year. I had to then say the same prayers that come out of the same five pages of the same book that hasn't been updated since 1950. (Okay, so I also went to Anglican services.) It was the stuff I knew by rote, and it didn't mean a thing to me. I just couldn't live like that.

The final thing that pushed me into Wicca was that they don't care one hoot if you are gay, or unmarried, or have leprosy, or pick your nose, or whatever. Their relationship with their Deity(-ies) is personal and not for judging by others, and this is respected. Instead of going by written law, they are guided by the spirit. They have a strong moral code and endeavor to respect everyone's path of spirituality. To my mind, Wiccans respect the Holy Spirit far more than does the average Christian because they listen to the Spirit, they celebrate the Spirit, they embrace the Spirit rather than getting out a book which is at least 2,000 years out of date and possibly really mucked up.

I have never actually given up the idea that Jesus died for my sins. I've doubted it a few times, but it's not something I can reject, especially since I was baptized (the whole adult full-immersion variety). I knew that inherently my spirit was guiding me that it was the right thing to do. Now I have read an article that really understands why dissatisfied Christians wander into and find their spiritual answer in Wicca (and other related pagan paths).

Am I still a Christian? I don't know, I really don't. I find God far easier to connect with through dance and song and self-guided prayer, meditation, whatever, than formalized prayer. I see my own personal God, not as a big bully that wants me to follow rules and regulations, but as a loving guide. The God I have always known loves everyone indiscriminately, and doesn't reject him or her because that person finds love with the same gender or connects with God by wearing orange and chanting. The God I know doesn't condone rape (Num. 31) or slavery or the submission of women to men. The God I know doesn't have an issue with me praying standing up, hands outstretched. I was hounded continually until I prayed "properly" on my knees with hands clasped together in the "proper" way. The God I know also loves the rest of creation and there is as much soul in the least of the animals as there is in me.

This God that I know appears in bits of the Sacred Writings. But there is another fierce, tyrannical, unforgiving God in there too. There's a god that allows men to be unfaithful to their wives, a god that condones slavery, a god that tells women to be quiet, and a God that says not to scream while being raped in the country. There is a God that makes deals with the devil to test the faith of one man. I do not want to know this God. This is not the God I have always known.

So how can I call myself a Christian, when I cannot in all honesty, love, honor and worship the God of the Sacred Writings? I believe Jesus really had the right idea, but his later apostles and the church, to my mind, are so foreign to what Jesus was trying to do. I cannot bring myself to be included in a congregation. I'm not sure that I'd be all that welcome either. I will worship with Christians on occasion, as I'm sure many are sincere of heart, and I really do think we are praying and worshiping the same thing. But I would also pray with Buddhists and Pagans and Hindus and Muslims if they let me.

I like Wicca-style paganism. I find its whole life-affirming, non-bigoted, self-empowering, spirit-in-everything, "trust your spirit" attitude refreshing and simple. Should I mention Occam's razor now?

I couldn't find this in any church, and I've been to many, seeking the very things Wicca is all about. The only thing stopping me dedicating my life to the Wiccan path is my belief that Jesus died for me, and sometimes I wish I could stop believing that. Can Jesus fit into Wicca? I don't really think so. But if the church could embrace the things that have been missing from it, the very same things that your article looks at and discusses, then maybe just maybe I could return to church again.

In the meantime, I'll just keep praying to the Deity that I have always known, and will endeavor to be always guided by my spirit. I will continue to do my celebrations out in nature, and will continue to believe that the spirit of the Creator dwells in each of us, and in every living thing. I will still know Jesus died for my sins and will always be thankful for his great sacrifice. I will continue to strive to be more Christlike.

I will leave the question as to whether I am a Christian or not up to God, for s/he alone can judge that one. Since I know how to worship in a Christian way, occasionally I will go to a church and worship with others, and to see if things have changed. But I don't think I'll call myself a Christian anymore. My "label" doesn't matter—it's what is in my heart that counts.

Case-study exercise

You can do this exercise either in a group format or on your own. You will need pen and paper to complete the exercise.

- What strikes you the most about Vicky's story?
- What do you feel are the main points she has raised about her experiences in the church? Which of these issues would you agree with and why? Which issues do you disagree with and why?
- What lessons have you learned from reading Vicky's story? Is there an underlying message in her story that the church needs to hear?
- On three occasions, Vicky says that she still believes that Jesus died for her sins. Would you see her as being someone who really believes in Jesus? Would you say, on the basis of her confession about Christ, that she is a Christian? In view of your answers, write down why you feel she is/isn't, and then spend some time discussing your reasons.
- If you had the opportunity to meet Vicky or someone like her, what would you say to her? What do you think her response to you would be?

Endnotes

Appendix II

[1] See the following:

- David G. Bromley (ed.) *Falling From The Faith: Causes and Consequences of Religious Apostasy*, Newbury Park, Beverly Hills and London: SAGE Publications, 1988;
- Michael J. Fanstone, *The Sheep That Got Away*, London: MARC, 1993;
- William D. Hendricks, *Exit Interviews*, Chicago: Moody, 1993;
- Janet Liebman Jacobs, *Divine Disenchantment: Deconverting from New Religions*, Bloomington and Indianapolis: Indiana University Press, 1989;
- Alan Jamieson, *A Churchless Faith*, Wellington, NZ: Philip Garside Publishing, 2000;
- David O. Moberg, *The Church as a Social Institution*, second edition, Grand Rapids: Baker, 1984;
- Rodney Stark and William Sims Bainbridge, *The Future of Religion: Secularization, Revival and Cult Formation*, Berkeley, Los Angeles and London: University of California Press, 1985;
- Bruce Wilson, *Can God Survive in Australia?* Sutherland NSW: Albatross, 1983;
- Bryan R. Wilson, *The Social Dimensions of Sectarianism*, Oxford: Clarendon Press, 1990;
- Robert Wuthnow, *Rediscovering the Sacred: Perspectives on Religion in Contemporary Society*, Grand Rapids: Wm.B. Eerdmans, 1992; and
- Robert Wuthnow, *Christianity in the 21st Century*, New York and Oxford: Oxford University Press, 1993.

Appendix III
Detail of Holistic Therapies

- *Acupuncture and acupressure*: grounded in ancient Chinese concepts about the flow of chi, or energy, throughout the human body. Illnesses arise when the flow of energy is out of balance. The remedy is to insert needles at key pressure points (meridians) to interrupt the flow of negative energy and allow the chi to be harmonized. The needles trigger signals in the nervous system with respect to pain. Acupuncture is used for pain relief with chronic illnesses, injuries, and as an anaesthetic.

   Acupressure is a variant approach where the same pressure points as in acupuncture are worked on by using hands and fingers rather than needles to effect the same results. Shiatsu is a Japanese variant of acupressure.[1]

- *Applied kinesiology*: a system of diagnosis and treatment based on the concept of energy. It is believed that disease has a structural source found in muscle weaknesses. Poor muscles lead to imbalances in the flow of chi. Remedial treatment aims to promote the flow of chi through the body. As a form of bodywork therapy, it combines acupressure, chiropractic, and muscle testing and nutritional data to promote optimum health. Other approaches have developed out of applied kinesiology, including John Diamond's behavioral kinesiology, John Thie's touch for health and kinergy.[2]

- *Aromatherapy*: operates by using natural oils and essences (frankincense, lavender, myrrh, and ylang-ylang) to promote relaxation and healing. These essences may be added to warm bath water, mixed with oil and rubbed into the skin, be inhaled, or ingested in an elixir. Some aromatherapists speak about diluting these essences to a microscopic level so as to activate the universal life force or spirit energy within the substance to produce healing.[3]

- *Ayurvedic medicine*: "Ayurvedic" literally means "life knowledge." It is Hindu folk medicine that draws on a range of remedies, such as herbal treatments, massage, healing oils, enemas, meditation, and yoga. Some illnesses are attributed to astrological conjunctions and demons. Other treatments involve wearing amulets, chanting mantras, and incantations to various deities. Ayurvedic medicine has been popularized in the West through Maharishi Mahesh Yogi's Ayurveda Health Centre and by Deepak Chopra in his book *Ageless Body, Timeless Mind*.[4]

- *Bach flower remedies*: Edward Bach (1886-1936) was a British immunologist and bacteriologist. In Bach's system, illness has its basis in emotional and mental states that make the body receptive to diseases. He believed that there are twelve basic personality types, each reacting to particular diseases according to their moods. His remedies address the ill state of mind using flower extracts. By treating the patient rather than the illness itself, the flower remedies can effect health-inducing states of mind. Bach's thesis builds, in part, on some ideas found in homeopathy. Some practitioners say the flower's spiritual essence is imparted to the solution the patient ingests.[5]

- *Chiropractic*: Daniel David Palmer (1845-1913) was the discoverer of chiropractic. It has two basic principles. First, the body is capable of healing itself. Second, for optimum health, the nervous system must be working properly. The nervous system malfunctions when the spinal column is misaligned. Palmer believed that there is a stream of energy flowing up the spinal column, and by manipulating this energy, he could effect healings. This is achieved by manipulating the spine to bring it back into correct alignment. Some chiropractors accept Palmer's view of energy and others do not.[6]

- *Crystals*: primarily seen as a tool for conducting energy to enhance healing or meditation. Crystals are often worn around the neck or placed on energy centers (chakras) located in different parts of the human body to generate an even flow of energy. Evidence for the power of crystals is seen first of all in the invention of crystal radio sets and computer chips. Second, it is believed that when a quartz crystal is squeezed, it will produce an electric charge (piezoelectricity).
- *Herbal remedies*: traced back to ancient China and Greco-Roman times. Hildegard of Bingen (1098-1179), the multitalented Christian nun, was an expert practitioner of herbal remedies. When it was discovered that the healing agents from herbs could be extracted, synthetic chemical mixtures developed into modern drugs. Herbal remedies were revived by Seventh-day Adventists such as Jethro Kloss (1863-1946). Some modern practitioners link herbal treatments to New Age spirituality, but not all do.[7]
- *Homeopathy*: Samuel Hahneman (1755-1843) was a German doctor who developed homeopathy. He was also a devotee of Swedenborg's teachings. As a system of treatment, homeopathy operates on the basis that like cures like. The remedies prescribed are in very small dosages, because Hahneman believed that a prescription is most effective when diluted. The dilution process is necessary to activate the spiritual energy or universal life force latent in the remedy.[8]
- *Iridology*: maintains that the human eye is a diagnostic map to our anatomy and health complaints.[9]
- *Magnetic therapy*: the use of magnets in medical treatment originated with the Swiss hermeticist Paracelsus (1493-1541). We know that magnetic forces affect the planet, as seen in the magnetic poles, so many affirm that magnetic energy affects the body. As iron is attracted to magnets and iron is a constituent of the human bloodstream, magnets are used to alleviate problems such as migraines.
- *Naturopathy*: rejects the germ theory of disease. Instead, dis-

ease arises from the accumulation of toxins and waste products inside the body. Treatments focus on cleansing the body of such toxins so that the body can heal itself. Remedies encompass acupuncture, aromatherapy, breathing exercises, colon cleansing, exercise, fasting, herbs, massage, reflexology, and vitamin supplements. Some naturopaths work within a Christian belief system, while others incline towards New Age beliefs about the universal life force.[10]

- *Reflexology*: a bodywork therapy where massage is applied to the feet to promote health. The soles of the feet are believed to be a map to our internal organs, and so, by massaging specific points, the parts of the body these relate to can be treated.

- *Reiki*: an energy-based system of healing. The reiki technique uses the laying on of hands to channel the universal life force into the body. The body has three basic areas for therapy—the head, front, and back. Other hand placements will be used for particular bodily ailments, as well as for emotional and mental problems. Students of reiki must go through four levels of training to cleanse themselves of negative energies before they can be vessels for the universal life force. Reiki originated with Mikao Usui, a Japanese teacher. Usui wanted to discover how Jesus healed people, but, after a frustrating search, turned to the Buddhist sutras. Usui entered a twenty-one-day retreat where universal energy was activated in him. He then enunciated five basic principles for reiki practitioners:
  - Just for today I will give thanks for my many blessings.
  - Just for today I will not worry.
  - Just for today I will not be angry.
  - Just for today I will do my work honestly.
  - Just for today I will be kind to my neighbor and every living thing.[11]

- *Sound medicine*: takes a variety of forms. Some practitioners employ music as a part of therapy for emotional, mental, and physical problems. Music may be used in a guided meditation to achieve relaxation or to delve into the subconscious mind where spiritual symbols may be accessed and interpreted according to Jungian analysis. Steven Halpern relates music therapy to kundalini yoga. Others speak of sound harmonics produced when chanting a mantra where the vibrations induce altered states of consciousness and a sense of well being.

- *Therapeutic touch*: this is a non-contact form of energy healing developed by Dolores Krieger, an American nurse. Therapists attune themselves to their patients by passing their hands across the body, but without touching them. Once a problem area has been identified, therapists then place their hand just above that area and channel an energy known as prana into the patient. This channeling of energy is meant to activate the patients' energy centers to heal themselves.[12]

Endnotes

Appendix III

[1] John J. Bonica, "Therapeutic Acupuncture in the People's Republic of China," *Journal of the American Medical Association*, 228, 1974, pp. 1544-1551; Peter Ky Lee, Thorkild W. Andersen, Jerome H. Modell and Segundina A. Saga, "Treatment of Chronic Pain with Acupuncture," *Journal of the American Medical Association*, 232, 1975, pp. 1133-1135; and Jon D. Levine, Joseph Gormley and Howard L. Fields, "Observations on the Analgesic Effect of Needle Puncture (Acupuncture)," *Pain*, 2, 1976, pp. 149-159.

[2] Donna Eden and David Feinstein, *Energy Medicine*, London: Judy Piatkus, 1999.

[3] On a biblical approach to aromatherapy, see Philip Johnson, "Energy Healing: A Christian Theological Appraisal" at www.ozemail.com.au/~ptcsyd/JohnsonPage/

[4] See Kurt A. Butler, *A Consumer's Guide to "Alternative Medicine,"* Buffalo: Prometheus, 1992, pp. 110-117.

[5] J. Gordon Melton, Jerome Clark, and Aidan A. Kelly (eds), *New Age Almanac*, Detroit: Visible Ink, 1991, pp. 184-186.

[6] J. Gordon Melton, Jerome Clark, and Aidan A. Kelly (eds), *New Age Almanac*, pp. 197-198; and John Ankerberg and John Weldon, *Can You Trust Your Doctor?* Brentwood: Wolgemuth & Hyatt, 1991, pp. 203-240.

[7] David Hoffmann, *The Elements of Herbalism*, Dorset: Element, 1990.

[8] For a positive view, see Alan Crook, *A Christian's Guide to Homeopathy*, London: Winter, 1996; and, for a negative view, Samuel Pfeifer, *Healing At Any Price?* Milton Keynes: Word, 1988, pp. 62-82.

[9] See Dorothy Hall, *Iridology*, Melbourne: Thomas Nelson, 1980; and Allie Simon, David M. Worthen and John A. Mitas, "An Evaluation of Iridology", *Journal of the American Medical Association*, 242, 1979, pp. 1385-1389.

[10] J. Gordon Melton, Jerome Clark and Aidan A. Kelly (eds), *New Age Almanac*, pp. 229-236.

[11] Paula Horan, *Empowerment through Reiki*, Wilmot: Lotus Light/Shangri-La, 1989.

[12] See L. Rosa, E. Rosa and S. Barrett, "A Close Look at Therapeutic Touch," *Journal of the American Medical Association*, 279, 1998, pp. 1005-1010; and Sharon Fish, "Therapeutic Touch: Healing Science or Psychic Midwife?", *Christian Research Journal*, 18, 1, 1995, pp. 28-38.

Select bibliography

Chapter 1

Background on New Age spirituality

Robert Basil (ed.), *Not Necessarily the New Age*, Buffalo: Prometheus, 1988.

Eileen Campbell and J.H. Brennan, *The Aquarian Guide to the New Age*, London: Aquarian, 1990.

Nevill Drury, *Exploring the Labyrinth: Making Sense of the New Spirituality*, Sydney: Allen & Unwin, 1999.

Marilyn Ferguson, *The Aquarian Conspiracy*, London: Paladin, 1982.

R.A. Gilbert, *Revelations of the Golden Dawn: The Rise and Fall of a Magical Order*, London: Quantum, 1997.

Rosemary Ellen Guiley, *Encyclopedia of Mystical and Paranormal Experience*, New York: HarperCollins, 1991.

Wouter J. Hanegraaff, *New Age Religion and Western Culture*, Albany: State University of New York Press, 1998.

Paul Heelas, *The New Age Movement: The Celebration of the Self and the Sacralization of Modernity*, Oxford and Cambridge, Massachusetts: Blackwell, 1996.

Irving Hexham and Karla Poewe, *New Religions as Global Cultures*, Boulder: Westview Press, 1997.

Richard G. Kyle, *The New Age Movement in American Culture*, Boston and London: University Press of America, 1995.

James R. Lewis and J. Gordon Melton (eds), *Perspectives on the New Age Movement*, Albany: State University of New York Press, 1992.

James R. Lewis, *Peculiar Prophets: A Biographical Dictionary of New Religions*, St Paul, Minnesota: Paragon House, 1999.

Jessica Lipnack and Jeffrey Stamps, *The Networking Book*, New York and London: Routledge & Kegan Paul, 1986.

Christopher McIntosh, *Eliphas Levi and the French Occult Revival*, London: Rider, 1972.

J. Gordon Melton, Jerome Clark and Aidan A. Kelly (eds), *New Age Almanac*, Detroit: Visible Ink, 1991.

Leslie A. Shepard (ed.), *Encyclopedia of Occultism and Parapsychology*, 2 Vols, New York: Avon, 1980.

Chrissie Steyn, *Worldviews in Transition: An Investigation of the New Age Movement in South Africa*, Pretoria: University of South Africa Press, 1994.

Rachel Storm, *In Search of Heaven on Earth: The Roots of the New Age Movement*, London: Aquarian, 1991.

Michael York, *The Emerging Network: A Sociology of the New Age and Neo-Pagan Movements*, Lanham and London: Rowman & Littlefield, 1995.

Christian responses to New Age spirituality

John Ankerberg and John Weldon, *Encyclopedia of New Age Beliefs*, Eugene: Harvest House, 1996.

Francis J. Beckwith and Stephen E. Parrish, *See the Gods Fall: Four Rivals to Christianity*, Joplin: College Press, 1997.

David Burnett, *Clash of Worlds*, Eastbourne: MARC, 1990.

Russell Chandler, *Understanding the New Age*, revised edition, Grand Rapids: Zondervan, 1993.

Constance Cumbey, *The Hidden Dangers of the Rainbow*, Shreveport: Huntington, 1983.

John Drane, *What is the New Age Still Saying to the Church?* London: Marshall Pickering, 1999.

Douglas Groothuis, *Unmasking the New Age*, Downers Grove: InterVarsity Press, 1986.

Douglas Groothuis, *Confronting the New Age*, Downers Grove: InterVarsity Press, 1988.

Karen Hoyt and J. Isamu Yamamoto (eds), *The New Age Rage*, Old Tappan: Fleming Revell, 1987.

Dave Hunt, *Peace, Prosperity and the Coming Holocaust: The New Age Movement in Prophecy*, Irvine: Harvest House, 1983.

Peter Jones, *The Gnostic Empire Strikes Back*, Phillipsburg: Presbyterian & Reformed, 1992.

Vishal Mangalwadi, *In Search of Self: Beyond the New Age*, London: Spire, 1992.

Texe Marrs, *Dark Secrets of the New Age*, Westchester: Crossway, 1987.

Walter Martin, *The New Age Cult*, Minneapolis: Bethany, 1989.

Kerry D. McRoberts, *New Age or Old Lie?* Peabody: Hendrickson, 1989.

Elliot Miller, *A Crash Course on the New Age Movement*, Grand Rapids: Baker, 1989.

John P. Newport, *The New Age Movement and the Biblical Worldview*, Grand Rapids: Wm.B. Eerdmans, 1998.

Michael Perry, *Gods Within*, London: SPCK, 1992.

Ted Peters, *The Cosmic Self*, San Francisco: HarperCollins, 1991.

Ron Rhodes, *New Age Movement*, Grand Rapids: Zondervan, 1995.

Charles Strohmer, *Wise as a Serpent, Harmless as a Dove*, Milton Keynes: Word, 1994.

Eldon K. Winkler, *The New Age Is Lying to You*, St Louis: Concordia, 1994.

Morag Zwartz, *The New Age Gospel: Christ or Counterfeit?* Melbourne: Parenesis, 1987.

Deconversion from New Age spirituality

Randall Baer, *Inside the New Age Nightmare*, Shreveport: Huntington House, 1989.

Tal Brooke, *Lord of the Air*, Eugene: Harvest, 1990.

Michael Graham, *The Experience of Ultimate Truth*, Melbourne: U-Turn Press, 2001.

Mark Phillips, *Truth Seeker*, Leicester: InterVarsity, 1998.

Assessing apologetics

David Clark, *Dialogical Apologetics*, Grand Rapids: Baker, 1993.

Ross Clifford, *The Mission of the Church and the New Age Movement*, Lilydale: Bible College of Victoria, 1995.

Douglas E. Cowan, "Bearing False Witness: Propaganda, Reality-Maintenance, and Christian Anticult Apologetics," Ph.D. thesis, University of Calgary, 1999/Ann Arbor: Bell & Howell Information & Learning, 1999.

John Drane, *Cultural Change and Biblical Faith*, Carlisle: Paternoster, 2000.

Avery Dulles, *A History of Apologetics*, Eugene, Oregon: Wipf & Stock, 1999.

Robert A. Guelich, "Spiritual Warfare: Jesus, Paul and Peretti," *PNEUMA: The Journal of the Society for Pentecostal Studies*, 13, 1, 1991, pp. 33-64.

Philip Johnson, "Postmodernity, New Age and Christian Mission: Mars Hill revisited," Lutheran Theological Journal, 31, 3, 1997, pp. 115-124.

Philip Johnson, "Apologetics and Myths: Signs of salvation in postmodernity," *Lutheran Theological Journal*, 32, 2, 1998, pp. 62-72.

Philip Johnson, "The Aquarian Age and Apologetics," *Lutheran Theological Journal*, 34, 2, 2000, pp. 51-60.

Alister McGrath, *Bridge Building*, Leicester: InterVarsity, 1992.

Harold Netland, "Toward Contextualized Apologetics," *Missiology*, 16, 3, 1988, pp. 289-303.

Timothy R. Phillips and Dennis L. Okholm (eds), *Christian Apologetics in the Postmodern World*, Downers Grove: InterVarsity, 1995.

Martin Robinson, *To Win The West*, Crowborough: Monarch, 1996.

John A. Saliba, *Christian Responses to the New Age Movement*, London: Geoffrey Chapman, 1999.

Incarnational mission

Joy Anderson, "Behold the Ox of God?" *Evangelical Missions Quarterly*, 34, 3, 1998, pp. 316-320.

David J. Bosch, *Transforming Mission*, Maryknoll: Orbis, 1991.

J. Daryl Charles, "Engaging the (Neo) Pagan Mind: Paul's Encounter with Athenian Culture as a Model for Cultural Apologetics (Acts 17:16-34)," *Trinity Journal* NS 16, 1995, pp. 47-62.

David Fetcho, "Disclosing the Unknown God: Evangelism to the New Religions," *Update*, 6, 4, 1982, pp. 7-16.

Ken Gnanakan, *Kingdom Concerns: A Theology of Mission Today*, Leicester: InterVarsity Press, 1993.

David J. Hesselgrave, *Communicating Christ Cross-Culturally*, 2nd ed., Grand Rapids: Zondervan, 1991.

Paul G. Hiebert, *Anthropological Reflections on Missiological Issues*, Grand Rapids: Baker, 1994.

Robert N. Minor, "Understanding as the First Step in an Evangelical Approach to World Religions: Some Methodological Considerations," *Journal of the Evangelical Theological Society*, 19, 2, 1976, pp. 121-128.

A. Scott Moreau (ed.), *Evangelical Dictionary of World Missions*, Grand Rapids: Baker, 2000.

Michael Nazir-Ali, *Mission and Dialogue*, London: SPCK, 1995.

H.L. Richard, *Following Jesus in the Hindu Context: The Intriguing Implications of N.V. Tilak's Life and Thought*, Pasadena: William Carey Library, 1998.

Garry W. Trompf, "Missiology, Methodology and the Study of New Religious Movements," *Religious Traditions*, 10, 1987, pp. 95-106.

Mike Wakely, "A Critical Look at a New 'Key' to Evangelization," *Evangelical Missions Quarterly*, 31, 2, 1995, pp. 152-162.

Chapter 2

Angel phenomena

Mortimer J. Adler, *The Angels and Us*, New York: Collier, 1982.

Matthew Bunson, *Angels A to Z*, New York: Crown, 1996.

Sophy Burnham, *A Book of Angels*, New York: Ballantine, 1990.

Duane A. Garrett, *Angels and the New Spirituality*, Nashville: Broadman & Holman, 1995.

Billy Graham, *Angels: God's Secret Agents*, revised edition, London: Hodder, 1995.

Hope Macdonald, *When Angels Appear*, New York: Harper, 1995.

Hope Price, *Angels*, London: Pan Macmillan, 1994.

Cherie Sutherland, *In the Company of Angels*, Sydney and New York: Bantam, 2000.

Chapter 3
Wicca—goddess worship revival

Margot Adler, *Drawing Down the Moon*, revised edition, Boston: Beacon, 1986.

Zsuzsanna E. Budapest, *Grandmother Moon*, San Francisco: HarperCollins, 1991.

David Burnett, *Dawning of the Pagan Moon*, Eastbourne: Monarch, 1991.

Vivianne Crowley, *Wicca: The Old Religion in the New Age*, London: Aquarian, 1989.

Nevill Drury, *The History of Magic in the Modern Age*, London: Constable, 2000.

Graham Harvey, *Contemporary Paganism: Listening People, Speaking Earth*, New York: New York University Press, 1997.

Craig S. Hawkins, *Witchcraft: Exploring the World of Wicca*, Grand Rapids: Baker, 1996.

Fiona Horne, *Witch: A Personal Journey*, Sydney: Random House, 1998.

Fiona Horne, *Witch: A Magickal Year*, Sydney: Random House, 1999.

Fiona Horne, *Life's a Witch!* Sydney: Random House, 2000.

Lynne Hume, *Witchcraft and Paganism in Australia*, Carlton South: Melbourne University Press, 1997.

Ronald Hutton, *The Triumph of the Moon: A History of Modern Pagan Witchcraft*, Oxford: Oxford University Press, 1999.

James R. Lewis (ed.), *Magical Religion and Modern Witchcraft*, Albany: State University of New York Press, 1996.

T.M. Luhrmann, *Persuasions of the Witch's Craft*, London: Picador, 1994.

Jeffrey B. Russell, *A History of Witchcraft*, London: Thames & Hudson, 1980.

Ceisiwr Serith, *The Pagan Family*, St Paul: Llewellyn, 1994.

Aida Besancon Spencer, Donna F.G. Hailson, Catherine Clark Kroeger and William David Spencer, *The Goddess Revival*, Grand Rapids: Baker, 1995.

Starhawk, *Dreaming the Dark*, revised edition, Boston: Beacon, 1988.

Kisma K. Stepanich, *Sister Moon Lodge: The Power and Mystery of Menstruation*, St Paul: Llewellyn, 1992.

Loren Wilkinson, "The Bewitching Charms of Neo-Paganism," *Christianity Today*, 15 November 1999, pp. 58-63.

Chapter 4
Myths and wisdom

Roelof van den Broek and Wouter J. Hanegraaff (eds), *Gnosis and Hermeticism: From Antiquity to Modern Times*, Albany: State University of New York Press, 1998.

Joseph Campbell and Bill Moyers, *The Power of Myth*, New York: Doubleday, 1988.

Patrick Curry, *Defending Middle-Earth: Tolkien: Myth and Modernity*, London: HarperCollins, 1997.

Mircea Eliade, *Myths, Dreams and Mysteries*, New York: Harper Colophon, 1975.

Michael Frost, *Seeing God in the Ordinary*, Peabody: Hendrickson, 2000.

Carl G. Jung (ed.), *Man and His Symbols*, New York: Dell, 1968.

John Warwick Montgomery (ed.), *Myth, Allegory and Gospel*, Minneapolis: Bethany, 1974.

Richard Noll, *The Jung Cult*, London: Fontana, 1996.

Timothy R. O'Neill, *The Individuated Hobbit: Jung, Tolkien and the Archetypes of Middle Earth*, London: Thames & Hudson, 1980.

Jeffrey B. Russell, *The Prince of Darkness: Radical Evil and the Power of Good in History*, London: Thames & Hudson, 1989.

Tom Snyder, *Myth Conceptions: Joseph Campbell and the New Age*, Grand Rapids: Baker, 1995.

Chapter 5
The zodiac revisited

John Ankerberg and John Weldon, *Astrology: Do the Heavens Rule Our Destiny?* Eugene: Harvest, 1989.

Michel Gauquelin, *Dreams and Illusions of Astrology*, Buffalo: Prometheus, 1979.

Fred Gettings, *Dictionary of Astrology*, London: Routledge & Kegan Paul, 1985.

Janis Huntley, *The Elements of Astrology*, Dorset: Element, 1990.

James R. Lewis, *The Astrology Encyclopedia*, Detroit: Visible Ink, 1994.

Cordelia Mansell, *Discover Astrology*, London: Aquarian, 1985.

Charles Strohmer, *What Your Horoscope Doesn't Tell You*, Wheaton: Tyndale, 1988.

Chapter 6
Psychotechnologies and complementary therapies

A Course in Miracles, London: Arkana, 1985.

Robert A. Baker and Joe Nickell, *Missing Pieces: How to Investigate Ghosts, UFOs, Psychics and Other Mysteries*, Buffalo: Prometheus, 1992.

Richard Carlson and Benjamin Shield (eds), *Healers on Healing*, London: Rider, 1990.

Deepak Chopra, *Ageless Body, Timeless Mind*, New York: Harmony, 1993.

Robina Coker, *Alternative Medicine: Helpful or Harmful?* Crowborough: Monarch, 1995.

Larry Dossey, *Healing Words: The Power of Prayer and the Practice of Medicine*, San Francisco: HarperCollins, 1993.

John Drane, Ross Clifford and Philip Johnson, *Beyond Prediction: The Tarot and Your Spirituality*, Oxford: Lion, 2001.

Abbe Gail, *Realize Your Psychic Power*, London: Guild, 1988.

Grillot de Givry (J. Courtenay Locke, translator), *Witchcraft, Magic and Alchemy*, New York: Dover, 1971.

Louise Hay, *You Can Heal Your Life*, Sydney: Specialist Publications, 1988.

Dan Korem, *Powers: Testing the Psychic and Supernatural*, Downers Grove: InterVarsity, 1988.

John Warwick Montgomery, *Principalities and Powers*, Minneapolis: Bethany, 1973.

Jonn Mumford, *Ecstasy Through Tantra*, St Paul: Llewellyn, 1988.

The New Age Catalogue, New York: Doubleday, 1988.

Stephen Parsons, *Searching for Healing*, Oxford: Lion, 1995.

Samuel Pfeifer, *Healing At Any Price?* Milton Keynes: Word, 1988.

Harold Taylor, *Sent to Heal*, Ringwood, Victoria: The Order of St Luke the Physician, 1993.

Chapter 7
Cosmic oneness paradigm

David Bohm, *Wholeness and the Implicate Order*, London and New York: Ark, 1983.

Ian Bradley, *God is Green*, London: Darton, Longman & Todd, 1990.

Fritjof Capra, *The Tao of Physics*, 3rd edition, London: Flamingo, 1991.

Deepak Chopra, *How To Know God*, Sydney: Random House, 2000.

Sydney L. Donahoe, *Earth Keeping: Making it a Family Habit*, Grand Rapids: Zondervan, 1990.

Matthew Fox, *Original Blessing*, Santa Fe: Bear, 1983.

Matthew Fox, *The Coming of the Cosmic Christ*, Melbourne: Collins Dove, 1988.

Dawn Hill, *With a Little Help from my Friends*, Sydney: Pan Macmillan, 1991.

Ken Keyes, *Handbook to Higher Consciousness*, 5th edition, Coos Bay: Love Line, 1975.

J.E. Lovelock, *Gaia: A New Look at Life on Earth*, Oxford: Oxford University Press, 1979.

James Lovelock, *The Ages of Gaia*, Oxford: Oxford University Press, 1988.

Ernest Lucas, *Science and the New Age Challenge*, Leicester: Apollos, 1996.

Shirley Maclaine, *Going Within*, New York: Bantam, 1989.

Elwood Norquist, *We Are One: A Challenge to Traditional Christianity*, Tucson: Cosmic Connection, 1995.

James Redfield, *The Celestine Prophecy*, New York and Sydney: Bantam, 1994.

James Redfield, *The Tenth Insight*, New York and Sydney: Bantam, 1996.

James Redfield, *The Celestine Vision*, New York and Sydney: Bantam, 1997.

James Redfield, *The Secret of Shambhala*, New York and Sydney: Bantam, 1999.

Jane Roberts, *The Nature of Personal Reality*, Englewood Cliffs: Prentice-Hall, 1974.

Rupert Sheldrake, *The Rebirth of Nature: The Greening of Science and God*, New York: Bantam, 1991.

Ken Wilbur (ed.), *The Holographic Paradigm and Other Paradoxes*, Boston and London: Shambhala, 1985.

Chapter 8
Near-death experiences
Bruce Elder, *And When I Die, Will I Be Dead?* Sydney: Australian Broadcasting Corporation, 1987.

Doug Groothuis, *Deceived by the Light*, Eugene: Harvest, 1995.

Tom Harpur, *Life After Death*, Toronto: McClelland & Stewart, 1991.

Gary R. Habermas and J.P. Moreland, *Immortality: The Other Side of Death*, Nashville: Thomas Nelson, 1992.

Robert A. Monroe, *Journeys Out of the Body*, London: Souvenir, 1972.

Raymond A. Moody, *Life After Life*, New York: Bantam, 1976.

Karlis Osis and Erlendur Haraldsson, *At The Hour of Death*, 3rd edition, Norwalk: Hastings, 1995.

Maurice Rawlings, *Beyond Death's Door*, New York: Bantam, 1979.

Cherie Sutherland, *Transformed by the Light*, Sydney: Bantam, 1992.

Ian Wilson, *The After Death Experience*, London: Corgi, 1989.

Carol Zaleski, *Otherworld Journeys*, New York and Oxford: Oxford University Press, 1987.

Chapter 9
Past lives
Mark Albrecht, *Reincarnation: A Christian Appraisal*, Downers Grove: InterVarsity, 1982.

Morey Bernstein, *The Search for Bridey Murphy*, New York: Doubleday, 1956.

J.H. Brennan, *Discover Reincarnation*, London: Aquarian, 1984.

Cassandra Eason, *Discovering Your Past Lives*, London: Foulsham, 1996.

Norman L. Geisler and J. Yutaka Amano, *The Reincarnation Sensation*, Wheaton: Tyndale, 1986.

Joseph Head and Sylvia Cranston, *Reincarnation: The Phoenix Fire Mystery*, Pasadena: Theosophical University Press, 1994.

Noel Langley, *Edgar Cayce on Reincarnation*, New York: Warner, 1967.

Wendy Doniger O'Flaherty (ed.), *Karma and Rebirth in Classical Indian Traditions*, Delhi: Motilal Banarsidass, 1983.

John Snyder, *Reincarnation vs Resurrection*, Chicago: Moody, 1984.

Chapter 10
The power of the mind and human potential
Charles Paul Brown, Berna Deane and James Russell Strole, *Together Forever*, Sydney: Pythagorean, 1990.

Tony Buzan, *Make the Most of Your Mind*, revised edition, London: Pan, 1988.

Nevill Drury, *The Visionary Human: Mystical Consciousness and Paranormal Perspectives*, Sydney: Bantam, 1991.

Wayne W. Dyer, *Real Magic*, Sydney: HarperCollins, 1992.

Wayne W. Dyer, *Your Sacred Self*, Sydney: HarperCollins, 1995.

Piero Ferrucci, *What We May Be: The Vision and Techniques of Psychosynthesis*, London: Aquarian, 1992.

Eric P. Jensen, *Superteaching*, Del Mar: Turning Point, 1988.

John Kehoe, *Mind Power*, Toronto: Zoetic, 1987.

Robert Kiyosaki, *If You Want to be Rich and Happy, Don't Go To School?* San Diego: Excellerated Learning, 1991.

Peter McWilliams and John Roger, *You Can't Afford the Luxury of a Negative Thought*, Los Angeles: Prelude, 1988.

Sheila Ostrander, Lynn Schroeder and Nancy Ostrander, *Superlearning*, London: Sphere, 1981.

Harry Palmer, *Living Deliberately: The Discovery and Development of Avatar*, Altamonte Springs: Star's Edge, 1994.

M. Scott Peck, *The Road Less Traveled*, New York: Simon & Schuster, 1978.

M. Scott Peck, *Further Along the Road Less Traveled*, New York: Simon & Schuster, 1993.

Anthony Robbins, *Awaken the Giant Within*, New York: Simon & Schuster, 1991.

Michael Domeyko Rowland, *Absolute Happiness*, Bondi Beach, New South Wales: Self Communications, 1993.

Jose Silva and Philip Miele, *The Silva Mind Control Method*, New York: Pocket, 1977.

Paul Solomon, *The Meta-Human*, Norfolk: Hampton Roads, 1990.

Chapter 11

Jesus' missing years

Paul Barnett, *Jesus and the Logic of History*, Leicester: Apollos, 1997.

Per Beskow, *Strange Tales About Jesus*, Philadelphia: Fortress, 1983.

F.F. Bruce, *The "Secret" Gospel of Mark*, London: Athlone Press, 1974.

Ross Clifford, *Leading Lawyers' Case for the Resurrection*, Edmonton: Canadian Institute for Law, Theology & Public Policy, 1996.

John Drane, *The Bible Phenomenon*, Oxford: Lion, 1999.

R.T. France, *The Evidence for Jesus*, London: Hodder, 1986.

Douglas Groothuis, *Revealing the New Age Jesus*, Downers Grove: InterVarsity, 1990.

Ronald Nash, *Christianity and the Hellenistic World*, Grand Rapids: Zondervan, 1984.

Ron Rhodes, *The Counterfeit Christ of the New Age Movement*, Grand Rapids: Baker, 1990.

N.T. Wright, *Who Was Jesus?* London: SPCK, 1992.

Chapter 12

Living meditation

Karen Armstrong, *The English Mystics of the Fourteenth Century*, London: Kyle Cathie, 1991.

Sheila Cassidy, *Prayer for Pilgrims*, Glasgow: Collins, 1980.

Ross Clifford and Philip Johnson, *Riding the Rollercoaster: How the Risen Christ Empowers Life*, Sydney: Strand, 1998.

The Cloud of Unknowing, Clifton Walters (translator), Harmondsworth: Penguin, 1964.

Rowland Croucher and Grace Thomlinson (eds), *High Mountains, Deep Valleys*, Sutherland, New South Wales: Albatross, 1991.

Richard Foster, *Celebration of Discipline*, revised edition, London: Hodder & Stoughton, 1989.

Richard Foster, *Prayer: Finding the Heart's True Home*, London: Hodder & Stoughton, 1992.

Nicky Gumbel, *Questions of Life*, Eastbourne: Kingsway, 1993.

Illuminations of Hildegard of Bingen, commentary by Matthew Fox, Santa Fe: Bear & Co, 1985.

Calvin Miller, *The Table of Inwardness*, Downers Grove: InterVarsity, 1984.

Lynda Rose, *No Other Gods*, London: Hodder & Stoughton, 1990.

R.C. Sproul, *Following Christ*, Wheaton: Tyndale, 1991.

Peter Toon, *What is Spirituality and Is It for Me?* London: Daybreak, 1989.

Peter Toon, *Meditating as a Christian*, London: Collins, 1991.

Appendixes

Mortimer Adler, *Truth in Religion: The Plurality of Religions and the Unity of Truth*, New York: Collier, 1990.

John Drane, *Faith in a Changing Culture*, London: HarperCollins, 1997.

John Drane, *The McDonaldization of the Church*, London: Darton, Longman & Todd, 2000.

Olive M. Fleming Drane, *Clowns, Storytellers and Disciples*, Oxford: BRF, 2001.

David Millikan and Nevill Drury, *Worlds Apart? Christianity and the New Age*, Sydney: Australian Broadcasting Corporation, 1991.

Harold Netland, *Dissonant Voices: Religious Pluralism and the Question of Truth*, Grand Rapids/Leicester: Wm.B. Eerdmans/Apollos, 1991.

Index

Index

Index

Index

Index

Index

Index

New Age spirituality
apologetic responses, 17
charting, 10–12
defined, 11
features, 11
Hermetic holism, 14
monist holism, 12–13
neo-gnostic holism, 13–14
neo-pagan/Wiccan holism, 14
New Consciousness, 3
New Edge, 3
New England Transcendentalists, 8
New Sense, 3
New Sight Community, 275
New Spirituality, 3, 4
New Thought, 8
Newton, 5, 152
Next Age, 3
Next Stage, 3
Nicene Creed, 10
Nicodemus, 181
Nine-to-five spirituality, 281–282
Nineteenth Century, journal, 220
Nirvana, 185, 205
Nityananda, Swami, 219
NLP (neurolinguistic programming), 202
Noah, 59, 74
Nock, A. D., 235
Non-disclosure contract agreement, 205
Non-dualistic Vedanta, 145
Norse traditions and Wiccans, 52
Nostradamus, 112, 125
Notovitch, Nicholas
inconsistency of data, 238
Jesus in India, 224–226, 228
Jesus in Tibet, 218–223
Novels, fantasy, 81
Numerology, 116, 128

O

Occam's razor, 292
Occult
background, 7, 9, 16
defined, 16
revival in New Age, 1, 9
Ofshe, Richard, 192

On Death and Dying, 158
O'Neill, Sharon, 270
Oneness. *See* Cosmic oneness paradigm
Operation Mobilization, 272
Orange People, 119
Order of St. Luke the Physician, 271
Order of the Golden Dawn, 7, 8
Order of the Star of the East, 8
Origen, 177, 183–184
Original Jesus, 228, 229
Orion, 92
Orphans, cosmic, 99
Osho (Bhagwan Shree Rajneesh), 119, 210, 224
Osiris male god, 49, 233
Osis, Karlis, 164
Otherworld Journeys, 159
Ouija board, 112, 124
Out of body experiences, 159
Out-of-space reincarnation, 184–185
Out of the Silent Planet, 99
Outing Christian astrologers, 95–97

P

Pacific Institute, 201
Pacino, Al, 77
Pacwa, Mitch, 126
Pagan myth, 233–234
Pagan symbols, 270
Paganism
Celtic, 77
Christianity, 64
Internet sites, 4
Wicca and, 53
Painting art in mission, 272–274
Palmer, Daniel David, 296
Palmer, Harry, 16, 205
Pan, 49
Panentheism
defined, 10, 100
Wiccans, 34
Panin, Ivan, 79
Pantheism
all is God, 146
defined, 12, 148

326

Index

Index

Index

New Age. *See* New Age spirituality

nine-to-five, 281–282

Sunday, 282

Sports champions and astrology, 100–101

Sprinkle, Annie, 119

Spurgeon, preacher, 276

Star of Jacob, 90–91

Star Trek Voyager television series, 4

Star Wars, movie, 72

Star Wars: The Phantom Menace, movie, 276

Stars

    precise measurements, 100–101

    role of, 106

Steiner, Rudolf, 9, 226

Stevenson, Ian, 191

Stewards of humans over nature, 59

Stonehenge, 115, 218

Stonehouse, Ned, 24

Stratford, Lauren, 55

Strauss, 228

Stress, handling of, 208–209

Strohmer, Charles, 98, 105

Studion, Simon, 7

Subliminal tapes, 202

Substantival monism, 145–146

Suffering and karma, 177, 186–187

Sumerian, ancient, and Wiccans, 53

Sun

    astrology sign, 88, 103

    center of solar system, 96

Sunday spirituality, 282

Supercamp, 201, 204

Superlearning, 203, 205

Superteaching, book, 204

Survey results, 266

Susanna, 62

Sutherland, Cherie, 159, 162, 163, 166

Sutphen, Dick, 37, 193, 283

Sutphen, Trenna, 193

Suzuki, Daisetz Teitaro, 15

Suzy and Kahuna, 261

Swann, Ingo, 211

Swedenborg, Emanuel

    background, 6

geomancy, 115

myths, 72

New Age influencer, 15

Swords (air) tarot suit, 120

Symbolic device (circle), 113

Symbols in myths, 71–72

Synagogues and zodiac mosaics, 93–95

Synod, 10

Szekely, Edmund Bordeaux, 232–233

T

Tacitus, 90, 238

T'ai chi, 118, 129–130

Takenouchi family papers, 227

Tales of transformation, 81

Talmud, 94

Tantra

    sacred sex, 118, 132

    yoga, 118, 122

Taoism

    atomic matter, 152

    background, 97

    dark spirits, 77

    feng shui and, 114

    influence on New Age, 15

    metaphysics, 130

    reincarnation, 190

    Wicca and, 53

Tara Centre, 9

Tarot

    angel depictions, 34

    background, 120–121, 133

    Crowley tarot cards, 48

    Devil card, 40, 133

    fortune-telling cards, 7

    function, 120–121

    gospel and, 269

    hermeticism, 14, 16

    history, 120–121

    Holy Grail, 116

    Internet sites, 4

    Judgment card, 34–35, 133

    Lovers card, 34, 133

    magazine articles, 3

    power and personal consciousness, 109

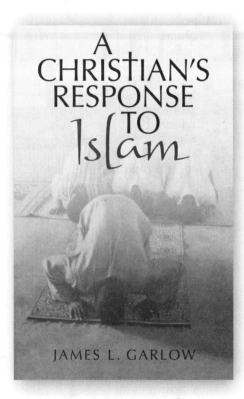

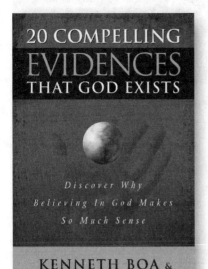

20 Compelling Evidences that God Exists

Kenneth D. Boa &
Robert M. Bowman, Jr.
Tackles the most profound
discussions from philosophy,
science, sociology, psychology,
and history, presenting 20 compelling
evidences that show the
reasonableness of faith in God.

ISBN 1-58919-306-7 ITEM #: 102645
6 x 9
Hardcover; 318P

Letters from a Skeptic

Dr. Gregory A. Boyd & Edward K. Boyd
Edward Boyd's agnosticism rested
"not [so] much on any positive position
...but rather on a host of negative ones."
It was this sincere struggle with the
intellectual challenges to Christianity
that led his son, professor Greg Boyd,
to enter into a heartfelt correspondence
with him—one in which "all of their
cards would be laid on the table." Out
of their unique dialogue, *Letters from a
Skeptic* was born. Follow along as father
and son, skeptic and believer, engage
the toughest questions about faith.

ISBN 1-56476-244-0 ITEM #: 58230
5-1/2 x 8-1/2
Hardcover; 192P

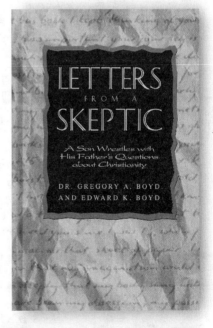

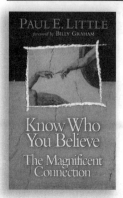
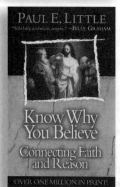
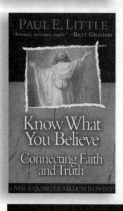